Ibn al-ʿArabī's *Barzakh*

Ibn al-ʿArabī's *Barzakh*

The Concept of the Limit and the Relationship between God and the World

Salman H. Bashier

State University of New York Press

Published by
State University of New York Press, Albany

Printed in the United States of America

For information, contact State University of New York Press, Albany, NY
www.sunypress.edu

Production by Marilyn P. Semerad
Marketing by Susan M. Petrie

Library of Congress Cataloging-in-Publication Data

Bashier, Salman, H., 1964–
Ibn al-ʿArabī's Barzakh : the concept of the limit and the relationship between God and the world / Salman H. Bashier.
p. cm.
Includes bibliographical references (p.) and index.
ISBN 978-0-7914-6227-0 hardcover (alk. paper)
ISBN 978-0-7914-6228-7 (paperback alk. paper)
1. Ibn al-ʿArabī, 1165-1240. 2. Intermediate state—Islam. 3. Creation (Islam) I. Title.

B753.I24B37 2004
181'.92—dc22

2003067308

10 9 8 7 6 5 4 3 2 1

To Peter Von Sivers

Contents

Acknowledgments xi
List of Abbreviations xiii
Introduction 1

1. Ibn al-ʿArabī's Liminal (*Barzakhī*) Theory of Representation: An Outlook from the Present Situation 11
   - Presentation and Representation: Complementary Elements in the Mystical Experience 11
   - Carter's View 15
   - Rorty's Antirepresentational Stand 19
   - Ibn al-ʿArabī's Stand 22
   - Wasserstrom's Criticism of Mystocentrism 25

2. Creation ex nihilo, Creation in Time, and Eternal Creation: Ibn Sīnā versus the Theologians 29
   - Creation ex nihilo in the Qur'ān 29
   - Creation ex nihilo, Creation in Time, and Islamic Theologians 31
   - Ibn Sīnā's Answers to the Theologians' Arguments 36
   - Ibn Sīnā on the Possible- and the Necessary-of-Existence 38
   - Ibn Sīnā's Distinction between Essence and Existence 40

3. Ibn Rushd versus al-Ghazālī on the Eternity of the World 43
   - Between *The Incoherence of the Philosophers* and *The Incoherence of the Incoherence* 43

The First Proof 45
The Second Proof 49
The Third Proof 51
Ibn Rushd's Doctrine of Eternal Creation: The Emergence of the Problem of the Limit 52

4. Mysticism versus Philosophy: The Encounter between Ibn al-ʿArabī and Ibn Rushd 59
Mysticism between Theology and Philosophy 59
An Interpretation of the Encounter between Khaḍir and Moses from Ibn al-ʿArabī's Perspective 60
The Encounter between Ibn Rushd and Ibn al-ʿArabī 66

5. The Barzakh 75
The Intermediate State (Barzakh) in the Qur'ān and in the Canonical Tradition 75
The Barzakh in the Exegesis of the Qur'ān and in Scholastic Theology 80
Plato's Theory of the Forms 83
Ibn al-ʿArabī's Definition of the Barzakh 86
Ibn al-ʿArabī versus Ibn Sīnā: Two Conceptions of the Relative 92

6. The Third Entity: The Supreme Barzakh 97
Plato's Form, The Muʿtazilites' Nonexistent, and Ibn al-ʿArabī's Fixed Entity 97
Plato's Introduction of the Receptacle 99
Ibn al-ʿArabī's Introduction of the Third Thing 102
The Problem of the Creation of the World Revisited 106

7. The Perfect Man: The Epistemological Aspect of the Third Thing 113
The Perfect Man as the Conclusion of Divine Love 113
The Perfect Man as the Possessor of Divine Knowledge 117
The Logic of the Knowledge of Perfection 122

8. The Limit Situation 129
On Knowing the Waystation of "In The Articulations is the Knowledge of the Stairs" 129

Acknowledgments

I am grateful to my mother Nazera who has been a source of divine inspiration to me, and to my late father Hamze. I like to think of him walking in the house chanting lines of classical Arabic poetry. The lines are still engraved in my memory and I often find myself chanting them in the way he did. I am grateful also to my MA teacher at the University of Haifa, the late professor Itzchak Klein. I remember he was very ill and did not say more than a few words in his last lecture. But then the lesson that he taught me in that hour was priceless: it is not the words but he who says them that makes the difference between absence and presence. I am grateful to professor Efraim Navon my MA supervisor who helped prepare me for more advanced research. I am also grateful to professor Sarah Sviri a true friend and intellectual partner, and to friends Dana Friebach-Heifetz, Muhammad Abu Salah, Kamal Hassan, James Chellis, and especially Irma Burgos. I will never forget her spiritual and intellectual support, her sharp mind and gentle soul.

I wish to thank professor Lois A. Giffen and my doctoral supervisor professor Bernard G. Weiss of the Middle East Center at the University of Utah, and also Beth Phillips, the secretary of the Center. During my doctoral studies I enjoyed their generous support and thanks to them I was able to complete the Eastern turn in my philosophical education. I wish also to thank the Herzog Center at Ben-Gurion University and the former head of the Center, Dr. Dror Zeeve, for granting me a postdoctoral award that allowed me to focus on preparing this book for publication, and the former head of the Middle East Department of Ben-Gurion University, Dr. Yoram Meital, and Aliza Uzan, the Secretary of the Department for allowing me to use the Department's facilities.

Finally, my special gratitude goes to professor Peter Von Sivers at the University of Utah. The least that I can say is that much of what I have said in this book and much of what I will be saying for the rest of my scholarly life is due to him. This book is dedicated to him.

Abbreviations

AV	Lenn Goodman, *Avicenna*. London, 1992.
BWA	Richard McKeon, ed. *The Basic Works of Aristotle*. New York, 1970.
DR	Ragnar Eklund, *Life between Death and Resurrection*. Uppsala, 1941.
F	Ibn al-ʿArabī, *Futūḥāt Makkiyya*. Beirūt, 1968.
PK	Harry Wolfson, *The philosophy of the Kalām*. Cambridge, Massachusetts, 1976.
RC	Robert Brandom, ed. *Rorty and his Critics*. Malden, Massachusetts, 2000.
RR	Steven Wasserstrom, *Religion after Religion*. Princeton, 1999.
SD	William Chittick, *The Self-Disclosure of God*. Albany, 1998.
SPK	William Chittick, *The Ṣūfī Path of Knowledge*. Albany, 1989.
TCD	Edith Hamilton and Huntington Cairns, eds. *Collected Dialogues of Plato*. Princeton, 1994.
TF	Ghazālī, *The Incoherence of the Philosophers*. Translated by Michael Marmura. Provo, Utah, 1997.
TT	Ibn Rushd, *The Incoherence of the Incoherence*, Translated by Simon Van Den Bergh. Oxford, 1954.

Introduction

In the year 1562 a Turkish aġa came to Istanbul. Six years later he became the watchman of the sultan's garden. One day he entered the garden and watched a musician demonstrating his skills before a group of people, bringing forth "laments like the nightingale and passions like a butterfly."[1] The gathering group applauded the musician and showed him great respect and admiration. When he was left alone the aġa implored him to be his instructor in the art of music. The musician brought forth a plectrum and handed it to the aġa, who locked himself in his room and, day and night, he practiced his hand. His skill increased so much that when he was practicing even the shadow of his hand could not be seen. Exercising his skill for many days and nights, the aġa was eventually overcome by sleep. He saw in a dream a group of gypsy musicians holding all kinds of musical instruments and playing sounds that "threw the universe in tumult." Then after showing the aġa great respect and reverence they said to him, "If you have liking for our art, if you want to learn it, God bless you!" The aġa turned to his teacher, the musician, and asked his help in interpreting the dream. The musician said:

> In truth this art is a gypsy art. But they are an ignorant tribe. What is a note [*naġme*]? What is time [*zamān*]? What is harmony [*mülāyemet*]? What is dissonance [*münāferet*]? What is melody [*laḥn*]? What is interval [*buʿd*]? What is tone [*ṣavt*]? What is song [*ġinā*]? They know not. A note is the same as a deliberate producing of the sound *ten*. *Ten* . . . consists of two letters. When a person produces it with a specific tone, that is a note. And this is the

> definition of time. Time is the sound of that interval between the voicing of the letter *ta* and the beginning of the letter *nūn* when a person pronounces the word *ten*. In the technical terminology of the science of music, a tone resembling *ten* . . . is called a tone. Harmony is that which is agreeable to nature. Dissonance is that which is offensive to nature. In the technical terminology of music, melody means to play the sound of notes high in some places and low in other places, that is treble and bass. Interval is what they call the space between two tones.[2]

Although the art of music is a gypsy one, the gypsies do not possess knowledge of it. They do not know the definitions of what music is made of, that is, the definitions of note, time, harmony, dissonance, melody, interval, tone, and song. The musician provides *liminal* definitions for these terms. For example, the "note" is defined as a liminal entity that separates between the *ta* and the *nūn*. A person may, with many specific tones, produce the (one) word *ten* in many different ways. This depends on the interval that he strikes between the letters *ta* and *nūn*, that is, on the sound produced when a variant interval is specified. Time is identified with the sound that is the product of striking that interval or the function of the space that separates between the two letters. A good musician is one who knows how to keep to harmony and away from dissonance; is one who knows how to strike a balance between the two components (letters) that constitute a specific tone and between two specific notes in a manner that is agreeable, or not offensive to nature.

By saying that the gypsies do not know what time is the musician does not mean that they do not know that time is the function of the space that separates between two letters. Acknowledgement of the literal definition of time does not guarantee real knowledge of it. For, like the relationship between the *ta* and the *nūn*, this knowledge is to remain relatively hidden as long as it is relatively determined. The moment the relationship is specified it is no longer the relationship the knowledge of which is of the musician's real concern. This knowledge is and remains nonmanifest, even as the musician who determines it, and is determined by it, is. This is, in my view, Ibn al-ʿArabī's mystical knowledge. In the year 1190 in Cordoba he witnessed a vision: "Know that when God showed to me and made me contemplate all the Messengers and prophets of the human species from Adam down to Muḥammad, in a scene [*mashhad*] in which it was granted to me to participate at Cordoba in 586, none of them spoke to me with the exception of Hūd, who explained to me the reason for their gathering."[3] Ibn al-ʿArabī does not tell us about the real reason behind the gathering of the Messengers and the Prophets of God either in this or in a more detailed account of the same vision, in which the prophet Hūd informed him that the Prophets and Messengers of God had come to visit a certain man.[4] However, as one of his modern biographers pointed out, Ibn al-ʿArabī confided the secret of the gathering to certain disciples of his, who transmitted it from generation to generation until the mystery was divulged by Jandī (d. 1330), the commentator on Ibn al-ʿArabī's *Fuṣūṣ al-Ḥikam*: The Prophets and the Messengers assembled to congratulate Ibn al-ʿArabī on being nominated the Seal of Sainthood, the supreme heir to the Seal of the Prophets.[5]

Ibn al-ʿArabī's notion of the Seal of the Sainthood has received a considerable amount of discussion by several of his scholars, the most important of which was provided by Michel Chodkiewicz.[6] It is also a notion that has come under serious attacks in both medieval and in modern times, especially the idea that sainthood encompasses the divine message (*risāla*) and prophecy (*nubuwwa*), and that in the person of each prophet the saint is superior to the prophet.[7] In the context of discussing the encounter between Khaḍir, one of God's saints, and Moses His prophet,[8] Ibn al-ʿArabī emphasizes that the saint possesses knowledge that is not available to the prophet:

> Imām of the Era, ʿAbd al-Qādir, said, "Assemblies of the prophets! You have been given the title, but we have been given what you were not given." As for his words, "You have been given the title," he means that the ascription of the word *prophet* has been interdicted to us, even though the general prophecy pervades the great ones among the Men. And as for his words, "but we have been given what you were not given," that is the meaning of Khaḍir's words, to whose rectitude and priority in knowledge of God has given witness. Moses, God's chosen speaking companion brought near to Him, went to the trouble of seeking Khaḍir, even though it is known that the ulama see Moses as more excellent than Khaḍir. Khaḍir said to him, "O Moses, I have a knowledge that God has taught me, and that you do not know." This is exactly the meaning of ʿAbd al-Qādir's words, "We have been given what you were not given."[9]

The knowledge that Khaḍir knew and Moses did not is knowledge of nonmanifestation. According to Ibn al-ʿArabī, this is the knowledge of the nonmanifest letter *waw,* which is between the manifest letters *kāf* and *nūn* in the divine word *kun* (be!). The word k[u]n consists of two manifest letters: *kāf* (k) and *nūn* (n), and a nonmanifest letter: *waw* (u). The word k[u]n, therefore, represents all that is manifest and nonmanifest. Thus, it signifies God, the Real, who is the liminal entity that brings the aspects of nonmanifestation and manifestation together. It also signifies the perfect human being, His deputy on earth and the configuration within which the Real manifests his words in the outside existence:

> He says, *Our only word to a thing, when We desire it, is to say to it "Be!"* [*kun*] [16:40]. Thus He brought three letters, two of which are manifest—the *kāf* and the *nūn*—and one of which [the *wāw*] is nonmanifest and hidden. . . . In this level, the perfect human being assumes the deputyship of the Real in differentiating between the prior word and the word that follows it. . . . The existence [*wujūd* in Chittick] of the letter in every point of articulation is its being engendered. If no one engenders it here, then who engenders it? Inescapably, the one who engenders it is between every two words or letters so as to give existence to the second word or the second letter and to attach it to the first. . . . In speech there is no escape from priority, posteriority, and order. So also, in the existent things, which are the entities of the divine words, there is priority, posteriority, and order. This is made manifest by the Aeon, and the Aeon is God, according to an explicit text. The Prophet said, "Do not curse the Aeon, for God is the Aeon." Within the Aeon, order, priority, and posteriority become manifest in the existence [*wujūd* in Chittick] of the cosmos.[10]

Dahr (Aeon) means "time."[11] According to Ibn al-ʿArabī, God applied to himself the word *dahr* and not *zamān* in order to distinguish his ruling property from the ruling property of the time that is imagined as a straight line with beginning and end. Instead, God's time is the Limit, which resembles any point that we may suppose on the circumference of the circle, and which can be considered both the beginning and the end of the circle.[12] Every point on the circumference of the circle resembles a limit between a preceding point and a following one. The circle itself has neither a beginning nor an end, but on its circumference there can be found endless points, as there can be found endless beginnings and ends. Like points on the circumference of the circle the words of God are infinitely many. But the infinitely many words of God originate from a single word. That word is the divine command *kun*, which consists of two manifest letters (*kāf* and *nūn*) and a nonmanifest letter (*wāw*). God engenders existence or brings his commands into manifestation by differentiating or setting limits between the letters or the words that are latent in his Essence. When God desires to make this affair known, he speaks within the configuration of the perfect human being. The perfect human being assumes the deputyship of the Real in differentiating between the engendered prior word and the word that follows it.

"Engendered existence," which comes to be through the divine command *kun*, translates *al-kawn* in Arabic. As William Chittick points out, it is possible that Ibn al-ʿArabī means by *al-kawn* "all that is," which is both God and the cosmos, and it is also possible that he means by it "everything other than God." Chittick thinks that Ibn al-ʿArabī has this second meaning in mind.[13] I think, however, that *al-kawn* may, perhaps paradoxically, be subject to both interpretations. This, I think, is what constitutes the definition of Ibn al-ʿArabī's most celebrated as well as most misinterpreted notion of the Oneness of Being (*waḥdat al-wujūd*), which he expresses in terms of unification that is not exclusive to differentiation. "Unification" is *tawḥīd* in Arabic. As Chittick points out, the grammatical form of the word involves an *active* stance of a person toward a certain object. Chittick writes, "Tawḥīd does not begin with unity, since that needs to be established. Rather, it begins with the recognition of diversity and difference. The integrated vision that *tawḥīd* implies must be achieved on the basis of recognized multiplicity."[14] This assertion is different if not perhaps only apparently from what Sachiko Murata says, "Undifferentiation and differentiation are often considered synonymous with the terms all-comprehensiveness (*jamʿ*) and dispersion (*farq or tafriqa*). As in similar pairs, the relationship is taken into account, not any absolute value attached to either side. What is differentiated from one point of view may be undifferentiated from another point of view. Undifferentiation is the higher, more powerful, more luminous, and prior dimension of reality. But it is able to manifest itself only through differentiation, which is lower, weaker, darker, and receptive toward its activity."[15]

Chittick is correct in thinking that being aware of difference is prior to or a condition for recognizing unity. However, unification, or, to use Murata's term, undifferentiation remains in a sense a prior dimension of reality, since a certain form of unity or identity is required before any recognition that is based on setting (rational) limits could be started. At any rate, the two interpretations can be applied to Ibn al-ʿArabī's doctrine of the Oneness of Being, which has been subject to serious misinterpretations both in medieval and modern times. Abū al-ʿIlā ʿAffīfī, for example, interpreted this doctrine on the basis of pantheism and in terms signifying a static unity rather than a dynamic actuality. In his interpretation, God and the world are reduced to one ineffective unity in which the element of variegation is absent. ʿAffīfī is aware of the dialectical element dominating Ibn al-ʿArabī's thought.[16] However, by presenting this dialectical element merely as a formal principle,[17] he overlooks the most fundamental notion of Ibn al-ʿArabī's thought, the notion of actuality that signifies the ceaseless unfolding of reality and its emergence into ever higher levels of unity. Consequently, he fails to grasp the true significance of the notion of *paradoxicality* intrinsic to Ibn al-ʿArabī's thought, ascribing the paradoxical expressions in his writings to lack of philosophical training and his failure to compromise monotheistic Islam with concessions to pantheism.[18]

ʿAffīfī wrote his work in a time in which the emphasis on rationalism was in its strongest phases.[19] As Phillip Rosemann points out, in the study of medieval thought this emphasis was characteristic of the Newscholastic methodology of research.[20] Rosemann's study of the history of medieval philosophy[21] raises interesting points, especially regarding the present increasing interest in emphasizing the mystical component in medieval thought. Rosemann says that the Newscholastic stance, which was the dominant paradigm until about thirty years ago, turned out to be paradoxical since it adopted the very rationalist assumptions of the project of modernity, which it set out to combat. The result was that Newscholasticism focused its attention on the most rational thinkers of the Middle Ages and had little interest in medieval mystics, always favoring the thinkers of Latin Europe over Arabic and Jewish medieval thinkers.[22] He explains the death of Newscholasticism as the outcome of a shift in the present time from the project of modernity, a shift that was caused by postmodernist emphasis on otherness and difference. This explains, according to him, the present day interest in mystical thinkers and in the mystical features of thinkers who were previously considered purely rational. This change of paradigm designates, according to Rosemann, an advance in our knowledge of the history of medieval philosophy. He insists, however, that the current postmodernist paradigm suffers from serious limitations, the most important of which is that it neglects the element of unity of the human knowledge and the social order and exaggerates difference. There is need for a new interpretation of the history of medieval philosophy, as this must relax its opting for partiality and difference by balancing it with serious reconsideration of wholeness and unity: "Philosophically, it is not enough to underline the multiplicity of coherent universes of discourse, analyzing each in and for itself, as this must inevitably lead to relativism. Relativism is logically untenable and self-destructive. Hence, we cannot content ourselves with parts, but rather need to move on to the whole, in which each of the parts finds its logical place."[23]

Thus, Rosemann thinks that the postmodern approach of analycity and relativism must be replaced by a new paradigm which gives equal weight to unity and universality. Among the scholars of Ibn al-ʿArabī are those who see in his thought the best potential for materializing this paradigm. Their voices, which speak in favor of restoring the values of unity and universality to a fragmented mind and world order, begin to sound so distinct that they sometimes verge on spiritual devotion. For example, Peter Young writes:

> Can it be that this knowledge which was brought down through Muḥyiddīn Ibn ʿArabī has a purpose and future beyond guiding to completion those who have such an aptitude to receive, and to pursue their spiritual destiny? As was said before, an idea that is true is of great effect. How much more so this idea of ideas, that existence is an absolute unity and totally present everywhere without division. Could this idea not become the real distinction of this age in which we live, its guiding principle and light with which it moves? If so it

> will be the greatest revolution in the general consciousness that has yet taken place in mankind's short history.[24]

Both Rosemann's and Young's words seem to be strongly in favor of unity and universality. We should keep in mind, however, that what seems to be a clear preference for unity over difference for those as well as for other scholars comes partially as a sort of reaction to a long Western philosophical tradition that has turned its back on the notion of the metaphysical unity of existence, and looked at the tendency toward metaphysical unity as a product of Oriental imagination. With its strong rationalistic trends Western intellectual tradition has rejected this tendency and, by doing so, pushed its rationalistic assumptions to their ultimate limits. What these thinkers seek is harmony and balance rather than exaggerating the value of unity in a manner that completely excludes difference. William Chittick expresses this point briefly in his introduction to the *Ṣūfī Path of Knowledge:* "Somewhere along the line, the Western intellectual tradition took a wrong turn. . . . Many important thinkers have concluded that the West never should have abandoned certain teachings about reality which it shared with the East. They have turned to the Oriental traditions in the hope of finding resources which may help revive what has been lost and correct the deep psychic and spiritual imbalances of our civilization. One result of this ongoing search for a lost intellectual and spiritual heritage has been the rediscovery of the importance of imagination."[25]

Imagination in Ibn al-ʿArabī is an intermediate reality, the reality of the Limit, or what Ibn al-ʿArabī calls *barzakh*. Barzakh is a term that represents an activity or an active entity that differentiates between two things and (paradoxically) through that very act of differentiation provides for their unity. Ibn al-ʿArabī's mystical concept of the Limit is contrasted with Aristotle's, according to which the Limit is the ultimate part of each thing, or the first part outside of which no part can be found, or the first part inside of which all parts exist. Aristotle says also that the Limit is the essence of each thing, since it is by their limits that things are known.[26] Ibn al-ʿArabī thinks that the Limit is the essence of each thing as well. But the Limit, according to him, is the essence of each thing not in the sense that it is the first or the last part of a thing, since this partial definition of the Limit turns it into a duality that consists of two parts, as one of its parts is identified with one limited thing and the other part with another limited thing. In this case, the existence of another limit will be called for to provide for the unity of the posited duality. This process can go on indefinitely until we arrive at a concept of the Limit that meets the two limited things, between which it differentiates, with *two* faces that are *one*. This will be Ibn al-ʿArabī's paradoxical definition of the Limit.

Ibn al-ʿArabī applies this paradoxical definition of the Limit to the antinomy[27] of the relationship between God and the world, or the antinomy of the finitude/infinitude of the world. Islamic scholastic theologians, who thought that the world was limited in space and in time, and Islamic philosophers, who thought that the world was limited in space but unlimited in time, are presented as the holders of the two theses of the antinomy. In their debate, the theologians and the philosophers developed in-between solutions to the antinomy, involving notions that might be considered precursors to Ibn al-ʿArabī's notion of the Limit. The Ashʿarite theologians, for example, advanced the notion of the "state" (*ḥāl*)—an intermediate entity between reality and unreality—a notion that underlined their theory of the perpetual renewal of the creation of the world. The Muʿtazilites, for another example, developed the notion of the "nonexistent thing," (*al-maʿdūm*) that signifies something between existence and nonexistence. Among the philosophers, Ibn Sīnā came out with the paradoxical conception of the possible-in-itself and necessary-through-the-other, and Ibn Rushd held a *complementarity thesis*,[28] according to which two different theses or accounts of the same substance matter may both be true even if their logical conjunction leads to a flat contradiction. The debate between the theologians and the philosophers and the in-between solutions that they had come out with are presented in chapters 2 and 3.

Ibn Rushd's complementarity thesis is presented as the culmination of the efforts of the theologians and the philosophers to solve the problem of the relationship between God and the world. It is also introduced in chapter 4 as the background for the emergence of Ibn al-ʿArabī's conception of the Limit. The chapter elaborates on the encounter that took place between Ibn Rushd and Ibn al-ʿArabī, the discussion of which is preceded by another discussion from Ibn al-ʿArabī's perspective of another encounter that took place, according to the Qur'ān, between Moses and Khaḍir. In both discussions the emphasis is laid on the contrast between the rationalistic and the mystical modes of thought.

Chapter 5 explores the roots of Ibn al-ʿArabī's notion of the Limit in the Qur'ān and the Islamic canonical tradition as well as in the Greek philosophical tradition. It focuses in particular on Plato's theory of the Forms and, to a certain extent, identifies the Platonic Form with Ibn al-ʿArabī's barzakh, the main example of which is the fixed entity (*ʿayn thābita*).

Chapter 6 provides a discussion of the ontological aspect of the barzakh. This aspect is represented through the notion of the Third Thing, which constitutes Ibn al-ʿArabī's representation of the paradoxical relationship between God and the world on the ontological level. Chapter 6 also extends the comparison between Ibn al-ʿArabī and Plato by comparing the former's introduction of the notion of the Third Thing with the latter's introduction of the notion of the Receptacle in *Timaeus*.

Chapter 7 presents the epistemological aspect of the Third Thing. This is the Perfect Man (*al-insān al-kāmil*), the possessor of perfect knowledge and the Supreme Limit between the Real (*al-Ḥaqq*) and creation (*khalq*). The discussion of the two aspects of the Third Thing, the ontological and the epistemological, comes to its conclusion in chapter 8 in the Limit-Situation, a situation in which the Real and his creation are represented as abiding in a mutual permeation and active interpenetration.

Despite its focus on Ibn al-ʿArabī's thought and, in particular, his concept of the Limit, this work attempts to provide a critical examination of rational philosophical thought in general. This explains its concern with examining one of the most recent of the modern philosophical criticisms to rationalism promoted by Richard Rorty. Rorty's stand is especially interesting since it provides comprehensive criticism not merely of this or that philosophical doctrine but rather of the whole philosophical enterprise. As I try to show in chapter 1 (which provides a critical introduction to Ibn al-ʿArabī's thought based on the examination of the shortcomings of the modern rationalist perspective), Rorty's pragmatist stand against rational thought bears a significant similarity to the mystical stand of Ibn al-ʿArabī. I attempt to show, however, that Rorty makes a mistake in abandoning the search for a universal methodology of knowledge and in promoting the sort of pragmatic contextualism that ignores the need for the unity of the human knowledge. In this work I try to show that, with the help of Ibn al-ʿArabī's unique methodology of acquiring knowledge, which is based on his unique concept of the Limit, we can provide an answer to Rorty's legitimate quest for a better approach to philosophical problems without actually having to quit the whole enterprise of the philosophical search for a unified theory of knowledge.

CHAPTER 1

Ibn al-ʿArabī's Liminal (*Barzakhī*) Theory of Representation: An Outlook from the Present Situation

Presentation and Representation: Complementary Elements in the Mystical Experience

The barzakh is an Arabized form of the Persian *pardah*.[1] It signifies a (hidden) barrier between two things. Such are, for examples, the barrier between this life and the life of the hereafter and the barrier of belief between doubt and certainty. Barzakh appears in three places in the Qur'ān, in all of which it signifies a limit or a barrier that separates two things, preventing them from mixing with each other. Q 25: 53, for instance, reads, "It is He Who has let the two bodies of flowing water: One palpable and sweet, and the other salt and bitter. Yet has He made a barrier (barzakh) between them, a partition that is forbidden to be passed."[2] The emphasis in the verse is on the role of the barzakh as a differentiator between two entities possessing opposite properties. The barzakh differentiates between the two bodies of water, the palpable and sweet and the salty and bitter. At the same time, by preventing the two entities from mixing with each other, the barzakh also provides for their unity. This synthetic activity that the barzakh performs is of a paradoxical nature. For, as a differentiator between two entities, the barzakh must be a *third thing*, separated from both, whereas as a provider for their unity, it must be related to both entities. Henry Corbin considers the paradoxicality involved in the notion of the barzakh as a mark that distinguishes Islamic theosophists and Ṣūfīs from Islamic philosophers and scholastic theologians. The theosophists and the Ṣūfīs, according to him, defended the notion of the World of the Barzakh, which designates an intermediate entity that relates God with the world, while the philosophers and the theologians rejected this notion on the grounds that it did not accord with the requirements of rational theory and logical argument.[3]

In this work, I present the controversy between Islamic philosophers and Islamic scholastic theologians over the problem of the origination of the world, or the problem of the relationship between God and the world. I also provide Ibn al-ʿArabī's solution to the controversy, which introduces the notion of the World of the Barzakh as an imaginal mirror that represents the eternal God as eternal and the temporally originated world as temporally originated, although in itself, it is neither eternal nor temporally originated.[4] The barzakh differentiates between God and the world. In virtue of this differentiating activity, God may be represented to our knowledge as eternal and the world as temporally originated. But the barzakh plays also the complementary role of a provider for the context of unity, in which context both God and the world can be represented as both eternal and temporally originated.

A considerable part of the treatment of Ibn al-ʿArabī's barzakh in this work will be conducted on the basis of examining the manner in which his reflections on the relationship between God and the world differed from those of the philosophers and the theologians. In following this perspective of difference, I will be conducting the discussion in accordance with Corbin's aforementioned statement. However, the work will also account for the element of continuity between the thoughts of the rationalistic thinkers and Ibn al-ʿArabī's mystical thought. The development of rational thought will be presented as culminating in Ibn Rushd's complementarity thesis, according to which two different theses or accounts of the same substance matter may both be true even if their logical conjunction leads to a flat contradiction.[5] In my view, this development provided a suitable background for the emergence of Ibn al-ʿArabī's mystical notion of the Limit, and enhanced his attempt at rationalizing this notion. In following this perspective of continuity, I will be working in accordance with Whitehead's statement that "the purpose of philosophy is to rationalize mysticism."[6] Thus, in examining the emergence of Ibn al-ʿArabī's notion of the Limit in the context of Islamic medieval thought, I will be combining two modes of reflection, as the one emphasizes separation and discontinuity and the other connection and continuity. This attempt at combining two contradictory yet complementary modes of reflection is largely inspired by the manner in which Plato describes the philosophical activity as consisting of the process of arrival of the rational thinker at the limits of rationality and the act of transcending these limits: "Hardly after practicing detailed comparisons of names and definitions and visual and other sense perceptions, after scrutinizing them in benevolent disputation by the use of question and answer without jealousy, at last in a flash understanding of each blazes up, and the mind, as it exerts all its powers to the limit of human capacity, is flooded with light."[7] In this passage there is a description of (a) an activity that practices setting limits, drawing comparisons, and creating concepts, which is characteristic of the rationalistic mode of reflection; and (b) an activity that transcends these limits and processes of concept formation, which is characteristic of the mystical mode of reflection. The question is what happens after achieving illumination, that is, after transcending the limits of rationality. One might consider that when that happens the mystical experience will have exhausted itself, leaving behind but immediate flashes of sudden apprehensions that cease to exist the moment they are perceived. Although not totally incorrect, this characterization is still incomplete, being responsible for the narrow-sighted depiction of the mystical experience as consisting of a sort of uncontrolled excursion into that which is not rational, and as a behavior that is based on feelings and instincts divorced from the good reasoning. Huntington Cairns, for example, makes the double mistake of identifying the mystical experience as a series of irrational apprehensions, and rejecting any identification between the mystical experience and what he considers as the purely rational Platonic procedure for acquiring knowledge:

> But the difference between Plato and the mysticism that has attached itself to his philosophy is essential. Plato's aim is to take the reader by steps, with as severe a logic as the conversational method permits, to an insight into the ultimate necessity of Reason. And he never hesitates to submit his own ideas to the harshest critical scrutiny; he carried this procedure so far in the *Parmenides* that some commentators have held that his own doubts in this dialogue prevail over his affirmations. But the beliefs of mystics are not products of critical examination and logical clarification; they are, on the contrary, a series of apprehensions, flashes, based on feeling, denying the rational order.[8]

In such characterizations of the mystical experience, as devoid of critical examination and logical clarification, an important element seems to be missing. This is the element of *representation* through which the mystic attempts, upon arriving at the limits of rational thought, to accomplish the (seemingly impossible) task of representing what has been presented to him.[9] In order to illustrate my meaning I will first cite an example of an experience of mystical presentation and then elaborate:

> All at once I *felt someone near me*, a Presence entered this little room of which I became immediately conscious. . . . Dazed, I knelt by the nearest chair and here is the physical phenomenon that has recurred many times since. Into my heart there came a great *warmth*. The only way I can describe it is in the words of disciples on their way to Emmaus: "our hearts burned within us." My hand raised in

> prayer also glowed from tips to wrist with a blessed warmth, never before experienced.[10]

William P. Alston relies on such reports of the experience of presentation, which reflect immediacy and sudden, overwhelming feelings of joy and warmth, in building a model of mystical awareness that is parallel to the model of sense perception in epistemology. Alston describes his model as follows: "The awareness is *experiential* in the way it contrasts with thinking about God, calling up mental images, entertaining propositions, reasoning, engaging in overt or covert conversation, remembering. Our sources take it that something, namely, God, has been *presented* or *given* to their consciousness, in generically the same way as that in which objects in the environment are (apparently) *presented* to one's consciousness in sense perception."[11]

First I would like to repeat a point that Sara Sviri thinks is worth highlighting, "since it is frequently overlooked by adepts and scholars of mysticism: essentially, according to the Ṣūfī outlook, it is not the mystical experiences which are of the highest importance, but *transcending* them."[12] Second it should be noted that, in contrast to Alston's model, the mystical experience consists not only of the moment of immediacy, and the joy that is joined to it, but also of the complementary moment of mediation, which is characterized by the mystic's constant attempt to represent the moment of presentation. This is an attempt that brings suffering rather than joy, due to the accumulating recognition in the mind of the mystic that the moment of representation can never bring the process of presentation to a closure. Consequently, the mystic becomes the locus of a constant shift between closure (attempted representation) and disclosure (renewed presentation).[13] The moments of closure and disclosure are complementary aspects of every genuine mystical experience. Each of the moments becomes a limiting case for the other moment, while the experience as a whole becomes an experience of Disclosure that contains closure and disclosure as *transcended* moments. Ibn al-ʿArabī's work, as characterized in Chittick's following words, might be an excellent exemplification of this experience of Disclosure: "To get to the point is to bring about closure, but there is no closure, only *dis*closure. Ibn al-ʿArabī has no specific point to which he wants to get. He is simply flowing with the infinitely diverse self-disclosures of God, and he is suggesting to us that we leave aside our artificialities and recognize that we are flowing along with him. There is no 'point', because there is no end."[14]

There seems to be some inconsistency in defining the task of philosophy as rationalizing (setting rational limits to) mysticism on the one hand, and, on the other hand, presenting the mystical knowledge as knowledge of disclosure. The apparent inconsistency, however, is nothing but the expression of a deeper tension that is the outcome of attempting to represent the moment of presentation, which is identified with unlimited Truth, through the (limited) discursive or linguistic medium. In the Islamic tradition, this tension was expressed explicitly in the literature of poets and mystics and implicitly in the works of theologians and philosophers. In order to elaborate on this point, I will make a somewhat extensive but, I hope, worthy reference to Michael G. Carter's "Infinity and Lies in Medieval Islam."

Carter's View

Carter opens his article by saying that there was a strong relationship between infinity, truth, and lies in medieval Islam and that measures were taken to restrict the role of infinity, since the existence of various kinds of infinity was recognized as a threat to the Islamic doctrine.[15] Carter mentions various dimensions of the Islamic cultural tradition in which the threat of infinity creates a reality of limitation. In Islamic theology, for example, the notion of the spatial or temporal extension of the universe infinitely posed a threat to God's standing as the First Cause. Although the philosophers were aware that exploring the nature of infinity was unavoidable for examining the notion of creation, they were also aware that orthodox Muslims considered the assertion of infinity in the created world heretical. Ibn Rushd, for example, attempts to solve the problem of the eternity of the world by arguing that it is a problem that originated in terminological ambiguity. Carter writes:

> We should perhaps take this more seriously than simply regarding it as proof of his commitment to Aristotle even at the risk of appearing heterodox: as a Muslim who believed in the reality of the Arabic revelation it may have struck him that since all truth and all reality were contained within Arabic by virtue of the Qur'ān, then the ultimate nature of infinity was no more accessible through human language than the ultimate nature of God. From this perspective Ibn Rushd remains closer to the style of the *mutakallimūn* that he is refuting than to a pure philosopher or scientist.[16]

According to Carter, Muslims distinguished between the divine language of the Qur'ān, through which absolute truth is revealed, and the human language, through which relative truth is conveyed. He insists that Ibn Rushd, who shared this understanding with the rest of the Muslims, was convinced that the human language is limited and that the nature of infinity, like the nature of God, can never be revealed through it.[17] He holds that this feature of limitation seems to have pervaded all the dimensions of the Islamic culture, with the exception of poetry, through which "an elegant compromise has been reached between the constraining requirements of a finite religion and the irresistible human urge for the infinite exercise of the imagination."[18] The assumption was that by means of poetry anything could be said, since by virtue of the very definition of its poetic form of expression none of it was to be taken seriously. While the Qur'ān was considered of divine origin and thus being necessarily true, poetry was considered fallible and never necessarily true.[19]

Carter does not think that Islam is unique in attempting to reach a compromise between divine truth and the human drive for creative imagination, a drive that Muslims satisfied through the creative activity of lying. He insists, however, that "given its logocentric nature and consequent vulnerability to linguistic corruption," Islam seems to be especially conscious of the problem and determined to eliminate it.[20] In addition to poetry, there were other literary devices by means of which Muslims could satisfy their need for creative activity. One of these devices was the mystical literary form of expression, which could be excluded from the reality of religious truth, "either because it deliberately excludes itself or because by definition it is unislamic."[21] Carter states that the parallelism between the divine Qur'ānic discourse and the poetic and mystical discourses reflects his main premise concerning infinity and truth as the relationship between these is conceived of in the Islamic tradition in the following manner: "Absolute truth is not in this world but is glimpsed through the *finite* text of the Qur'ān, while relative truth is found in all other human language, of which poetry represents the highest aesthetic form, and in which an *infinite* variety of untruth is possible."[22]

In order to properly evaluate Carter's view I will say first a few words about the paradox of the Liar. Carter does not mention the paradox in his article but it seems clear from his discussion that he has it in mind.[23] In its simplest form, the paradox can be stated in the form of a declaration of a person that he is saying something false: If it turns out that the person who is making the declaration is telling the truth, then he must be lying, since that is what he is declaring. If the person is lying, then he must be telling the truth. Muslims might be understood to have employed the paradox as a sort of protective means, in the sense that they allowed for the existence of some groups (poets, mystics, and so forth) activating certain language games declared as such. When the participants in these language games make a controversial declaration, they are often protected through their declaration that it is merely within the boundaries of their specific language game that relative truth is issued and that this truth possesses no validity outside the boundaries of *this* language game. According to Carter, Islamic tradition made use of certain contexts of discourse (poetic, mystic) in order to avoid the threat of the notion of infinity. When poets and mystics say something that is considered a lie, according to orthodox religious truth, they are protected by their own declaration that they are only dealing with relative truth, as it is determined in the relative context of their own form of discourse. This is how, Carter thinks, a compromise was made in the Islamic tradition between the requirement of the absolute religious Truth, which was revealed through the Qur'ān, and the needs of the human creative imagination that Muslims satisfied through the use of a contextual conception of truth justification.

Carter's view has a certain undeniable appeal due to the fact that it addresses a real problem (the problem of the limitation that characterizes the Islamic tradition), and provides an ingenious explanation for it. Nevertheless, this view fails to do justice to the relevant parties whose positions it seeks to explain. This is so not only in relation to mystics, like Ibn al-ʿArabī, who made explicit use of the paradox of the liar, but even in relation to philosophers, like Ibn Rushd, who made implicit use of the paradox. For, to say that Ibn Rushd remains closer to a scholastic theologian than to a philosopher or to a scientist because he resolved the problem of the origination of the world by declaring the limitations of human language is to overlook the real impact of his solution to the problem. As I am going to show in this work, although it is true that Ibn Rushd was reluctant to write down philosophical solutions to problems that pertain to religious truths, he made it very clear that such solutions could be provided in a philosophy book.[24] The fact that he was not just a follower of Aristotle does not mean that he was closer to a scholastic theologian than to a philosopher or scientist. This work will attempt to show that Ibn Rushd's declaration of the limitation of language was an indication of the limitation of the rational thought of theologians and philosophers alike and that it can be considered the outcome of the critical attitude of an original thinker, rather than that of a dogmatic theologian or a rational philosopher.

Few would disagree with the view that the notion of infinity posed a threat to the Islamic tradition, and that Muslim thinkers sought ways to cope with this threat. However, it is highly questionable whether the solution that they had elaborated for the problem, which consisted of declaring the limitation of certain linguistic forms, was merely a protective means for safeguarding them against the threat of infinity and the criticism of their critics. As I will make explicit in several places in this work, Ibn al-ʿArabī made extensive use of the Liar, or the declaration of the limitation of language. He did so especially in those places where he provided an examination of the liminal (barzakhī) nature of things. The following passage is one such example in which he introduces his paradoxical representation of the nature of reality:

> The barzakh is nothing but Imagination. If you possess the power of reasoning and you perceive the image you realize that you have perceived an affair of existence, on which your sight has fallen. But you immediately know, with manifest certainty, that originally there was

> nothing there to be witnessed. Then what is the thing for which you have affirmed *entified* existence, and that you negated even in the very state of affirming it? Imagination is neither existent nor nonexistent, neither known nor unknown, neither affirmed nor negated. A person who sees his image in the mirror knows decisively that he has perceived his form in some respect and that he has not perceived his form in some other respect. Then if he says: "I saw my form I did not see my form," he will be neither a truth teller nor a liar. What is then the truth of the perceived form? The form is negated and affirmed, existent and nonexistent, known and unknown. God manifested this truth to the servant as a sign so that he realizes that once he has become incapable of recognizing the truth of [the liminal nature of the image], although it is an affair of this world, then he knows that he is even more incapable in relation to the knowledge of its Creator.[25]

Our representation of the image in the mirror is paradoxical. For in a certain respect, we know that it *is* our image that we perceive in the mirror and, in another respect, we know that it *is not* our image. If our representation of the image, which is an affair of the world, is paradoxical, our representation of the Maker of the world must be even more so. Still, it will be a mistake to think, following the general thrust of Carter's argument, that Ibn al-ʿArabī employed the consideration of this paradoxical representation for merely distinguishing our knowledge of God (Absolute Truth) from our knowledge of the world. On the contrary, our incapacity to set a rational limit (definition) for the liminal cases that make their appearance in the world should be considered an indicator for our incapacity to set limits for the Truth of the appearances of the world. The paradoxical representation of liminal cases provides for the unity of our knowledge, even as the reality that is represented by this knowledge possesses paradoxical characteristics.[26] The consideration of the paradoxical representation of liminal cases represents a threshold over which the reality of the divine and the reality of the world, or the Truth and its appearances interact and, through that very interaction, restore the unity of the human knowledge, not for the sake of perpetuating the split in the human consciousness.[27]

The unity of the human knowledge is based, according to Ibn al-ʿArabī, on a liminal conception of representation, which depicts reality in terms of difference through unity rather than mere separation or empty unification. Ibn al-ʿArabī's representational theory is similar to the classical representational theory of knowledge in some respects and is different from it in some other respects. In order to introduce Ibn al-ʿArabī's representational theory of knowledge, and explain its difference from the classical theory of representation, I will make a digression to one of the most serious recent criticisms of the representational theory of knowledge made by Richard Rorty. The rationale for making such a rather lengthy digression will become clear in the process of the discussion. Here it suffices to note that in recent years philosophical investigation (especially but not only in the field of the theory of knowledge) seems to have arrived at the limits of (rational) thought. Some thinkers have declared that philosophical thought has come to its end, and that philosophy has to give up searching for Truth and satisfy itself with a social or pragmatic conception of epistemic justification.[28] Others have gone, in my opinion, a little farther by recognizing the paradoxical nature of the limits of thought,[29] although they seem to have been incapable of drawing the full implications from this recognition. The spirit so to speak of these philosophical reflections was not foreign to Ibn al-ʿArabī, whose focus on the notion of the limits of thought has, in my opinion, very few parallels in human intellectual history. Like many modern thinkers, Ibn al-ʿArabī emphasizes the significance of knowing the limits of human thought. Unlike most of them, however, he does not understand this in terms of rationally reflecting on the limits of thought or staying within these limits. For him, to know the limits of thought is to realize them and to realize the limits of thought is to transcend them. Hence, representation must be transcendent even as the thing that is represented is. It is this feature of transcendence that distinguishes Ibn al-ʿArabī's theory from the classical theory of representation.

Rorty's Antirepresentational Stand

The representational theory of knowledge states that knowledge is a true representation in the mind of the external reality if there is a correspondence between the mind-independent objects and their representations. Closely related to the representational theory of knowledge is the correspondence theory of truth, according to which a statement is considered true if it corresponds to the mind-independent facts. As Hilary Putnam points out, most philosophers hold some version of the correspondence theory of truth, as they believe that abandoning it amounts to the denial of the objectivity of truth and the adherence to hopelessly subjective points of view.[30] Putnam identifies the correspondence theory of truth with the externalist approach in epistemology, which holds that the world consists of fixed, mind-independent objects and that there is exactly one true description of objects, which is determined through the correspondence between words and things. Although Putnam finds a close connection between the notions of truth and rationality,[31] he does not think that rational representation is to be determined by means of fixed methodological verification principles, as the analytic tradition in philosophy and especially the Logical Positivists, who worked within the context of this tradition, had surmised. Like other scholars, he emphasizes that the principle of verification is self-refuting, since it is neither analytic nor empirically testable.[32] Despite his explicit rejection of the Logical Positivists' rational principle of verification, Putnam expresses his awareness of the risk of adopting the other extreme alternative of the rational model, which is relativism. On the basis of this view, Putnam launched his criticism against Rorty's anti-representationalism, regarding it as a gesture of skeptical despair.[33] The following is a concise statement of Rorty's argument against epistemological representationalism: "(a) The very notion of representation—the idea that our thought is representational—is historically linked to the idea that it can represent what is *outside* our language and thought. But (b) since the idea of such representation is incoherent, we can either embrace idealism or simply give up on the idea that thought and language are representational at all. Since classical idealism is presumably not an option for Rorty, he concludes that the pluralist must abandon the notion of representation itself."[34]

Rorty holds that no real or ideal correspondence can be found between the words of language and the things that the words describe. Rather, what determines the truth of the use of words (or sentences) is the social context, or the language game, in which they are used. In his criticism to Rorty's view, Putnam applies a skeptical argument as old as skepticism itself: "How can Rorty so much as use *words* to tell us that kicking a rock involves a particular rock if those very words do not relate particularly to kicks and rocks?"[35] Putnam's argument, it should be indicated, is but another modern version of the argument leveled against a skeptic believing in a Heraclitean world in which nothing is fixed and everything is in constant flux. For, how can the skeptic hold a thought and build a skeptical argument in such a constantly fluctuating world? It must be clear that both arguments rest on rational assumptions to the effect that a rational order in the world is a necessary condition for (explaining) the very possibility of the (corresponding) rational activity that occurs in the mind reflecting on such a world. It should be clear, however, that such arguments have no power over the skeptic who does not share these rational assumptions with his critic. In my opinion Rorty represents this sort of skepticism. In what follows, I will elaborate on his antirepresentational position regarding epistemological representation. I will then compare it with that of Ibn al-ʿArabī. In the attempt, I will bring the considerations that led me to believe that employing Ibn al-ʿArabī's conception of representation can assist us in (a) avoiding Rorty's extreme antirepresentational view, which denies that truth is correspondence to reality or that reality possesses an intrinsic or essential nature,[36] and (b) relaxing the rather extreme rational demands that modern epistemology imposes on representational theories of knowledge or correspondence theories of truth.

The assumption underlying my discussion is that the modern epistemological characterization of the rational as what corresponds to a given or fixed reality makes Rorty's skepticism about all representational theories of knowledge unavoidable. In order to escape the Rortian predicament, we must introduce, or rather reintroduce, a more adequate conception of rational representation, a conception that has, in my view, preserved its original meaning in Ibn al-ʿArabī's mystical thought. Jürgen Habermas provides an excellent account of Rorty's "narrative of maturation," or the account of his arrival at his antirepresentational stand:

> The existential background to Rorty's neopragmatism is his rebellion against the false promises of philosophy: a philosophy that pretends to satisfy aesthetic and moral needs in satisfying theoretical ones. Once upon a time, metaphysics wanted to instruct its pupils in spiritual exercises involving a purifying contemplation of the good in the beautiful. But the youthful Rorty, who had allowed himself to be filled with enthusiasm with Plato . . . painfully comes to realize that the prospect of contact with the reality of the extraordinary . . . although possibly attainable in the more definite forms of prayer, cannot be achieved along the path of philosophy. . . . The realization that everyday reality conceals no higher reality, no realm of being-in-itself to be disclosed ecstatically, and that everyday practices have no room for a redemptory vision, cures the sobered Rorty of his Platonic sickness.[37]

In 1967 Rorty edited *The Linguistic Turn*, a reader that summed up the triumphant progression of analytic philosophy and, at the same time, marked a break in its history.[38] Rorty considered analytic (or linguistic) philosophy as signifying one of the greatest stages in the history of philosophy.[39] He came to realize, however, that analytic philosophy shared the fundamental (false) premise with the metaphysical tradition that "there are philosophical truths still to be discovered." Hence, the only remaining option for him was to bed farewell to all philosophy.[40] Rorty made full use of the new ideas that had been developed in the philosophy of language. He adopted Wittgenstein's view that what determines the truth of language is the context of communication, or the language game that relates speaker, interpreter, and the world.[41] He also made use of Peirce's replacement of the two-place relation between the object that is represented and the subject that performs the representation with a three-place relation that is a "symbolic expression, which accords validity to a state of affairs, for an interpretive community." The world became, for Rorty, a symbolic point of reference rather than something to reflect, as the communicated facts were not separated from the process of communication or interpretation.[42]

Rorty's next important work, *Philosophy and the Mirror of Nature* (1979), aimed to complete the linguistic turn by showing the futility of the adherence to the *pathos of distance*, "the sense of something non-human toward which we reach but which we may never grasp." The pathos of distance, which was created by Plato's attempt at representing what is most universal and least material, was given a new turn in the seventeenth century when philosophers began to look for the foundations of human knowledge not in higher Platonic truths but rather in what underlies the human knowledge:[43]

> One of the big questions I was trying to answer for myself when I wrote *Philosophy and the Mirror of Nature* was: how did philosophy survive the New Science? Why didn't the success of corpuscularian physics make philosophy obsolete? How did philosophy extricate itself from what the eighteenth century called "natural philosophy," and set up in business on its own? My answer ("because they invented the veil of ideas, and thereby produced a new field of inquiry to replace the one that physics had taken over") had some merit, but it dodged around an important topic. That was the topic of how philosophy managed, among the educated classes, to take over some of the functions of religion.[44]

According to Rorty, the emergence of epistemology (the theory that searches for the foundations of knowledge) as first philosophy should be seen as a new attempt to cross the abyss that perpetuated the pathos of distance by promoting the conception of mental representation as a new "veil of ideas."[45] Since he wrote *Philosophy and the Mirror of Nature*, Rorty has persevered in his attempt to dissolve all representational theories of knowledge and correspondence theories of truth and provide further supporting demonstrations for his anti-representational stand.

Ibn al-ʿArabī's Stand

Like the younger Rorty Ibn al-ʿArabī was filled with enthusiasm for Plato's thought. However, he never ceased to draw inspiration from Plato, insisting that he was perhaps the only philosopher who deserved the title "lover of wisdom."[46] Ibn al-ʿArabī was among the very few exceptions to a long Islamic philosophical tradition that regarded Aristotle rather than Plato as the authority in philosophical inquiries. Paul Walker ascribes the difficulty of Muslim scholars in dealing with the Platonic writings to the symbolic form of his language, which added obscurity to his dialectical method.[47] I think, following Walker's view, that the symbolic form of Plato's language, which signified a certain tendency to transcend the limits of the rational, was mainly responsible for the fact that Muslim scholars did not receive his works with the same enthusiasm that they received the works of Aristotle. In later stages, when Islamic philosophical thought arrived at maturity and as rationalism began to exhaust itself, some thinkers, such as Shihāb al-Dīn Yaḥyā al-Suhrawardī (d.1191) and Ibn al-ʿArabī, began to search for philosophical truth in Plato rather than in Aristotle.

Like Rorty, Ibn al-ʿArabī regards the words of language as symbolic expressions, subject to the interpretive effort. However, what the two thinkers understand by *symbolic expression* and *interpretive effort* differs considerably. According to Rorty, the validity of the interpretive effort requires an interpretive community and a certain social context of discourse, which alone may provide justification for the use of language and the interpretive effort that is attached to it. Rorty dismisses the talk about the truth or the reality that corresponds to the knowledge of the communicated symbolic expressions, admitting only the contextualist justification of *this* knowledge. Since the only ideal of discourse for Rorty is "to justify your beliefs to a competent audience," it follows that "if you can get agreement from other members of such an audience . . . you do not have to worry about your relation to reality."[48] For Ibn al-ʿArabī, interpretation (*taʿbīr*) is what the term signifies in Arabic: the act of crossing over. The truth of the interpretive effort presents itself in the act of crossing over from one state to another. Hence, any adequate representation of this truth must also be carried out through a corresponding act of crossing over.[49] Moreover, true knowledge about the nature of the symbolic expression can be considered an adequate representation of all existent beings (words, ideas, things), since all existent beings are words that signify a state of crossing between affirmation (of existence) and denial (of existence).[50] Under this interpretation, difference becomes the root of all things,[51] since for the thing to be in a constant state of crossing is for it to be constantly differentiated not only from other things, but also from itself. Ibn al-ʿArabī shows awareness of the use that skeptics make of the view that difference is the root of all things to argue that things do not possess any kind of reality and that, consequently, the truth about the nature of things must remain unknown.[52] Although he admits the skeptics' depiction of the nature of things as abiding in constant fluctuation, he refuses to accept their conclusion that things do not possess any sort of reality. Things do possess reality but theirs is a symbolic, or, imaginal reality. It is not the reality of the affirmation of reality or the reality of the denial of reality, but rather a liminal reality, characteristic of liminal objects. Nor does he accept the skeptics' conclusion that the truth about the nature of things must remain unknown, a conclusion that is based on the realization that things do not posses fixed realities:

> If the faulty nature of this knowledge is revealed to them, they say that there could be no knowledge altogether to rely on. If they were told, however, that their statement is based on the knowledge that there could be no knowledge and that their statement, therefore, could

> not be supported because of their denial of the very possibility of knowledge, they would say: "And that is exactly what we say, namely, that our statement is not based on knowledge and that it is erroneous." Then, it must be said to them: "You *knew*, then, that your statement was not based on knowledge and that it was erroneous. Hence, you affirmed what you denied."[53]

Following Ibn al-ʿArabī's paradoxical conception of representation, we can argue that Rorty failed to see how philosophy could be the mirror of nature, that is, provide a representation of reality, because he failed to see the true nature of mirroring. Under this interpretation, Rorty's failure stems from the dogmatic assumption that representation must be of a given reality, an assumption that he seems to have in common with the analytic tradition of which he is critical. It should be remembered that Rorty criticized analytic thought for sharing with the metaphysical tradition, which it devalued, the assumption that there are given truths waiting to be discovered.[54] Once he realized that the arguments of analytic philosophers had resulted in analyzing the idea of the given to death, he thought that the notion of representation must give way as well. It can be said, therefore, that Rorty was, after all, still reacting to and working within the context of the tradition of analytic philosophy, a tradition that was incapable of realizing that a conception of representation that does not account for the paradoxical element of reality must be dismissed as inadequate. In the following passage, which brings us back to the paradox of the liar, Ibn al-ʿArabī explicates on the aspect of paradoxicality involved in knowing reality:

> Realize the Gnosis of the Attributes which has arisen in you, and take heed: You have never at any time discovered any Attribute [as it is] in accordance with the Reality of your Lord, but, rather, you have come to know the Qualities which you infer from the primary elements of your [own] being. You have not ceased being yourself, nor have you gone out of yourself, while [God's] Attributes closely adhere to His Essence, transcending any connection with your [discursive] knowledge of their essential quiddity—although, regarding this, they *are* connected to your Gnosis of their Essence. But you are quite unable to attain unto them—standing in the Way of Realization you do not know your Lord by every means—while, at the same time, [it can be said that] you know nothing *except* Him—and deem no Being transcendent besides Him. For if you say that you know Him, you have spoken the actual truth, and have "succeeded"; and if you say that you have not known Him, [again] you have told the sincere truth, and "preceded"! So choose [either] negation for yourself or affirmation—the Attributes [of God]

> are far beyond connection with accidental knowledge of them, even as [His] Essence is.[55]

According to Ibn al-ʿArabī, to know something is to find it and to find something is to set conceptual limits to it. Reality is unlimited and, therefore, it cannot be found. If it cannot be found, then it cannot be known. One who thinks that he knows Reality is veiled and his veil is nothing other than his own thought. "Standing in the Way of Realization," one can never know except one's own reality. Thus, if he says that he does not know Reality, he will be telling the truth. But then, Ibn al-ʿArabī states that one who says that he knows Reality, that is, that he has found Reality, is also telling the truth. Actually, he says more than just that. He says that one knows nothing *except* Reality. Ibn al-ʿArabī thinks that Truth is transcendent. However, he thinks that the transcendence of Truth implies transcending not only the limitation of the language that represents it, but also transcending the limitation of its non-limitation. Having clarified this point, I will now turn to Steven Wasserstrom's criticism of Henry Corbin's study of the history of religion and Ibn al-ʿArabī's mystical thought. The reader will soon realize that there are several parallels between Wasserstrom's attack on Corbin's study of mysticism and Rorty's attack on philosophy.

Wasserstrom's Criticism of Mystrocentrism

Wasserstrom understands Corbin's hermeneutics of Islam as constituting a religion after religion. According to him, Corbin's depreciation of society and social theory demands myth and symbol. Hence, in his reflections on history as the unfolding of a great myth and in his attempt to tell a unified symbolic story, Corbin tends to diminish the little differences among the participants of the religious community and close up the gap of contradictions in the society of believers.[56] Corbin must be brought back to the challenge of difference and living otherness. It is this very challenge that must be met when dealing with Ibn al-ʿArabī:

> If History of Religions is to remain a broadly communicable intellectual operation, we teachers should resist mystocentrism. . . . The historiography made conventional by Corbin, which accepts Ibn al-ʿArabī's theosophical break-through as a great step forward, tacitly privileges "Akbarian" gnosis as pinnacle, or quintessence, of the entirety of Islam as a religion. The essence of religion thus is assumed to be found in religious experience; by a process of concentric essences, the essential kind of religious experience in turn is seen to be mystical experience.

> This is, in effect, an inheritance from Ibn al-ʿArabī himself. The problem is not that, in this way, we take the tradition as a guide; the problem is that we do so uncritically. . . . In the case of Ibn al-ʿArabī, it seems altogether plausible, if not imperative, to study him in all possible contexts. Following the model of a pioneer like Michel de Certeau, one can hope for a History of Religions inquiry into mysticism that is integrated with all kinds of inquiries—sociological, psychological, historical, theological. Ibn al-ʿArabī is too important to be left to a scholasticism.[57]

Wasserstrom's talk about "all possible contexts" and "all kinds of inquiries" and his emphasis on the importance of social differences and on staying "within the limits of human knowledge"[58] is a striking reminder of Rorty's contextualism and the latter's rejection of anything that transcends socially contextualized knowledge. Wasserstrom thinks that Corbin's representation of Ibn al-ʿArabī's mystical thought precludes the sort of rational communication that takes into consideration the socially differential context in which communication takes place. This is, again, a striking reminder of Rorty's emphasis on the significance of considering different justifications of meanings of sentences for different audiences, instead of attempting one universal conception of justification that cuts across all social settings.[59]

Wasserstrom seems to be aware that it might be hard, if not impossible, to study Ibn al-ʿArabī in the socially contextualized manner that he is suggesting. Perhaps this awareness explains his rather apologetic statement that although Corbin's study of Ibn al-ʿArabī implies certain rejection to the notion of being a historian, "we historians are entitled (if not obliged) of assess him in historical terms."[60] Wasserstrom, it seems, has failed to take Claude Addas' following words into account:

> In a sense his entire work is nothing but the record of his inner experience: visions, dialogues with the dead, ascensions, mysterious encounters in the "Imaginal World" (*ʿālam al-khayāl*), miraculous journeys in the celestial spheres. Whether they are a psychopath's fantasies, as Asin believed, or genuine spiritual perceptions as Corbin claimed, the fact is that for Ibn ʿArabī they were not only as real but much more real than the Andalusian earth on which he walked as a child. Everyone who devotes himself to studying the Shaikh al-Akbar—whether as a biographer or as a historian of ideas—must take this into account.[61]

Wasserstrom blames Corbin for being a prophetic philosopher who set forth a visionary history of the world[62] that was the projection of his own symbolic imagination rather than the true reflection of the reality of the world, which is a reality of difference. He complains that the history of the religion of Islam suffers from mystocentrism, which explains the frustration of scholars who seek to establish a communicative history of religion of "believers, in the public life of believers." [63] In my view, studying Ibn al-ʿArabī in the manner suggested by Wasserstrom might do to mysticism what the analytic philosophers have done to philosophy. To stay within the limits of the human rationality, that was the great achievement of Kant that was responsible for creating the analytic tradition and eventually bringing about the sort of Rortian contextualism in philosophy.[64] "To stay within the limits of human knowledge,"[65] that is what Wasserstrom wishes to begin in the study of mysticism, and by doing so commit mystical thought to the same destiny as philosophical thought.

Wasserstrom claims that the antisocial or antihistorical study of Ibn al-ʿArabī creates a religion after religion [66] exactly as Rorty claims that the emergence of epistemology as the core of philosophy serves to take over the role of religion in preserving the pathos of distance.[67] But, while Rorty's claim seems to make some sense, Wasserstrom's does not seem to make any. Rorty is criticizing a philosophy (analytic philosophy) that took upon itself the task of ridding us of all metaphysical or religious notions of transcendence, but found itself sharing with metaphysics and religion the effort of creating veils of ideas and preserving the pathos of distance. Hence, Rorty seems to make some sense in accusing analytic philosophy of defeating its own principles. Mystical thought, however, is innocent of the crime that Wasserstrom tries to frame it with. Mystical thought never aspired to ridding itself of the belief in higher truths. On the contrary, mystics, and Ibn al-ʿArabī in particular, have always declared that their thought is at the heart of the religious. If they are using their declaration in the special context of the mystical language game in order to hide a big lie, as Carter's view presumes, this must be left for careful examination. But one cannot blame the mystics for contradicting a principle that was never part of their declaration.

CHAPTER 2

Creation ex nihilo, Creation in Time, and Eternal Creation: Ibn Sīnā versus the Theologians

The controversy between Islamic theologians and Islamic philosophers is presented in this work as consisting of two major parts. The present chapter covers the first part while the next chapter, which deals with the controversy between Ibn Rushd and Ghazālī, covers the second part. The problem singled out as central in the debate is the problem of the creation of the world, which is the problem of the relationship between God and the world. The general trend of the discussion will be toward revealing the creative tension in the positions of the parties involved in the debate and preparing the stage for the sort of resolution of the tension proposed by Ibn al-ʿArabī through his unique concept of the Limit (barzakh).

Creation ex nihilo in the Qur'ān

Richard Netton counts the capacity to create ex nihilo among the four basic characteristics ascribed to the Creator in the Qur'ān.[1] According to the Qur'ānic "Creator Paradigm," God is a being who (1) creates ex nihilo, (2) intervenes in historical events, (3) guides his people, and (4) can be known through his creation. Netton believes that despite the wide range of the exegesis of Scriptures, the majority of the interpreters of the Qur'ān agreed upon these characteristics.[2]

The commentators on the Qur'ān in general insist that creation ex nihilo is a Qur'ānic doctrine. To support this view, Bayḍāwī (d. 1286) cites Q 40:57, which asserts that creating the heavens and the earth is greater than creating man. This is so, according to Bayḍāwī, because God made man from a previously existing material, while the heavens and the earth he created out of nothing.[3]

This explanation seems to be inconsistent with other verses in the Qur'ān that depict the creation of the world from a preexistent matter. Wolfson mentions, for example, Q 41:11: "Then He applied Himself to the [creation of] heaven and it was smoke." But he explains that according to Zamakhsharī (d. 1144), the preexistent smoke itself was created, for the smoke proceeded from the water under the throne of God and the throne of God is one of the things created before the heavens and the earth.[4] Wolfson takes note of the passage in the Qur'ān that seems to imply that creation was ex nihilo, namely Q 52:35: "Where they created *min ghayri shay'in*?" The phrase *min ghayri shay'in* can be taken to mean "from nothing." But, it can also be taken to mean "Were they created by nothing?" or "Were they created for no purpose?" Wolfson concludes by saying that the position of the Qur'ān on the nature of creation is vague.[5]

Several scholars have maintained the view that there is no decisive evidence in the Qur'ān in favor of creation ex nihilo. Oliver Leaman says that the language of the Qur'ān is not precise enough to come down clearly on one side or another with respect to the nature of creation, and that even texts which might seem to point in the direction of creation ex nihilo can easily be interpreted otherwise.[6] Dominique Urvoy supports Roger Arnaldez's statement that the idea of creation ex nihilo is not stated explicitly in the Qur'ān, and that it has to be projected on the Qur'ānic text in order for one to find it there.[7] Similarly, David Burrell says that when scholars seek to remind us that the Scriptural texts should not be invoked in support of the notion of creation ex nihilo they are making a stand against reading later conceptual refinements into these texts.[8] Ibn Rushd's following words might be a suitable summary of the views of the above-mentioned scholars:

> It will be evident from the verses which give us information about the bringing into existence of the world that its form really is originated, but that being itself and time extend continuously at both extremes, i.e. without interruption. Thus the words of God the Exalted, "He it is Who created the heavens and the earth in six days, and His throne was on the water," taken in their apparent meaning imply that there was a being before this present being, namely the throne and the water, and a time before this time. . . . Thus the theologians too in their statements about the world do not conform to the apparent meaning of Scripture but interpret it allegorically. For it is not stated in the Scripture that God was existing with absolutely nothing else: a text to this effect is nowhere to be found.[9]

Ibn Rushd claims that by interpreting the Qur'ānic account of creation allegorically the theologians are in effect admitting the importance of rational interpretation. His opinion is that it is not merely permissible to interpret the

Qur'ānic account of creation along rationalist lines, but that it is in fact an intellectual duty to do so, rendered obligatory by Islamic Law. Without it, it would be impossible to draw the unknown, or the hidden from the known, or the apparent in the Scriptures. Ibn Rushd's emphasis on the significance of interpretation is consistent with the line of thought of Islamic philosophers who sought to establish a proper harmony between religion and philosophy by interpreting religious ideas as symbols of philosophical truth.[10]

The majority of Islamic theologians did not object to the view that rational interpretation is important for understanding the meanings of the words of the Scriptures. The strong emphasis on the importance of reason (*'aql*) in the Qur'ān alone would render such an objection self-defeating.[11] The theologians suspected, however, that the philosophers were applying their reasoning for the sake of justifying philosophical theories borrowed from ancient authorities, which they considered a threat to the teaching of the Scriptures.[12] That is why, well before the time of Ghazālī, the theologians came to acknowledge the importance of learning rational argumentation for refuting the arguments of their opponents. In the following, I will discuss two of the theologians' arguments against what they conceived as the most threatening of the philosophers' doctrines, namely, Aristotle's doctrine of the eternity of the world.

Creation ex nihilo, Creation in Time, and Islamic Theologians

Etienne Gilson points out that the first question that early Greek thinkers asked themselves was about the most fundamental stuff of which the world was made. In their search for the single underlying reality, they reduced the world to water, then to air, then to fire, until Parmenides came out with his contention that the ultimate reality consists of Being. Gilson writes:

> When he made his discovery, Parmenides of Elea at once carried metaphysical speculation to what was always to remain one of its ultimate limits; but, at the same time, he entangled himself in what still is for us one of the worst metaphysical difficulties. It had been possible for Parmenides' predecessors to identify nature with water, fire or air, without going to the trouble of defining the meaning of those terms. If I say that everything is water, everybody will understand what I mean, but if I say that everything is being, I can safely expect to be asked: what is being? For indeed we all know many things, but what being itself is, or what it is to be, is an extremely obscure and intricate question.[13]

One of the most serious difficulties entailed in Parmenides' position is that his notion of Being precludes the possibility of becoming or change. As Gilson explains, a cause of the existence of Being, or of its destruction, is inconceivable, because a cause must *be* first before it *becomes* a cause. The notion of Being is, therefore, prior to the notions of causality and becoming. Moreover, any fundamental modification in the structure of Being is inconceivable, since this would imply that something that was not *is* beginning to be, or is becoming.[14] F. M. Cornford reduces the premises of Parmenides' theory of Being to three:

1. That which is, is, and cannot not-be; that which is not, is not, and cannot be.
2. That which is can be thought or known; that which is not, cannot.
3. That which is, is one and cannot be many.[15]

Although Parmenides does not address the problem of creation as a religious question, I think, following Ruhi Afnan, that his theory of Being implies the denial of the notion of creation as it was conceived by Islamic theologians.[16] Following Lenn Goodman, I think also that, in contrast to the theologians, Islamic philosophers were good Parmenideans, as was Aristotle, their first authority.[17] As Goodman explains, Islamic philosophers rejected the notion of pure non-being, emphasized the identity of being and intelligibility, and disapproved of causeless, unprecedented happenings, such as creation ex nihilo, as illogical.[18] To state that the world is created out of nothing means that being was generated from nonbeing, a statement that is inadmissible in Aristotle, since it infringes upon the principles of intelligibility.[19]

Following Aristotle, Islamic philosophers claimed that to think that the world comes to be from unqualified nonbeing is to think something unintelligible; is to think nothing.[20] However, for Islamic theologians, who represented the orthodox view, the philosophers' adherence to Aristotle's distinction between qualified and unqualified nonbeing was only another attempt to subvert the words of the Scriptures, since creation ex nihilo was precisely what the Qur'ān taught. For example, Q 19:8 reads "That is what your Lord says: 'That is easy for Me: I did indeed create you before, and you had been nothing (*walam taku shay'an*).'" We may interpret the verse as implying that God made man when he was nothing of what he is now. Still, there seems to be in this verse a miraculous dimension that is assigned to the notion of creation and that does not fit neatly in the rational scheme of the philosophers. Creation out of pure nonbeing is a miraculous event. God alone is the author of miracles, and it is a main feature of a miracle (*muʿjiza*) that it renders reason incapable of comprehending the manner of its transpiring. The notion of creation ex nihilo was considered a serious challenge[21] to human rationality, one that is especially designed to compel humans to acknowledge the limitations of their rational faculty so that they may believe in God unconditionally. Indeed, to demonstrate the limitation of reason as a way for preparing people for the unquestionable acceptance of the notion of creation ex nihilo was Ghazālī's main strategy in his polemics against the philosophers in *The Incoherence of the Philosophers*.

In an earlier period of the theological polemic, the Muʿtazilites, due to their strong commitment to rational explanation, seemed to have a problem with the conceivability of the notion of creation ex nihilo. Wolfson brings Ibn Ḥazm's statement that (almost) all Muʿtazilites believed that the nonexistent (*al-maʿdūm*) is something (*shay'*), and emphasizes that this view about the nonexistent was evidently contrary to the view that prevailed among the orthodox.[22] According to Wolfson, the Muʿtazilites' belief in the existence of the nonexistent goes back to Greek origins. The Muʿtazilites became acquainted with Plato's theory of the creation of the world out of a preexistent eternal matter in *Timaeus*, and with Aristotle's theory that nothing can come out of nonexistence in an absolute sense. They also learned about Aristotle's principle that matter is not nonexistent in an absolute sense but only accidentally. As Muslim thinkers, faithful to the apparent teaching of the Qur'ān, the Muʿtazilites could not accept Aristotle's doctrine of the eternity of the world in time, but they could find no evidence in the Qur'ān against the notion of preexistent matter. And so, Wolfson concludes, they accepted Plato's account of the creation of the world in time from a preexistent matter.[23]

The question whether the nonexistent is something or nothing was a major dividing line between the Muʿtazilites and the Ashʿarite theologians.[24] However, due to the influence of the apparent teaching of the Qur'ān, and despite their disagreement with the Ashʿarites over the problem of the nonexistent and other related issues, the Muʿtazilites protested against the philosophers' doctrine of the eternity of the world and provided arguments in its refutation. Wolfson mentions eight theological arguments in favor of the createdness of the world.[25] The argument that is relevant to the discussion of the creation of the world in time is the Argument from the Impossibility of an Infinite by Succession. Different versions of this argument were utilized by Muʿtazilites and Ashʿarites, but the argument in its original form is based on John Philoponus's refutation of Aristotle's doctrine of the eternity of the world.[26]

Aristotle defines the infinite as "What is incapable of being gone through, because it is not its nature to be gone through."[27] He argues that there cannot exist a body that is actually infinite.[28] If it does, "any part of it that is taken will be infinite, if it has parts: for 'to be infinite' and 'the infinite' are the same. . . . Hence it will be either indivisible or divisible into infinities. But the same thing cannot be many infinities."[29] He admits, however, that to suppose that the infinite does not exist in any way leads to impossible consequences. One of these consequences is that time, which is infinite, will be finite.[30] To avoid this difficulty Aristotle draws a distinction between actual and potential infinites. Only the potential infinite (time, for example) does exist in the sense that its parts exist successively, that is, one after another and not simultaneously as in the case of the parts of the actual infinite.[31]

Philoponus advanced two arguments against the concept of the infinite by succession, or the potential infinite, on the basis of which Aristotle established his doctrine of the eternity of the world. The interesting point is that Philoponus's arguments are based upon two principles established by Aristotle himself. The first principle is that no infinite can be traversed in a limited time, and the second principle is that nothing can be greater than the infinite. It follows from the second principle that it cannot be the case that one infinite can be greater than another infinite.[32] In his first argument, Philoponus says that, under the assumption of the eternity of the world, the number of the generated individuals of any species must be actually infinite. For if we suppose a finite number of individuals, then each individual of the species must have its existence in a finite time and the whole time will be finite. If then the succession, advancing from one individual to another, arrives at things now existing through an infinite number of individuals, the infinite has to be traversed, which is impossible according to Aristotle's first principle. Thus, on the basis of the principle that an infinite cannot be traversed, if the number of individuals was infinite in the past, no individual could have come into existence.[33] Philoponus's second argument against Aristotle's doctrine of the eternity of the world is based on Aristotle's principle that one infinite cannot be greater than another. The argument reads, "If the world has no beginning in time, then the generated number [of men] up to the time of Socrates, for instance, would be infinite; but if to that number were added the men generated from the time of Socrates to the present time, there would be something greater than the infinite, which is impossible."[34]

In addition, Philoponus argues that the assumption of the eternity of the world leads to the following absurdity: We know that the sphere of Saturn completes its revolution in thirty years, while the sphere of Jupiter completes its revolution in twelve years. Given the assumption that the time of the world is infinite, the revolutions of Jupiter and Saturn must be equally infinite. Yet, we know that the sphere of Jupiter completes almost three times as many revolutions as the sphere of Saturn. This is impossible, however, if time is infinite, since one infinite cannot be greater than another infinite.[35]

Islamic theologians employed different versions of Philoponus's arguments against the eternity of the world. Naẓẓām (d. 845), a Muʿtazilite, introduced two arguments. In the first argument, he states that if the revolutions of the celestial bodies are infinite they can have no first. But that which has no first revolution could have no succession of revolutions up to some given day. The fact that whatever has passed does arrive at some end is a proof that it has a first, that is, it is a proof that it is finite. Naẓẓām's second argument states that, under the assumption of the eternity of the world, adding the number of the revolutions of one planet to the number of the revolutions of another planet creates an infinite number of revolutions that is greater than the infinite number of the revolutions of each planet. Yet, this cannot be the case, since one infinite cannot be greater than another infinite.[36]

Juwaynī (d. 1065), an Ashʿarite, advances the following argument for the impossibility of the existence of an infinite by succession. He says that the believers in the eternity of the world maintain that an infinite number of revolutions must have elapsed prior to any given revolution in a given time. But that which is infinite, through the succession of one unit after another, cannot come to an end. But it is a fact that the revolutions, which preceded the revolution in a given time, have come to an end and, therefore, they must be finite.[37]

As we can see, establishing the conception of the finitude of time played a crucial role in the theologians' refutation of the philosophers' doctrine of the eternity of the world, which was established on the basis of a conception of time that was exactly the opposite of that of the theologians. This was Aristotle's conception according to which every moment of time is a limit between two times, each one of which is also a limit between two times ad infinitum. Thus, time consists potentially of an infinite number of limits with no first limit in which the process begins or a last in which it ends.[38] On the basis of this conception of time, Ibn Sīnā argued in favor of the eternity of the world by demonstrating that the very postulation of the notion of a first to the time of the world entails the expression *before*, which indicates the prior and necessary existence of time.[39] Ibn Sīnā's conception of time as continuous was essential for establishing the actuality of the causal relation between God and the world. Apart from this conception, an unbridgeable gap would separate God, the First Cause, from the world, his immediate effect. Ibn Sīnā considered postulating such a gap as indicating a logical fault in the way of thinking of the theologians.

In their part, the theologians were concerned with the preservation of a separating limit between the creative activity of God and its temporal effect. That is why they adhered to a discontinuous (atomistic) conception of time. Maimonides states that the theologians inferred their view about the atomistic nature of time from Aristotle's claim that space, time, and motion have a close correspondence to each other. They argued that if bodies consisted of indivisible particles, then, by applying Aristotle's correspondence principle, time must consist of indivisible particles as well.[40] The theologians' eagerness to emphasize the independence of God from the world, their insistence on denying the notion of the concomitance of creation with the eternal existence of God, and their adherence to the atomistic conception of time led them to a doctrine of continuous creation (*al-khalq al-mutajaddid*), according to which the existence of the world is an immediate product made possible each instant anew. The world consists of atoms that cannot endure for two instants of time so that nonbeing belongs to them essentially. The atom endures only through

God's imparting to it the accident of duration, which also cannot endure for two instants.[41]

This atomistic conception of the world led the theologians to an occasionalist stand, most critical of the philosophers' depiction of the necessity of causal relationships between things in the world. As Michael Marmura points out, the theologians' occasionalist criticism of natural causation was in conflict with the position of Ibn Sīnā, who was involved with the Ashʿarites in a serious debate concerning such matters as the manner of the creation of the world and the related issue of the necessity of the laws of nature.[42] The thing that bothered Ibn Sīnā most about the theologians' position was the consequences of their occasionalist view, which depicted the world as consisting of separated atoms created by God in disconnected instants. Such a depiction of reality seemed to defy the very purpose of rational reflection, since this is conditioned on observing regularities and establishing laws of nature that govern the manner of the existence and the causal interactions of things in the world. Nonetheless, in his disagreement with the theologians, Ibn Sīnā seemed to have been involved in a serious predicament. For the theologians developed their occasionalist view in the context of their attack on the Aristotelian doctrine of the eternity of the world, in which context they applied Aristotelian principles. And so, when Ibn Sīnā sought to reconcile the Aristotelian position with that of the theologians, this was not, as Ibn Rushd protested later, because of his forced yielding to the dogma of the theologians of orthodoxy. Far from it, the curious tension in Ibn Sīnā's position was due to an inherent tension in the very Aristotelian rationalism that he was trying to defend.

Ibn Sīnā's Answers to the Theologians' Arguments

Ibn Sīnā provides a brief summary of the theologians' arguments against the eternity of the world in the *Ishārāt* ,[43] followed by the following responses: (1) What applies to the parts of a whole does not apply to the whole itself. Each one of the parts of an infinite number is limited, but the infinite number itself is not limited. The theologians observed the coming to be and the ceasing of existence of individuals of species, and inferred that the whole species begins in time. This cannot be the case, however, since there is a contradiction in assuming that an infinite number can exist in actuality.[44] (2) No impossible consequences follow from adding to or subtracting from the number of the instances of an infinite, if the infinite in question is nonexistent. For example, the assumption of an infinite number of revolutions in the circular celestial motion does not contradict the fact that the number of revolutions may be more or less.[45] (3) The occasion of the coming to existence of a given instance *a* is witnessed to be dependent on the existence of another instance *b*. The existence of *b* does not depend on an infinite number of instances, but only on one specific instance, which preceded it in existence. There is no impossibility in continuing this process ad infinitum.[46] Concerning this last point, it is worth bringing Ibn Sīnā's full response:

> As for the argument concerning the dependence (*tawaqquf*) of one thing for its occurrence on an infinite number of occurrences or the need (*iḥtiyāj*) of one thing for an infinite number of occurrences to be traversed up to [the time of] its occurrence, [we say that] it is a false argument. For the meaning of our saying that something depended on another is that the two things are characterized as nonexistent, and that the second nonexistent thing would not become existent until the first nonexistent thing enters into existence. The same thing can be said about the need [for traversing the infinite]. Moreover, it is not correct to say at any time that the last was dependent on the existence of an infinite number of occurrences or that it required an infinite number of occurrences to be traversed up to the time of its occurrence. . . . If you mean by dependence that the last thing did not exist before the existence of things each one of which occurred in a different time and that the times must be therefore uncountable, then your meaning must be absurd. [After all] this is what is disputed, namely, whether or not the thing is possible, and how can the assumption of its possibility be used to refute itself?[47]

In addition to these refutations of the theologians' arguments, Ibn Sīnā provides his positive argument for the preexistence of the world in time: If the world was created in time, then its existence must have occurred after its nonexistence in a prior time, in which case the time of its present existence is the antecedent of a preceding time in which it did not exist. Hence, there can be no such thing as a beginning of the world in time.[48] On the basis of this conception of time, Ibn Sīnā establishes his view of the nature of the causal relationship between God and the world. God is a perfect cause and, as such, he must not be separated in time from the immediate effect of his causation. The perfect conditions for the creation of the world were there from eternity and no time was better than another for God's acting. Hence, the notion of creation does not signify a priority of God to the world in time, but only the ontological priority of God to all things. God is prior to the world only essentially or ontologically and not temporally.[49] As Goodman points out, this nontemporal reading of the notion of creation was, for Ibn Sīnā, the only logically coherent reading of the Scriptural story of creation and the only plausible understanding of God's (absolute) imparting of existence on the world, since temporal stories of absolute creation in time undermine the very absoluteness which they seek to establish.[50]

One may wonder, however, whether Ibn Sīnā's doctrine is inconsistent with the very meaning of the notion of creation. If the world has been, is, and will eternally coexist with God, does not this amount to saying that creation is a term that signifies an act that has and will never occur? This was, indeed, one of Ghazālī's main points of criticism to Ibn Sīnā's account of creation. Ghazālī insisted that the Qur'ānic notion of the world's creation and Ibn Sīnā's doctrine of eternal creation were two mutually exclusive accounts of the world's origination, as the affirmation of the one leads necessarily to the negation of the other. Ibn Sīnā, according to Ghazālī, ignored this fact and exploited the notion of creation to disguise his philosophical belief in the uncreatedness of the world.[51]

Ibn Sīnā, however, employed the notion of eternal creation as a means to bridge the gap between the Aristotelian teaching of the eternity of the world and the apparent teaching of the Qur'ān. His notion of eternal creation proposed a synthesis between the Aristotelian account, which depicted necessity in the world that each kind of being bears within itself, and the theologians' account, which stressed the contingency and dependence of finite beings on the creative act of God. As Goodman explains, it was this synthesis of seeming opposites that enabled Ibn Sīnā to identify eternal creation as the true meaning of creation.[52] I think that Goodman is correct in saying that eternalist philosophers did not readily give up the language of creation; that they saw eternal creation not as an alternative to but as an interpretation of creation.[53] The nature of Ibn Sīnā's synthetic system of thought demanded the notion of creation, but it demanded that it be interpreted. The myth of creation symbolized for him the reality of ontological dependence of all beings upon God, a dependence that cannot be absolute if creation is temporal.

The ontological dependence in question is the dependence of the world, which may or may not exist, on God, who cannot not exist. Like the theologians, Ibn Sīnā reflected on the world as contingent and, consequently, as dependent on the necessary being of God. He complicates his view, however, as he claims that although the world may or may not exist it still exists necessarily, due to its eternal relationship with God. Ibn Sīnā's fusion (or confusion) between the doctrine of the contingency of the world and the doctrine of its eternity yielded a third possibility of a world possible-of-existence-in-itself and necessary-of-existence-by-the-other.

Ibn Sīnā on the Possible- and the Necessary-of-Existence

Richard Frank points out that in their reflections on the categories of possibility and necessity, as these categories bear upon the relation between God and the world, Islamic philosophers and theologians shared a common understanding.[54]

In both philosophy and theology the contingent is characterized as the possible that exists instead of its contrary. This, Frank says, is an Aristotelian doctrine based on the principle that the union of contraries is impossible in the same substrate at the same time. Both philosophers and theologians define the eternal as that whose nonbeing is impossible, which is also a common conception in the Aristotelian tradition.[55] Thus, both philosophers and theologians owe their definitions of the conceptions of the possible and the necessary to the Aristotelian rational principles of thought. This is so despite the fact that theologians often attacked Aristotle's logic,[56] or tried to minimize its significance.[57]

Ibn Sīnā shares with the theologians the Aristotelian rationalist assumption that an existent entity is possible *if* no logical contradiction follows from its nonexistence.[58] At this juncture, however, he parts company with the theologians. For, as Oliver Leaman explains, Ibn Sīnā introduces not one but two types of necessity. The first type is posited when a contradiction follows from assuming the nonexistence of the necessary, while the second type designates an entity which "regarded in respect to its essence, is possible but, regarded with respect to its actual relation to its cause, it is necessary."[59] Leaman emphasizes that this distinction between two types of necessity is curious, since it contradicts the conventional approach, which distinguishes between the possible which can, but does not exist, the possible which does exist in actuality, and the necessary which cannot not exist.[60] Ibn Sīnā claims that the possible cannot not exist, since in that case it would be impossible of existence: "The possible cannot not have existence for in that case it would be impossible. Thus it is now clear that everything necessary of existence by another thing is possible of existence by itself. And this is reversible, so that everything possible of existence by itself, if its existence has happened, is necessary of existence by another thing; because inevitably it must either truly have an actual existence or not truly have an actual existence—but it cannot not truly have an actual existence, for in that case it would be impossible of existence."[61]

Ibn Sīnā says that if the existence of the possible-of-existence has happened then it must be necessary of existence by another. But he says also that the possible-of-existence cannot not have existence, for in that case it would be impossible. One may conclude, therefore, that the possible-in-itself and the necessary-by-the-other are identical. Yet Ibn Sīnā refuses to admit this. For, according to him, the possible-in-itself and the necessary-by-the-other are two different conceptions signifying two different meanings.[62] The meaning of the possible-in-itself is that the thing by itself is neither existent nor nonexistent, whereas the meaning of the necessary-by-the-other is that the thing exists necessarily. One may protest, however, that from a metaphysical point of view this difference in meaning does not make any difference to the way things are in actual reality. There seems to be a contradiction inherent in Ibn Sīnā's view about the nature of beings, and to try to explain this contradiction away through differentiating between meanings may be perceived as an attempt to escape the contradiction rather than resolving it. There is, therefore, a tension in Ibn Sīnā's position, which is augmented by another distinction that he makes between the essence of a thing and its existence.

Ibn Sīnā's Distinction between Essence and Existence

Ibn Sīnā makes a clear distinction between the essence of a thing, or its proper nature (*ḥaqīqa*), and its existence (*wujūd*), and refers to this distinction throughout his work.[63] Was the distinction between the essence of a thing and its existence an original contribution of Ibn Sīnā? Scholars differed considerably on this question. David Burrell at one time held that no Greek thinker nor pagan commentator had explicitly stated the distinction and that one was justified in attributing it to Ibn Sīnā.[64] In *Knowing the Unknowable God*, however, he traces the roots of the distinction back to Aristotle's statement in *Posterior Analytics* that the definition of a thing and its existence are not the same thing.[65] Soheil Afnan maintains the same view, asserting that the logical distinction existed already in Aristotle's discussion of definitions, but that Ibn Sīnā developed the distinction in an original manner and within a system of thought, which he made his own.[66] Other scholars insist that Ibn Sīnā only borrowed a logical distinction that he found in Aristotle, and that he never put it forth as his own invention.[67]

Etienne Gilson has an especially interesting view: Ibn Sīnā's claim that existence is an accident added to the essence of a thing stems from his religious drive to justify the account of creation of the monotheistic religion of Islam. According to him, the importance of the distinction comes from recognizing that if the world has been created, then *to be* is the first thing that happened to it. The existence of beings in the world is something that *happens* to them, that is, is an accident added to their essence.[68] On the basis of Gilson's analysis, I think that although the roots of Ibn Sīnā's distinction can be traced back to Aristotle's logical discussion of definitions, the distinction becomes notably original when situated in the context of Ibn Sīnā's attempt to establish harmony between Greek philosophy and Islamic religion. In elaborating on this point, I will rely on Goodman's discussion of Ibn Sīnā's metaphysics.[69]

Goodman explains that although Aristotle was aware of the distinction between essence and existence, the distinction for him was only logical, since for a thing to be is for it to have the essence that it has. Beings are substances whose existence is identical to their essence. Their nature allows for accidental change but preserves continuity through the change.[70] Ibn Sīnā allowed for the logical distinction between essence and existence to have a profound impact on metaphysics. He thought that even in the category of substance, where being is conceived in its primary sense, a distinction must be made between the essence of a thing and its existence.[71] Substances are essentially possible in themselves, but are necessary only through the act of the existence-giving of God. What makes beings necessary is what gives them existence. This applies to beings in the cosmos as well as to the cosmos itself as a whole. For according to Ibn Sīnā, even if the cosmos is eternal or infinite, its existence is still necessary not in itself but through the existence giving of God. Thus, there is no self-contradiction in denying the existence of the entire world even though it has always existed.[72] Goodman cites Fazlur Rahman's comment on this reasoning: "This is the true meaning of the famous metaphysical dictum 'Existence is accidental to essence.' It means that the contingent is never rid of its contingency and never becomes self-necessary like God."[73] This conclusion is the opposite of the one we arrived at in the previous discussion. We have seen how, by rationally analyzing the concept of the possible-in-itself, Ibn Sīnā had to conclude that the possible-in-itself is a thing that must come into existence. This is certainly a conclusion that fits in the system of thought of Aristotle, for whom beings in the world and the world as a whole exist necessarily. Here, however, we come to the conclusion that the possible things in the world, and the world itself as a whole, are never rid of their contingency. This conclusion fits more in the system of thought of Islamic theologians.[74]

By drawing the distinction between the essence of a thing and its existence, Ibn Sīnā sought to describe a cosmos that is a middle entity between the cosmos of Aristotle and the cosmos of the theologians. The cosmos is contingent in the sense that its existence is imparted on it by God, but is necessary in the sense that God's imparting of existence on it is eternal.[75] The important difference between Ibn Sīnā and the theologians in this respect is that according to Ibn Sīnā, the imparting of existence on the cosmos does not take place through a temporal process. Goodman emphasizes Rahman's assertion that for Ibn Sīnā existence is not posterior in time to the essence of things, but is prior only logically and ontologically to the determination of their essences.[76] Following Rahman, Goodman asserts that when it comes to Ibn Sīnā's distinction between essence and existence, thinking in terms of posteriority is one of the most prominent misinterpretations of his doctrine of the contingency of being.[77] He concludes by saying that creation for Ibn Sīnā is not the imparting of existence to what previously lacked it, since the temporality invoked by such a notion precludes the absolute or eternal nature of God's creative act. Moreover, he insists against critics, who accuse him of denying creation in favor of the Aristotelian doctrine of the eternity of the world, that he was as motivated by the doctrine of absolute creation as by Aristotle's doctrine of the eternity of the world.[78]

It must be clear, however, that what Goodman means by absolute creation in Ibn Sīnā has little, if anything, to do with absolute creation, as the theologians perceived it. What the theologians regarded as a true account of the creation of the world in time is for Ibn Sīnā a mythical or an explanatory tool to the effect that the world would not have come into existence without God's imparting of existence on it. The relationship between God and the world is ultimately an intellectual one, and Goodman seems to be correct in saying that Ibn Sīnā's rationalism was based on the assumption that the world can be made intelligible by way of explanations.[79]

By introducing the formula of the "possible-of-existence-in-itself, necessary-of existence-by-the-other," Ibn Sīnā sought to provide a rational synthesis of two contradictory accounts of the relationship between God and the world. His synthesis, however, proved to be problematic. For it seems to have contained two contradictory propositions: the world is possible in itself; the world is necessary by the other. Reconciling these two propositions must be inconsistent with Ibn Sīnā's rationalist assumption that a thing considered *in itself* is something different altogether from a thing considered *in relation* to the actuality of its causes.[80] It turns out that Ibn Sīnā's rational explanation of the relationship between God and the world rests on a notion (the notion of the thing as possible in itself and necessary by the other) that is not intelligible in itself. Jacob L. Teicher assigns this notion to the intuitive part of Ibn Sīnā's thought. He points out that Ibn Sīnā attempted in his metaphysical account of creation to combine the rationalistic and the intuitive components of his thought, but that he ended up with a body of thought most of which is derived from rationalistic philosophy, whereas the soul of the body, which consists of the concept of the possible-of-existence-in-itself and necessary-of-existence-by-the-other, is based on intuition.[81]

Ibn Sīnā's rational analysis led him to the conclusion that the only way to account for the relation between God and the world is to reflect on the world as possible of existence in itself and necessary of existence by the other. Nonetheless, he continued to insist that the world-in-itself is totally different from the world as necessary by the other. Ibn Sīnā's rational analysis led him to a synthesis that is not rational according to his own analytical standards. The tension in Ibn Sīnā's position is characteristic of his metaphysical account of eternal creation, which seeks to provide a synthesis between the assumed creationist teachings of the theologians and the Aristotelian doctrine of the eternity of the world. This tension was fully exploited by Ghazālī in his attack on the theory of eternal creation in *The Incoherence of the Philosophers*. In *The Incoherence of the Incoherence* Ibn Rushd undertakes the task of defending philosophy, attempting to rid it of the tension created by Ibn Sīnā, but ending up lifting Ibn Sīnā's rather problematic synthesis to a higher and more sophisticated level.

CHAPTER 3

Ibn Rushd versus al-Ghazālī on the Eternity of the World

Between *The Incoherence of the Philosophers* and *The Incoherence of the Incoherence*

Much has been said about the debate between Ghazālī and Ibn Rushd, or between the *Incoherence of the Philosophers* and the *Incoherence of the Incoherence*. My concern is not merely with the details of the debate, although some crucial moments of it are accounted for in this chapter. Rather it is about introducing the debate in such a manner as to highlight the significant role that the notion of the Limit plays in it. In this sense, this chapter continues the same strategy adopted in the previous chapter by revealing the paradoxical development in the thought of the parties involved in the debate, as the notion of the Limit becomes the locus of the evolution of this development.

Abū Ḥāmid al-Ghazālī (d. 1111) lived in a time in which Islamic philosophical and theological traditions had reached a very advanced stage. He wrote an autobiography[1] in which he described his struggle with skepticism on his way to liberation from the shackles of both theology and philosophy by means of mystical knowledge. It is believed that Ghazālī wrote *The Incoherence of the Philosophers* in this period of skepticism.[2] Ghazālī's attitude toward theology seems to be marked by a certain ambivalence. On the one hand, he launched his attacks on the philosophers in *The Incoherence of the Philosophers* on the basis of theological assumptions. On the other hand, however, he believed that engaging in theological disputations engenders controversy and results in a loss of morality.[3] The same ambivalence surrounds his attitude toward philosophy, as careful readers of *The Incoherence of the Philosophers* can sense beneath the surface of his attack on philosophy the great passion that he had for philosophical polemic. Oliver Leaman has appropriately characterized Ghazālī's relationship with philosophy as a love-hate relationship.[4] Moreover, as William Chittick states, Ghazālī's objection was not to the sort of training of the mind that philosophers advocated but to certain conclusions that they reached.[5]

Ghazālī was described by Ibn Rushd as a man who "adhered to no one doctrine in his books but was an Ashʿarite with the Ashʿarites, a Ṣūfī with the Ṣūfīs and a philosopher with the philosophers."[6] He was also described by Ibn Ṭufayl (d. 1184) as a man whose works "bind in one place and loose in another."[7] Ibn Ṭufayl expresses his wonder at Ghazālī's providing an apology for his inconsistent practice, saying, "If my words have done no more than to shake you in the faith of your fathers, that would have been reason enough to write them. For he who does not doubt does not look; and he who does not look will not see, but must remain in blindness and confusion."[8] To shake the believer in the faith of his fathers was what Ghazālī set out to do in *The Incoherence of the Philosophers*, declaring that his objective was to alert those who think well of the philosophers. Thus, he insists that in his argument with them he does not claim and affirm but only demands and denies.[9] Ghazālī plays the role of the skeptic, who concerns himself solely with revealing the contradictions in the position of the philosophers. It is a fact, however, that he wrote his *Incoherence* as a theologian affirming theological convictions. Hence, Van Den Bergh's characterization of Ghazālī as a great dogmatist is appropriate.[10] Nevertheless, as Michael Marmura explains, when Ghazālī argues on the basis of theological assumptions in *The Incoherence of the Philosophers*, he does this as part of his polemic to refute, and does not attempt to develop in a positive way a theological system.[11]

Ibn Rushd believed that exposing the untutored masses to theoretical discussions runs the risk of undermining their religious faith and generating conflict instead of harmony in the community. At the same time, he considered it a transgression to withhold theoretical discussions from philosophers-to-be. Thus he was, on the one hand, reluctant to respond to Ghazālī's *Incoherence*, regarding most of its arguments as merely dialectical and as devoid of demonstrative truth. On the other hand, however, he found it mandatory to defend philosophy against Ghazālī's attack. In doing so, he was working with great caution, as he still believed that exposing the genuine opinions of the philosophers might cause harm to the masses.[12] This was one methodological difficulty that he encountered. Another difficulty arose from the fact that Ghazālī's attack on philosophy was directed mainly against Ibn Sīnā, with whom Ibn Rushd was in much disagreement in the first place. Thus, Oliver Leaman is correct in saying that in *The Incoherence of the Incoherence* Ibn Rushd was fighting with one hand tied behind his back.[13]

In *The Incoherence of the Philosophers* Ghazālī attacks the philosophers on twenty problems.[14] He discusses the problem of the eternity of the world first and devotes to it about a quarter of his book. Islamic thinkers attributed the doctrine of the eternity of the world to Aristotle. Van Den Bergh identifies the contradiction that Ghazālī detected in Aristotle's position: Aristotle affirmed, on the one hand, that the motion of the cosmos is eternal. On the other hand, he believed in the finitude of causes, as there must be a First Principle from which movement is derived. Hence, Aristotle held both contradictory propositions: that time and movement are infinite, and that every causal series must be finite.[15] According to Van Den Bergh, Islamic philosophers further accentuated the contradiction in Aristotle by reflecting on God not only as the First Mover of the universe but also as the Creator from whom the universe emanates eternally. He introduced the difficulty in the philosophers' position in the form of the following question: "Can there be a causal relation between an eternally unchangeable God and an eternally revolving and changing world, and is it sense to speak of a creation of that which exists eternally?"[16]

Ghazālī introduces the philosophers' theory of the eternity of the world as established on the basis of four proofs. He gives a detailed account of the philosophers' arguments, followed by his own counter arguments. I will devote the next three sections of the discussion to the philosophers' proofs for the eternity of the world,[17] Ghazālī's objections to them and Ibn Rushd's response to Ghazālī's objections. I will devote the last section to a fuller exposition of Ibn Rushd's doctrine of eternal creation as well as the difficulties that stem from his position.

The First Proof

The philosophers' argument in the first proof for the eternity of the world is based on the assumption that before the existence of the world all moments of time are identical and that, in such a circumstance, there is no sufficient reason for determining the origination of the world in a specific time.[18] Ghazālī introduces two objections to this argument.[19] His first objection is that there is no impossibility in assuming that the world had been created by an eternal will, which had decreed its existence in the time in which it existed. He defines divine will as an attribute the nature of which is to differentiate between similar things, and asserts that even the human will is endowed with such a nature. For example, a hungry man may not be able to tell the difference between two dates, and still he can take the one and leave the other.[20] Ibn Rushd protests that Ghazālī's objection is based on the false assumption that things willed may be identical. This is impossible, however, since things willed are opposites and all opposites can be reduced to the opposition of being and not being. The man in Ghazālī's example does not prefer the act of taking one definite date to the other but the act of taking to the act of leaving. His will favors the existence of the act over its nonexistence.[21]

It should be clear that Ghazālī and Ibn Rushd's arguments are based on different standpoints from rational deliberation. Ghazālī thinks that reason is limited, as its activity consists of reflecting on whatever material the senses provide to it. When the senses fail to distinguish between objects that seem identical, reason's judgment is suspended. If reason displays such a limitation in relation to the decrees of man's will how much so should it be limited when it comes to the working of the transcendent decrees of God's Will? In the *Revival of the Sciences of Religion* he illustrates this point through the following example:

> I wonder how He will answer the Muʿtazilī in his statement that *al-aṣlaḥ* is obligatory upon Him, hypothesizing a debate in the Hereafter between a youth and a mature man, both of whom died Muslims; and God elevates the degree of the adult and prefers him to the youth. . . . And if the youth says, "Oh, Lord, why did you raise his rank over mine?" God will say, "Because he became an adult and exercised his judgment (*ijtahada*) in acts of obedience." So the boy will say, "You caused me to die young, while you should have prolonged my life so that I could grow up and exercise *my* judgment. . . . Then the Almighty will say, "Because I knew that if you grew up you would have been a polytheist or a sinner, so it was better for you to die in your youth"— this is the Muʿtazilī's excuse for God Almighty—and thereupon the unbelievers will call out from the lowest levels of Hell fire and say . . . "Why did you not cause *us* to die young?"[22]

The proper conclusion to be drawn from this example is that whatever reason (*ʿaql*) assesses has no necessary connection to transcendent assessments. According to Kevin Reinhardt, this statement summarizes the view of the Ashʿarites, the epistemological opposites of the Muʿtazilites.[23] Following the broad thrust of this view, Ghazālī states that the world existed in the way it existed in the time in which it existed by a divine will, and questions about why it was created now and not at some other time only entangle reason in unsolvable contradictions.

For Ibn Rushd this conclusion must be inappropriate since it negates the very essence of rational knowledge, which consists of knowing the causes of things or their ultimate principles: "Another example is His saying, 'Have they not studied the kingdom of the heavens and the earth, and whatever things God has created?' This is a text urging the study of the totality of beings."[24] Hence, he thinks that it is obligatory to inquire not only about things in the cosmos, but also about the cosmos itself as a totality. This inquiry belongs at the heart of metaphysics (*ilāhiyyāt*), the essence of Islamic philosophy, and the realm of its chief contribution,[25] which is, in part, what rendered Ghazālī's criticism especially threatening in the philosopher's eyes. Another important reason that urged Ibn Rushd to not let Ghazālī's challenge go unanswered was the latter's claim that rational argument is what led him to his critical convictions.[26] One such argument is that the assumption of the eternity of the world implies that an infinite number of revolutions of the spheres have expired, although their number in limited time can be divided by six, four, and two.[27] Moreover, the number of the revolutions of the spheres must be either even or uneven. If it is infinite, however, the philosophers will have to draw the absurd conclusion that it is neither even nor uneven.[28]

Ibn Rushd's answer to this argument is basically identical to Ibn Sīnā's answer for the same argument,[29] but the conclusions that he draws differ drastically from Ibn Sīnā's. Like Ibn Sīnā, he distinguishes between potential (accidental) and actual (essential) infinite, emphasizing that only the former is acknowledged by the philosophers. Consequently, there cannot be a proportion between two movements in their totality, since they are both potentially infinite, although there can be a proportion between their actual parts.[30] Ibn Rushd states that the distinction between potential and actual infinites provides an answer to the greatest of the objections leveled by the theologians against the doctrine of the eternity of the world: If we assume that the movements in the past are infinite, then it is impossible for a movement in the present to take place, unless an actual infinite number of preceding movements is terminated.[31] The argument consists of the following hypothetical syllogism:

1.1. If the series of temporally originated things has no beginning, then it has no end.
1.2. But the series of temporally originated things has an end.
1.3. Therefore, it is false that the series of temporally originated things has no beginning.[32]

Ibn Rushd says that the philosophers do not admit the minor premise in the syllogism. No philosopher allows the existence of an infinite number of causes, since this would imply the existence of an effect without cause and a motion without a mover. Once the minor premise is rejected, the argument is rendered invalid. The infinite that the philosophers admit has neither a beginning nor an end and, therefore, one cannot say that it has ended or that it has begun. This, says Ibn Rushd, can be understood from the notion that beginning and end are correlatives.[33] Beginning and end are correlatives in the sense that the affirmation of the one entails the affirmation of the other and the negation of the one entails the negation of the other. The finite must be limited in two directions, whereas the infinite must be unlimited in two directions.[34] According to Ibn Rushd, the theologians' error is based on assuming that time is essentially a continuous, straight line with no beginning. On the basis of this (false) assumption, it was possible for them to show the impossibility of traversing an infinite linear series to reach the present.[35] He concludes his answer to this part of the argument with the following rather unexpected statement: "It will be clear to you that neither the arguments of the theologians for the temporal creation of the world of which Ghazālī speaks, nor the arguments of the philosophers, which he includes and describes in his book, suffice to reach absolute evidence or afford stringent proof."[36] Ibn Rushd is saying here that the arguments of the theologians and the philosophers are equally unpersuasive. He provides a partial explanation for his meaning in his answer to the second part of Ghazālī's argument. Ghazālī asks whether the infinite number of the revolutions of the spheres is even or uneven, and Ibn Rushd explains that of the number that exists only potentially it cannot be said that it is even or uneven. For what exists potentially falls under the law of nonexistence.[37] What he says next is especially important, as it explains what was, according to him, the source of the error not only of the theologians but also of the philosophers: "The cause of this mistake is that it was believed that, when something possesses a certain quality in the soul, it must possess this quality also outside the soul, and, since anything that has happened in the past can only be represented in the soul as finite, it was thought that everything that has happened in the past must also be finite outside the soul."[38]

The theologians reflect on the world as existing in a time that resembles a line having a beginning, while the philosophers represent the time of the world as a line that has no beginning. In both cases what is conceived or imagined as possessing a certain quality in the soul is thought of, mistakenly, as possessing the same quality in reality. "Therefore," says Ibn Rushd, "someone who claims that the world is everlasting, thinking that it is in a time which has no beginning, errs with respect to a decisive statement concerning the principles of the Peripatetics, just as someone who says that it is in a time which has a beginning necessarily errs."[39] As Barry Kogan points out, this conclusion is peculiar, since it not only rejects the position of the theologians, but also appears to repudiate the philosophers' view that the world is eternal in the sense that it has no temporal beginning.[40]

Ghazālī's second objection to the philosophers' first proof consists of affirming that the philosophers must acknowledge the possibility of the creation of the temporal being by an eternal, since no intelligent person can believe in the existence of events that lead to other events ad infinitum. There must exist a limit for these events and this limit will be the eternal itself from which the temporal proceeds.[41] Ibn Rushd answers Ghazālī's objection by saying that the temporal arises from the eternal through a median (*wāsiṭa*) whose being is eternal in its totality, although temporal in its particular movements.[42] This was another attempt by Ibn Rushd to explain the contradiction involved in the positions of the theologians and the philosophers. By arguing that the world is a kind of median, eternal in one respect but temporal in another respect, he seems to be endorsing both positions of the theologians and the philosophers. Ghazālī was familiar with the view that the world can be represented as a median originated in its parts but eternal in its totality. This is a view that he ascribed to Ibn Sīnā and which he criticized by insisting that positing a median, which is partially temporal and partially eternal, creates another problem concerning the relationship between the eternal and the temporal parts of the posited median. Another median will be called for, as we will have infinite regress.[43]

Ibn Rushd's answer to this challenge consists of briefly repeating his claim that the temporal does not proceed from the median in so far as it is eternal, but only insofar as it is temporal.[44] This restatement does not constitute a satisfactory answer to Ghazālī's legitimate demand for a further unifying principle to account for the relatedness between the finite and the infinite aspects of the proposed median. It becomes clear that positing the median served Ibn Rushd only in neutralizing a tension that was growing larger in the rational stand of the philosophers. Ibn Rushd, it might be argued, did not succeed in establishing a connection between the eternal and the temporal, but only in neutralizing the contradiction inherent in the relationship between them. But what if the relationship between the finite and the infinite aspects of reality possessed the very contradictory nature that Ibn Rushd was seeking to neutralize? In this case, distancing the finite aspect of reality from its infinite aspect amounts to dividing the one reality against itself and, by doing so, striking deeper roots for the contradiction.

The Second Proof

The second proof for the eternity of the world is based on the argument that the priority of God to the world and to time is essential, not temporal, in the sense that the movement of the man, for example, is prior to the movement of his shadow. To assume that God is prior to the world not essentially but temporally implies that there must have been before time an infinite time, which is self-contradictory. Thus, the assertion that time had a beginning is absurd. Moreover, time is the measure of motion as motion and the world, the thing in motion, must be eternal.[45] Ghazālī insists, however, that time is created with no time prior to it. God existed without the world and then he existed with the world, and there is no need to assume a third essence, such as the essence of time, although the imagination cannot resist the temptation to make this assumption.[46]

In his turn, Ibn Rushd says that what Ghazālī reproduces as the philosophers' proof for the eternity of the world does not really constitute a valid proof. This is because it is of the nature of the world, not its Creator, to be in time. God is not simultaneous with or prior to the world in time.[47] If not in time, then in what sense is God prior to the world? According to Ibn Sīnā, God is prior to the world not temporally but essentially and by a priority of causation. Ibn Rushd rejects this type of priority: God is not prior to the world, neither by a priority of time, nor by a priority of causation. His position seems to suffer from a certain inconsistency. He says that there are two kinds of existence, one in the nature of which there is motion, and which cannot be separated from time, which is the existence of the world, and another which is timeless and belongs to God. He states that the entity in the nature of which there is no motion and which is free from time is the *cause* of the entity that cannot be separated from time.[48] Nevertheless, he refuses to admit that the priority of God to the world is based on the priority of cause to effect. This is because the temporal priority of cause to effect belongs to the nature of things in motion and in time, while God, the Unmoved Mover, is free from motion and is timeless.[49] Yet, in the same context of the discussion, he says that "the posteriority of the world to the Creator, Who does not precede it in time, can only be understood as the posteriority of effect to cause."[50] He also emphasizes in *A Discourse on the Harmony between the Belief of the Peripatetics and that of the Mutakallimūn* that the priority of God to the world is a "priority of the unchanging, timeless, existence to the changing existence, which is in time."[51] To make things even more complicated, he says in the same work, "It is not characteristic of the world to be in time. Rather, time is something that arises with the world's being."[52] To say that time is something that arises with the world is to repeat Ghazālī's view that time was generated together with the world. What is intriguing is that Ibn Rushd arrives at this conclusion, which is identical with Ghazālī's, through "arrogating unquestioned superiority to the conclusions of intellectual inquiry," to borrow David Burrell's description of Ibn Rushd's reasoning.[53]

The paradoxical tendency in Ibn Rushd's position becomes more apparent in his answer to Ghazālī's next attempt to refute the philosophers' doctrine of the eternity of the world. Ghazālī draws on a parity thesis between the time of the world and its space: if the philosophers admit that space is finite, because it is the property of bodies which are finite, they must also admit that time is finite, because it is also a property of the finite movement of bodies in space.[54] The philosophers cannot imagine a limit of a body existing without anything outside it, but they are willing to suppose that this is possible. Likewise, a limit of time existing without a time outside it cannot be imagined, and still the theologians are willing to suppose that this is possible as well.[55] Ibn Rushd accuses Ghazālī of inappropriately comparing the limit of time with the limit of space. For one cannot imagine a time whose initial term is not the final term of another time. This, however, does not apply in the case of the point in space, for the point is the end of the line and one can imagine a point which is the beginning of a line without its being the end of another line.[56]

Ghazālī proceeds in presenting the philosophers' following argument. They say that the theologians believe that it was possible for God to create the world a year, ten years, and so on ad infinitum before he created it. This implies, according to them, that an infinite number of worlds should have existed before this world, which is absurd.[57] Ghazālī asks whether it was in God's power to create the world's highest sphere a cubit, two cubits, and so on ad infinitum, higher than he had created it. If the answer is "yes," impossible consequences must follow.[58] If, on the other hand, the philosophers hold fast to their claim that it is not possible for the world to be larger or smaller than it is, then they must admit that the world is necessary, not possible. Ibn Rushd says that Ibn Sīnā's distinction between two kinds of necessary-of-existence—that which exists necessarily by itself and that which exists necessarily through another—can be an appropriate answer to this argument.[59] The first kind applies to God, the absolute necessary-of-existence, while the second applies to the world, being a totality that exists *through* God. It is in the concept of the existent that exists necessarily through another that Ibn Rushd finds the link between the temporal and the eternal aspects of the world: "The nexus between temporal existence and eternal can only take place without a change affecting the First through that movement which is partly eternal, partly temporal. And the thing moved by this movement is what Avicenna calls 'the existence through another,' and this 'necessary through another' must be a body everlastingly moved, and in this way it is possible that the essentially temporal and corruptible should exist in dependence on the eternal."[60]

There seems to be some irony in the fact that Ibn Rushd establishes his answer to Ghazālī's challenge on the basis of a concept that he borrows from Ibn Sīnā, with whom he found himself in considerable disagreement. As I am going to show in the following discussion, Ibn Rushd's response to Ghazālī's objection to the philosophers' third proof for the eternity of the world intensifies the ironic tendency in his position, bringing it to bordering on the paradoxical.

The Third Proof

As Oliver Leaman points out, the philosophers' third proof for the eternity of the world[61] is based on the Principle of Plenitude, which establishes a conceptual connection between the eternally possible and the actual. Given infinite time, the possible-of-existence must, according to this principle, exist necessarily.[62] If it is possible that God could have created infinite worlds before this one, then it must be the case that these worlds will be created.[63] But then we would have to assume the actual existence of an infinite number of worlds before this world, which is absurd.

In his answer to the philosophers' argument, Ghazālī resumes his attack on the basis of his parity thesis. He says that in relation to the world's space the possible consists of the existence of an actual body of a limited surface, although the exact size of this body is not specified. Likewise, the possible in relation to the world's time is that the world must have a limit or beginning in time, although the exact time of the coming into existence of the world need not be specified.[64] Ghazālī thinks, therefore, that it is perfectly possible to think about the existence of alternative worlds that could have been created before this world. Ibn Rushd, however, thinks that if these alternative worlds were truly possible, then their existence must be necessitated eventually, which is absurd.[65] Leaman finds it ironic that Ghazālī employs a distinction between possibility and actuality that was originally established by Aristotle, while Ibn Rushd holds that possibility is coextensive with reality in the manner of Ashʿarite thinkers.[66] But the irony, in my opinion, pertains to the core of Ibn Rushd's position. For by identifying the eternally possible with the eternally existent, Ibn Rushd actually restates Ibn Sīnā's identification between the possible-of-existence-in-itself and the necessary-of-existence-by-the-other. Ibn Rushd, however, was extremely critical of Ibn Sīnā's concept of the possible-in-itself and necessary-by-the-other, as we read in the Eighth Discussion of *The Incoherence of the Incoherence*: "Ibn Sīnā affirms that the necessary existent through another is in itself a possible existent and what is possible needs something necessary—this . . . is to my mind superfluous and erroneous, for in the necessary, in whatever way you suppose it, there is no possibility whatsoever and there exists nothing of a single nature of which it can be said that it is in one way possible and in another way necessary in its existence. For the philosophers have proved that there is no possible whatsoever in the necessary; for the possible is the opposite of the necessary."[67]

Ibn Rushd thinks that Ibn Sīnā's position is self-contradictory, insisting that "the possible in itself and in its essence cannot become necessary through its author, unless the very nature of the possible were to change into the necessary."[68] It turns out that Ibn Rushd is in a situation that is similar, in a sense, to that of Ibn Sīnā. He also seems to have established his defense of the philosophers on the basis of a concept of which he seems to be severely critical.

Ibn Rushd's Doctrine of Eternal Creation: The Emergence of the Problem of the Limit

Mājid Fakhry asserts that through a striking paradox Ibn Rushd, "can rightly be reckoned as the staunchest exponent of the thesis of an eternal universe."[69]

The paradox in question is about a universe that is both eternal and created. Like Ibn Sīnā, Ibn Rushd thinks that the notion of creation of that which exists eternally is the only notion that is consistent with the principles of rationality. What renders the paradoxical tendency in his position more apparent than that of Ibn Sīnā is his rejection of the theory of emanation, which enabled the latter to mitigate the contrast between God and the universe. Fakhry explains that the theory of emanation was favored by Islamic Neoplatonist philosophers[70] because it appeared to bridge the gap between the material and the intelligible worlds and, at the same time, avoid the rather irrational ex nihilo account of creation.[71] Charles Genequand expresses the same view, adding that the purpose of the theory of emanation was to establish a link between the First Cause and the physical world, a link that was missing in Aristotle's system.[72] He provides the following summary of Ibn Sīnā's emanationist account of creation:

> All beings derive from the First, but not as a result of deliberate intention; the First cannot will anything other than itself, because this would be tantamount to an admission of its own imperfection. The First contemplates itself and this thought produces other things. By contemplating itself, it produces the First Intellect (that of the starless sphere). The First Intellect contemplates its own essence as possible in itself and from this intellection the first sphere results necessarily (*yalzam*). It also contemplates its own essence as necessitated by the First and from this intellection the soul of the first sphere results necessarily. Finally, by contemplating the First it produces the next Intellect, that which is immediately below itself. This ternary process repeats itself at the level of each of the ten heavenly spheres down to the Active Intellect.[73]

This brief account of the process of emanation demonstrates the significance of the distinction between essence and existence for a theory of creation that seeks to account for the unity of the Eternal One in his relation to a multiple world. The main significance of this distinction in the context of such a theory is to allow for the possibility of deriving the multiplicity in the world not directly from the One, but from the distinction between the essence and the existence of the world. Ibn Rushd was a believer in the theory of emanation when he wrote the epitome (*talkhīs*) of Aristotle's *Metaphysics*, but by the time of writing *The Incoherence of the Incoherence*, he became a serious opponent of the theory.[74] Scholars offer different explanations for this critical change of mind, as most of them seem to agree that in one way or another it had something to do with Ghazālī's criticism of Ibn Sīnā's philosophy. Genequand alludes to the idea that Ibn Rushd rejected the notion of emanation because it was established on the basis of the controversial distinction between the possible-in-itself and the necessary-by-the-other, a distinction that seemed self-contradictory to him.[75] He provides another significant rationale for explaining the change in question: Ibn Rushd rejects the theory of emanation because it presupposes the existence of the One *above* the Mover of the universe; the One in the theory of emanation is so distanced from the world that his existence becomes unwarrantable.[76] Genequand insists that Ibn Rushd rejects the presupposition of the existence of the One beyond the Mover of the universe not because he is a doctrinaire Aristotelian, as is commonly asserted, but because of his belief that the eternity of the world and the primacy of motion are two notions that are closely related.[77] God is eternal in the sense that he is a pure actuality. It is not enough for such a God to give the initial push to the world, and then cease to act. If God ceases to act, the universe will enter a state of chaos, or even vanish:[78] "If movement were to come to a standstill, the Prime Mover would be unable to cause [the sphere] to acquire continuous movement beyond [the point of its] corruption, in as much as its movement would be corruptible [in principle]. Now if its movement were to have been corrupted, *it would itself have been corrupted through rest and [likewise] all entities whose existence consists in movement would have been corrupted.*"[79]

God, as the Prime Mover, must produce the *best act*. The best act, Barry Kogan explains, is such that its existence cannot carry within itself any predetermined limit. Thus, to be the effect of the act of a Perfect Mover, the world must be eternal, for only a finite God would produce a finite act.[80] Creation for Ibn Rushd is a continuous process, pertaining to each and every occurrence that takes place in the universe, rather than a single occurrence that brings the world into existence and ceases to be. The substance of the world is being-in-motion as the world consists of potentialities that attain to their actuality not in the form of a finished product, but in the form of a continuous process of pure motion.[81]

If the act of God cannot contain within itself any predetermined limit, and if the world is produced continuously and eternally, then what sense does Ibn Rushd make of the notion of the createdness of the world? Kogan finds the answer to this question in Ibn Rushd's distinction between the parts of the world's movement and the totality of this movement. The former would have the characteristic of finitude, that is, temporal origination, while the latter would be characterized by infinitude, that is, pre-eternity:[82] "Praised then be the God who exercises providence over this world by the creation of this mobile body which is characterized by finite motion in accordance with one part and infinite motion in accordance with the other."[83]

The world is the totality of motion. Motion as a totality is the actuality not the actualization, of the movable. Motion as actualization, is a process that eventually comes to an end, since it has a predetermined (temporal) limit, whereas as actuality motion is the unlimited end of limited potentialities to move or come to be.[84] The difference that Kogan finds in Ibn Rushd's thought between motion as actuality and motion as actualization corresponds to the difference discerned by Teicher between *essential* and *spatialized* time. Teicher mentions this distinction in the context of dealing with the controversy between theologians and philosophers over the problem of the origination of the world. He formulates the controversy in terms of an antinomy. The thesis of the antinomy states that the world is finite in time, while the antithesis states that the world is infinite in time. Teicher explains that in his solution to the antinomy Ibn Rushd made use of the concept of essential time in contrast to the spatialized time of the theologians and the philosophers:

> Both the thesis asserting the beginning of the universe and the antithesis proclaiming the eternity of the universe presuppose, Averroes contends, the same notion of "nonessential time." Both the thesis and the antithesis conceive time abstractly, in a manner contrary to its true nature, for both of them conceive time as a straight line. The only difference between the thesis and the antithesis is that the former conceives time as a finite and the latter as an infinite line; but the fundamental notion of time assumed in either case is not that of duration but that of "spatialized" time. The true nature of time is, Averroes concludes, like the true nature of the Universe, incessant change and movement.[85]

Spatialized time is the finite actualization of essential time, which is represented in the soul either in the form of a finite line with a beginning or an infinite line without a beginning. The infinite actuality of time, like the infinite actuality of motion, cannot be comprehended except in terms of priority or posteriority. The Essence of time, however, is not a prior or a posterior time, since it is the Present, the Instant (*al-ān*) that defines priority and posteriority:[86] "Concerning time, we seek to know its essence, since its existence seems to be self-evident . . . in our saying that some of it *is* past time and some of it *is* future time, and that the Instant (*al-ān*) is a shared Limit between past and future times. Existence does not belong to the Present time [the Instant] by nature but by positing, since a portion of time [the Instant] cannot *come to be in act*. Time is, therefore, interrelated, and any limited time exists only as Limit between two instants of time."[87]

Prior and posterior times exist as instances that are interrelated with other instances in an infinite totality of time. The infinite totality cannot be actualized, since this renders it finite. Time cannot, therefore, become an actual infinite. Can time become an actual finite? It turns out that what pertains to the totality (the maximum) of time pertains also to the Instant, which is the finite portion (the minimum) of time. Thus, time cannot *become* an actual infinite or an actual finite. Both philosophers and theologians missed the true meaning of time, since the nature of time, like the nature of the universe, consists of motion. Borrowing Bergsonian concepts, Teicher characterizes Ibn Rushd's conception of time in terms of *duration* and *creative evolution*. He expresses the view that this intuitive notion of time, which was implicit in Ibn Sīnā and explicit in Ibn Rushd, brought about the overthrow of the Aristotelian *Physics* and *Metaphysics* in the twelfth century.[88]

It must be noted, however, that Ibn Rushd's conception of time as consisting of limits marked in terms of before and after is found in Aristotle.[89] Hence, to say that Ibn Rushd's notion of reality as being-in-motion brought about the overthrow of Aristotle's *Physics* and *Metaphysics* must be an exaggeration. Nevertheless, his statement is not entirely incorrect, since it can be said that Islamic thinkers made manifest a tension that was latent in the Aristotelian doctrine of the eternity of the world. For although Aristotle insisted that time must be eternal due to the fact that it is always a limit between before and after,[90] he insisted that the Limit is "the ultimate part of each thing, or the first part outside of which no part can be found, or the first part inside of which all parts exist."[91] Aristotle's theory required this definition of the Limit in order to confirm the finitude of the world's space. In a world that is infinite in space there can be no first principle from which movement in the world can commence and, therefore, no derivation is possible of the series of causes and effects. Thus, although the time of the world must be potentially infinite, as it consists of limits related to other limits ad infinitum, the space of the world must be actually finite, otherwise the world will exist as an actual infinite in every respect, which is impossible.

The tension that Islamic theologians detected in Aristotle was accentuated by Islamic philosophers due to the special context in which they debated the doctrine of the eternity of the world against a conception of a God who creates ex nihilo. Ibn Rushd was able to explain how an infinite time could exist by claiming that time is a matter of moving from a prior motion to a posterior motion, and insisting that this does not pose a problem to the notion of the infinity of time, since motion is something that is in the mind.[92] The notion of the infinity of time did not seem to him an unsolvable problem, since it was the potential infinite and not the actual infinite that he conceived of as the true infinite. However, the real problem remains in finding out how the potentially infinite can become actually finite. For from Ibn Rushd's analysis of the notion of time it becomes clear that although he believed that time can exist as an actual finite in the form of prior or posterior times, the *essence* of time cannot exist as an actual infinite or as an actual finite. Following Ghazālī, we can extend the same analysis to space and ask, If the essence (the Limit) of time cannot exist either as an actual infinite or as an actual finite why not say the same thing about space? To treat space differently requires some rational justification. What rational justification do we have for insisting upon two contradictory conceptions of the Limit, one that pertains to time, depicting the essence of time as a limitless limit, and another that pertains to space, depicting the essence of space as the end beyond which there is nothing? With Ghazālī and Ibn Rushd the debate between the theologians and the philosophers over the problem of the origination of the world reached a new level, as the whole debate boiled down to the question, How can a synthesis between the finite and the infinite conceptions of the Limit be possible? In order to answer this question, we have to address a more direct question: What is the Limit? In the following chapters I will provide an examination of Ibn al-ʿArabī's answer to this question.

CHAPTER 4

Mysticism versus Philosophy: The Encounter between Ibn al-ʿArabī and Ibn Rushd

Mysticism between Theology and Philosophy

William Chittick follows scholarly convention in dividing Islamic thinkers into three groups: philosophers (*falāsifa*), scholastic theologians (*mutakallimūn*), and mystics (*Ṣūfīs)*, stating that the difference between the three groups comes down to the methodologies that they applied for acquiring knowledge and not to their objects of investigation.[1] He indicates that the philosophers' emphasis was on the universality and the communicability of truth, as they insisted on observing the laws of logic so that the rational conclusions of the intellect might be clearly explained and comprehended on the discursive level.[2] Oliver Leaman expresses a similar view, noting that the philosophers' emphasis on the universality and communicability of truth was behind their insistence that only the abstract use of reason was capable of convincing anyone of the truth, regardless of their religious affiliations.[3]

In the Islamic philosophical tradition the emphasis on universality and communicability reached its culmination in the philosophical thought of Ibn Rushd. It was, in my opinion, one of Ibn Rushd's greatest achievements and yet his most misunderstood discovery that truth is one and universal, even though it may be expressed in contradictory ways.[4] Ibn Rushd argued that in their discussion of the world's origination, theologians and philosophers believed in the same truth, but in different ways or from different perspectives. Theologians, who believed in the finitude of the world, and philosophers, who believed that the world was infinite, were both correct, since the world can be considered as both finite and infinite from two different perspectives, or according to two different rational interpretations. Furthermore, in *The Incoherence of the Incoherence and On the Harmony of Religion and Philosophy* Ibn Rushd claimed that neither the argument of the theologians nor the argument of the philosophers, each on its own, may express more than half the truth and that the two arguments combined provide a suitable resolution to the problem of the world's origination.[5] One can say that for Ibn Rushd, rational interpretation had become a supreme judge, not only over the texts of scriptures but also over the authoritative philosophical texts of Aristotle.

The philosophers' adherence to the superiority of rational interpretation was the opposite of the theologians' insistence that a person may not come up with any conclusions that may be explicitly or implicitly opposed to the revealed text. When reasoning leads to such conclusions, these must be rejected or interpreted for the sake of harmonizing them with the revealed text.[6] In Chittick's view, the position of the Ṣūfīs regarding the revealed texts was, in a sense, similar to that of the theologians. For the Ṣūfīs also maintained that all knowledge must be judged according to the standards provided by the revealed texts. Chittick points out, however, that the Ṣūfīs held that a true understanding of the revealed texts could be attained only through the method of unveiling (*kashf*), which was considered by them the only adequate method of ascertaining the true meanings of the revealed texts.[7] The method of unveiling distinguished Ṣūfīs not only from the theologians but also from the philosophers. Against the philosophers, the Ṣūfīs held that the human intellect alone was insufficient for achieving the ultimate truth and that a personal knowledge that comes directly from God is needed for achieving this aim.[8] In order to be ready to receive this knowledge, the Ṣūfīs had to remove the veils that separated them from God. They regarded the philosophers' belief that rational thought was sufficient by itself to achieve ultimate knowledge as just another veil that had to be removed before such knowledge was obtained.

In my opinion, the conclusion that reason is just another veil that has to be removed before perfect knowledge is obtained is the most important lesson that we learn from the encounter between Ibn Rushd and Ibn al-ʿArabī. I will discuss this encounter in the following sections of this chapter. First, however, I will discuss an encounter that occurred, according to the Qur'ān, between Khaḍir and Moses.[9] Ibn al-ʿArabī mentions Khaḍir in the same chapter in which he mentions his encounters with Ibn Rushd. From the context of his discussion it becomes clear that Moses and Ibn Rushd represent in his account the knowledge of the Law, whereas he and Khaḍir represent the knowledge of the Saints.

An Interpretation of the Encounter between Khaḍir and Moses from Ibn al-ʿArabī's Perspective

In chapter fifteen of the *Futūḥāt*, entitled "On The Poles and the Realizers in the Knowledge of Breaths and their Secrets," Ibn al-ʿArabī identifies Khaḍir with the Realizers (*muḥaqqiqūn*) in the Knowledge of Breaths (*anfās*), which is the knowledge of Creative Imagination.[10] Ibn al-ʿArabī compares God's act of creation to breathing. Before they come into existence, the entities of the possible things exist as fixed entities or essences (*aʿyān thābita*) in God's Essence. The essences of the possible things long and press for manifestation and this longing and pressure create a certain constraint. God relieves this constraint by an act of breathing, through which he gives manifestation (existential formulation) to the essences of the possible things. To know the manner in which this occurs, a special knowledge is needed and this is the Knowledge of Breaths or the Knowledge of Creative Imagination.[11]

Ibn al-ʿArabī says that Khaḍir was known for his capacity for renewing life, so much so that, "whenever he settled in a barren place God would make that place fertile and prosperous."[12] He explains that those who are Realizers in the knowledge of Khaḍir are the masters in the art of "setting souls in bodies and dissolving bodies and bringing them together by removing forms from them, or, clothing them with forms."[13] The Realizers possess knowledge through Imagination (*al-khayal*). This knowledge is rooted in the World of Imagination (*ʿālam al-khayāl*), which is the root of the spiritual and corporeal worlds and the Barzakh within which the two worlds are brought together although, at the same time, they are kept apart. Hence, as Chittick explains, the World of Imagination must not be described in terms of either/or (this world or that world), but rather in terms of neither/nor or both/and.[14] Rational thinkers consider it impossible that a thing should be characterized by opposite attributes, but Ibn al-ʿArabī insists that it is in the unlimited power of Imagination to synthesize extreme opposites.[15] He says that only the possessors of the knowledge of Khaḍir, namely the knowledge that synthesizes the corporeal and the spiritual aspects of reality, are capable of knowing the real nature of God's work, which is the same as the knowledge of the world.[16] He considers the acquiring of this knowledge a special favor bestowed by God on persons like Khaḍir, "since for every knowledge there are people suitable for it, and since time, circumstances and the various configurations of minds do not allow that knowledge be singled out equally for all."[17] This warning seems to have eluded Moses's attention in his search after Khaḍir's knowledge. Moses set out on a long journey and was determined not to give up until he had reached the Meeting of The Two Seas (*majmaʿ al-baḥrayn*).[18] There he found one of God's Servants (Khaḍir),[19] to whom God had granted mercy from himself and whom God had taught knowledge from his own Presence.[20] Moses asks permission to become Khaḍir's follower so that he might learn something of the special knowledge that God had taught him. Khaḍir warns Moses that he will not have patience with him. For how can he have patience about things that his understanding fails to encompass (*ʿalā mā lam tuḥiṭ bihi khubran*)? Moses insists and Khaḍir stipulates that the prophet should not ask any questions about anything that he witnesses until he speaks to him concerning it.[21]

> So they both proceeded: until, when they were in the boat, he scuttled it. Said Moses: "Hast thou scuttled it in order to drown those in it? Truly a strange thing hast thou done!"(16:71) He answered: "Did I not tell thee that thou canst have no patience with me?"(16:72) Moses said: "Rebuke me not for forgetting, nor grieve me by raising difficulties in my case."(16:73) Then they proceeded; until, when they met a young man, he slew him. Moses said: "Hast thou slain an innocent person who had slain none? Truly a foul (unheard-of) thing hast thou done!"(16:74) He answered: "Did I not tell thee that thou canst have no patience with me?"(16:75) (Moses) said: "If ever I ask thee about anything after this, keep me not in thy company: then wouldst thou have received (full) excuse from my side."(16:76) Then they proceeded: until, when they came to the inhabitants of a town, they asked them for food, but they refused them hospitality. They found there a wall on the point of falling down, but he set it up straight. (Moses) said: "If thou hadst wished, surely thou couldst have exacted some recompense for it!"(16:77)

At this point Khaḍir announces that it is time for departure. He explains to Moses the hidden secret behind his strange acts. As for the boat, it belonged to poor people. By rendering it unserviceable he wished to save it from a cruel king who seized on every boat by force. As for the youth, his parents were faithful people. Knowing that he would grieve them by unbelief, he wished to give them in exchange a pure and affectionate son. As for the wall, it belonged to two youths, orphans, in the Town; there was beneath it a buried treasure to which they were entitled. God desired that they reach the age of full strength and get out their treasure. Khaḍir concludes the encounter by saying, "I did it not of my own accord. Such is the interpretation of (those things) over which thou wast unable to hold patience" (16:82)[22]

In his study of Ibn al-ʿArabī's treatment of the figure of Khaḍir, Ian R. Netton points at the dual nature of Khaḍir's actions. Each action has a constructive aspect, which is known only to God and which is revealed, in this case, only to Khaḍir, and a destructive aspect imagined by Moses. Each action, therefore, can be regarded as signifying a paradox within the overall paradoxical nature of the encounter.[23] Following the *Oxford English Dictionary*, Netton defines *paradox* as a seemingly absurd though perhaps well-founded statement. What seemed absurd and irrational to Moses turned out to be well founded and fully rational after Khaḍir had revealed the hidden meanings of his actions. In Q 16:71 Moses says, "Hast thou scuttled it in order to drown those in it? Truly a strange thing hast thou done!" What Khaḍir had done seemed strange to Moses's familiar ways of understanding. It was not what he would have done in the same circumstances. Moses's way of understanding was based on an opinion (*doxa*) limited by his own domain of acceptability. The way of paradox, however, is always beyond the boundaries of familiarity and acceptability.[24] It can be said that, in comparison to Moses, Khaḍir possessed the capacity to see through both ways, that is, discern the limits of opinionated consideration and also see beyond that. It is the knowledge of the paradoxicality involved in perceiving the same thing from two incompatible and even contradictory perspectives that distinguished Khaḍir's level of consciousness from that of Moses.

One might wonder how Moses could have reacted otherwise to Khaḍir's scuttling the boat, for example. How could he possibly perceive the paradoxical notion that to have the boat saved is to have it destroyed? For Khaḍir's actions seemed to be inconsistent not only externally, that is, inconsistent with the external conditions in which they were located, but also internally. For in his first act Khaḍir returned bad for good whereas in his third act he returned good for bad. In such absence of external and internal consistency there seemed to be no way to predict the kind of action to be committed in novel situations. The way to rational knowledge was blocked, since predictability, which is a cardinal factor in obtaining rational knowledge, was simply unavailable.

In the story of the encounter, Moses's position symbolizes the predicament of the rational thinker whose system of beliefs interferes with his intended goals. Moses's insistence upon analyzing Khaḍir's acts according to rational principles induced interference. He struggled to neutralize this interference. But by doing so, he was only making it more persistent. It turns out that the struggle to dissolve the paradox is what renders it even more unsolvable and the position of the rational thinker even more pressing. The impression is created that what is needed is not merely the dissolution of the paradox but the understanding of it. Understanding the paradox requires that we refrain from seeing it, through all kinds of rational neutralizations, as a frustrated product of some "bad" reasoning. In order to illustrate this point I will make a reference to Carl Jung's following statements:

> It is therefore understandable . . . that . . . the psychic should be as stable and definite as possible. . . . But this involves a certain disadvantage: the quality of directedness makes for the inhibition or exclusion of all those psychic elements which appear to be . . . incompatible with it. . . . But how do we know that the concurrent psychic material is "incompatible"? We know it by an act of judgment. . . . This judgment is partial and prejudiced, since it chooses one particular possibility at the cost of all the others. The judgment in its turn is always based on experience, i.e., on what is already known. As a rule it is never based on . . . what is still unknown, and what under certain conditions might considerably enrich the directed process. . . . Through such acts of judgment

> the directed process necessarily becomes one-sided, even though the rational judgment may appear many-sided and unprejudiced. The very rationality of the judgment may even be the worst prejudice, since we call reasonable what appears reasonable to us. What appears to us unreasonable is therefore doomed to be excluded because of its irrational character. It may really be irrational, but may equally well merely appear irrational without actually being so when seen from another standpoint.[25]

There is a psychological choice involved in our adherence to the rational. This choice yields a one-sided judgment even though the rational judgment may appear to us many-sided and unprejudiced. It appears that our rationality is determined in such a manner as to exclude all the "irrational" contents from the psyche without actually perceiving this as an act of exclusion. Whenever a certain content of thought arises that seems to be incompatible with our rational mode, our first response is to find rational ways of dismissing it, without actually being aware that we are dismissing what would be regarded as fully rational under different circumstances. This built-in mechanism of rational determinism is responsible for producing the aporiatic way of thinking or acting described by Brian Martine as follows:

> We are puzzled less by the phenomena than by the way that they seem to continue to wriggle out of the categorical nets that we weave to contain them. Our most common response has been to assume that some tighter weave will make a difference, that some more careful method of observation and the corollary production of more highly refined categories will solve the problem. And in one sense, this has proved extremely fruitful. . . . But in another sense, we seem to have made little progress indeed. The ancient standoff between the One and the Many, the play between sameness and difference as we try to reconcile our experience of plurality with our desire for unity, leads to as many logical puzzles and theoretical battles now as it did then. . . . The fact that these basic ontological tensions and conflicts remain despite enormous advances on other fronts leads me to believe that there must be something that lies neglected at the most fundamental level of our practice in thought.[26]

We are not making real progress regarding such intellectual activities that keep puzzling us today as before because we have not been able to free ourselves from our common response, which has been to tighten the weave of our categorical nets. Instead we should try "to free ourselves from the concerns of immediate experience, and explore the ontological structure of the thinking that developed out of those concerns."[27] Martine adds another statement that brings us back to our discussion of Ibn al-ʿArabī. He states that we need to expose the foundation of our bias toward "the determinate dimensions of thought and being," and our continuing to neglect the significant component of *indeterminacy* in the structure of both dimensions.[28]

Ibn al-ʿArabī calls the possessors of Khaḍir's knowledge "Realizers in the Knowledge of Breaths." God acts by breathing. God never ceases to breathe and, consequently, the cosmos never ceases to undergo perpetual transmutation (*taḥawwul*). The cosmos is never the same for two moments, since it is the immediate outcome of the unceasing activity of God.[29] To acquire the knowledge of Khaḍir, one has to be able to perceive the perpetual transmutation of the cosmos, which corresponds to the perpetual self-disclosure of God. To acquire this sort of perception, one must be capable of realizing the difference between actuality and actualization. An action comes close to actuality when it identifies this as indeterminacy and is an actualization when it adheres to a determined form of the actuality. To perceive the true nature of the totality of existence, which is identical with the actuality of God's work, we have to allow for more indeterminacy in our thought. A form of thinking that is determined by a closed system of beliefs or opinions (*doxa*) corresponds only to a determined form of being, that is, to a determined form (an actualization) of God's (paradoxical) action. The truth value of the action is determined by its correspondence to a reality that is a whole, not to a limited segment of it. But reality as a whole is the actuality that does not have a predetermined limit. Hence, the truth value of any action depends on how effectively it relates to a reality that is always undergoing an actual becoming.

Hence, a true action becomes a symbol for the present moment, which is a limit between the past, which has been actualized, and the future, which is yet to be actualized. In his concluding words to Moses, Khaḍir says that he did what he did not of his own accord. His action designated an Instant that could be assigned both to himself and to God. Such an action reflects the reality of creation, since creation is the link between the reality of the world and the reality of God. It should be recalled that, according to Ibn al-ʿArabī, creation is not something that God chooses. God creates because of the constraint that the essences of the possible things (*aʿyān thābita*) create in Him. Thus, if God were to speak, he would also say: "I did it, not of my own accord." This does not mean that God's Will is restrained. On the contrary, the one-sided conception of creation is what restrains God's unlimited actuality, since this conception leaves the reality of the world unaccounted for. Thus, Khaḍir's saying, "I did it, not of my own accord" signifies a reality that is a cocreative synthesis, unifying affirmation (I did it) and negation (not of my own accord), without nullifying the element of differentiation intrinsic to this actuality.[30] In their first encounter, Ibn al-ʿArabī confronted Ibn Rushd with this reality and Ibn

Rushd was shocked. For he came to realize that what explained reality, that is, the creative tension between its two opposing poles, is what the rational thinker strove to explain away.

The Encounter between Ibn Rushd and Ibn al-ʿArabī

> The Breath of Life (*rūḥ*), from whom I received what I have committed to this book, informed me that one day, he gathered together his companions . . . and said to them: "Understand my allusions in this my Station. . . . Not all that is known can be divulged. There are special people for each kind of knowledge . . . and by [people] I mean one person in particular, in whose hands is the opening key to my symbol. . . . I swear by the Light of Light and by the Spirit of Life and the Life of the Spirit that I am turning away from you to where I came from and returning to the root of my origin. . . . Truth (*ḥaqīqa*) is Truth; the Path (*ṭarīqa*) is the Path. This life and the Garden [in the hereafter] consist of the same bricks and the same structure, even though the one is made of clay . . . and the other of gold." . . . This was part of his counsel to his children, and it is a great matter. One who knows it finds peace. I entered one day in Cordoba to its judge Abū al-Walīd bin Rushd. He desired to see me because of what he heard and what had reached him concerning what God had opened to me in my Retreat (*khalwa*). He was showing wonder at what he heard. Then, my father sent me to him on purpose, so that he might meet me, since he was one of his friends. When I entered . . . he embraced me and said to me: "Yes." I said to him: "Yes." His joy in me increased, since I understood his meaning.
>
> But then I realized the [real] motive of his pleasure therein and said to him, "No!" With this, [Ibn Rushd] was taken aback, his color began to change, and he seemed to have misgivings about what he was thinking. Then he asked me, "How have you found the matter through Illumination and Divine Inspiration (*al-kashf wa-l-fayḍ al-ʾilāhī*)—is it the same as what we [Philosophers] acquire through Speculation (*al-naẓar*)? "Yes [and] no," I replied, "and between the 'Yea' and the 'Nay' the spirits shall take flight from their matter, and heads go flying from their shoulders!" At this, [Ibn Rushd] turned pale, trembling seized him, and he fell to repeating the phrase, "There is no Power and no Strength save in God!" for he had understood what I was alluding to.[31]

According to Ibn al-ʿArabī this was not the only encounter that occurred between him and the philosopher. He mentions another two or three.[32] Notice how he develops the trend for separation between the rational, symbolized by Ibn Rushd's presence *or* absence, and the mystical, symbolized by his own person, through the remaining encounters. First he tells us about a certain desire of the philosopher to meet with him one more time, but he does not make it perfectly clear whether this second meeting occurred in actual fact. After that he tells us about an encounter that seemed to have occurred in an ecstasy (*fī l-wāqiʿa*). Finally, he speaks about an encounter with the body of the philosopher at the time of his funeral:

> After that [meeting, Ibn Rushd] requested of my father [another] interview with me. . . .[33] And he thanked God (Exalted be He!) That he had lived in such a time that he could behold one who had entered upon his Retreat in ignorance (*jāhil*^{*an*}) and emerged in this Condition—without lesson or examination, with no study or reading. "We had affirmed the possibility of this Condition (*ḥālah*)," he averred, "but we had never actually seen anyone who had mastered it."[34] Thereafter, on another occasion I formed the desire to meet with [Ibn Rushd], so, by God's Mercy, he was made to appear before me in an ecstasy (*fī l-wāqiʿa*) in such a form (*ṣūrah*) that between him and me there was a fine veil (*ḥijāb raqīq*), so that I could see him but he could not perceive me nor know that I was present—so preoccupied was he with himself! I said to myself, "Truly, he is not intended for that which we are!" I never met him again until he passed away. . . . When the coffin containing his body was loaded on the back of a beast of burden, his books were placed on the other side to balance it. . . . I uttered [the following verse]:
>
> *On the one side the Master, on the other side his Works–*
> *How I wonder if his hopes have found their fulfillment!* [35]

As Chittick points out, Ibn al-ʿArabī had little respect for most of the learned masters of rational deliberation as scholastic theologians and philosophers, but great respect for Ibn Rushd.[36] For, as Ibn al-ʿArabī says, Ibn Rushd was aware of the possibility of the Knowledge of Mysteries:

> We have met very few truly intelligent men. . . . They know the veneration due to God's majesty, and they are aware of the knowledge about Himself that God gives only to His servants—the prophets and those who follow them—through a special divine effusion that is outside ordinary learning and cannot be acquired through study and effort or reached by reason through its own reflective powers. I met one of the great ones among them. He had seen what God had opened up to me

> without rational consideration or reading, but through a retreat in which I was alone with God, even though I had not been seeking such knowledge. He said, "Praise belongs to God, that I should have lived in a time in which I saw one whom God has given mercy from Him, and taught him knowledge from Him."[37]

Ibn al-ʿArabī distinguishes between two types of philosophers, the philosopher-infidel and the philosopher-believer. Ibn Rushd was a philosopher-believer and, needless to say, he was considered by Ibn al-ʿArabī superior to the philosopher-infidel. Still, as Claude Addas points out, Ibn al-ʿArabī thought that Ibn Rushd's possibilities were limited, and that he would never attain to the knowledge possessed by the Saint.[38]

The knowledge of the Saint is the Knowledge of the States (*aḥwāl*). The State (*ḥāl*) in theology (especially Ashʿarite theology) is a quality (*ṣifa*) that belongs to an existent thing, but that in itself is neither existent nor nonexistent.[39] In mysticism, it is a mental condition that is given to the recipient immediately by divine grace and is not gained by application or effort.[40] The States (*aḥwāl*) are characterized by constant alteration in comparison with the Stations (*maqāmāt*) that are characterized by persistence. With Ibn al-ʿArabī the notion of the State gains further depth, as he furnishes it with an ontological in addition to its epistemological implication. As Suʿād al-Ḥakīm explains, for Ibn al-ʿArabī the State (*ḥāl*) signifies a link that connects the created with the Creator.[41] This link undergoes constant change, as in this lies the secret of the perpetual transmutation (*taḥawwul*) in the cosmos: "The whole cosmos never ceases to change for all eternity, ad infinitum, because of the change of the root which replenishes it. The root of this change is the divine self-transmutation in the forms of the cosmos."[42] The cosmos never ceases to change due to its Imaginal foundation. In Chittick's words, "Cosmic imagination refuses to be fixed. As manifest in the Breath of the All Merciful, the cosmos is 'the dream of the Real' and 'Unbounded Imagination' (*al-khayāl al-muṭlaq*). It undergoes constant 'transmutation' (*istiḥāla*), which means to change from one state (*ḥāl*) to another."[43] To say that the cosmos is imaginal does not mean that it is not real. The cosmos is real, but its reality consists of the fact that it is/is not the Real. As Chittick points out, according to Ibn al-ʿArabī, the Realizers' answer to every question concerning God and the world is "Yes and no," or, "He/not He" (*huwa lā huwa*).[44] This is "because the cosmos is imagination, and imagination is that which stands in an intermediary situation between affirmation and denial. About it one says 'both this and that,' or, 'neither this nor that.' The universe is neither Being nor nothingness, or both Being and nothingness."[45] It is a synthesis of opposites; a creative synthesis, since it constantly undergoes transmutation (*taḥawwul*). Those who realize the true nature of the cosmos are able to discern the true nature of the Real, since the world is the work of the Real. Those who realize this become themselves a creative synthesis of opposites:

> Nothing in the cosmos brings together the opposites save the Folk of God specifically, because He whom they have realized is He who brings together opposites, and through Him the gnostics know. For He is the First and the Last and the Manifest and the Nonmanifest [57:3] in respect of one entity and one relation, not in respect of two diverse relations. Hence they have departed from what is rationally understood, and rational faculties do not bind them. Rather, they are the divine ones, the Realizers. The Real has given them realization in what He has given them to witness, so they are and they are not.[46]

The Realizers have been given realization of the States (*aḥwāl*), which are neither existent nor nonexistent. They have departed from what is rationally understood, since what is rationally understood must be either existent or non-existent, and since a synthesis between extreme opposites is impossible according to rational principles. The rational faculties cannot bind the Realizers, for, like the Real, they cannot be found.[47]

The epistemological opposites of the Realizers are those who are entirely unaware of the true nature of the world's constant transmutation from one state to another. They have adhered to their reflection on a world that is inactive and unchanging. Such a limited reflection can hardly yield any true knowledge of the true identity of the Real's form of action, which abides in perpetual self-transmutation. These thinkers misinterpreted the Real's words, "Have they not reflected?" (Q 7:184) For when reason makes itself a slave to reflection it misses the real meaning of reflection, that the Real ordered reason to reflect in order to arrive at the conclusion that knowledge comes from God alone.[48]

Thus, Ibn al-ʿArabī speaks about three types of thinkers. There are those who make their reflection their own guide and, by doing so, they fail to properly interpret the signs that God has appropriated for them in order to know Him. To this category belong most of the theologians and the philosophers. Ibn al-ʿArabī does not include Ibn Rushd in this category of thinkers. Ibn Rushd belongs to the group of thinkers who seem to be applying their reflection in a proper manner and to have achieved the kind of awareness that pertains to the knowledge of Reality, but who are, nevertheless, still confined by their own rational limitations. Lastly, there are those thinkers who have been enabled not only to discern the limits of rational deliberation, but also to ascend to a higher level of knowledge, the level of the Knowledge of the States.[49]

Corresponding to these three types of thinkers there are three Paths of knowledge. The first is identified with Being, the second with Nonbeing and the third with the Limit:

> There is a First Path, the extreme limit of which is the Real the Being (*al-ḥaqq al-wujūd*).[50] There is a Second Path that has no designated limit so that it drives the Wayfarer into Nonbeing. In this Second Path the Wayfarer wanders aimlessly. For, Nonbeing cannot be determined or tied by a limit, contrary to the Real the Being, Who can be delimited even in His very nondelimitation, since His nondelimitation is the same as His delimitation. Between these two there is a Third Path. This Path is liminal (barzakhī), like the States in the science of *kalām*. The extreme limit of this Path cannot be characterized by Being or Nonbeing. As for the Path the extreme limit of which is the Being the Real (*al-wujūd al-ḥaqq*),[51] it is entered by those who are the Professors of the Oneness of God as well as the believers, the polytheists, the infidels and all followers of the doctrines of Being. As for the Second Path, it is entered only by those who divest God of His attributes (*muʿaṭṭila*). This Path does not lead the Wayfarer to any definite point. As for the liminal (barzakhī) Path, it is entered only by those who know God especially, whom God obliterated in His affirming them, and preserved them in the state of their annihilation. They are those who neither die nor are they kept alive (Q 20:74) until God passes His judgment between his servants. Then they will follow the Right Path to the Path of the Being the Real (*al-wujūd al-ḥaqq*), having been invested from the reality of the Right Path with an attribute and acquired from it a form that appears on them in the waystation of the Being the Real (*al-wujūd al-ḥaqq*), by which they know each other, and which is not recognized by the people of the other two Paths.[52]

One must notice the resemblance between Ibn al-ʿArabī's first two Paths of knowledge and Parmenides' Two Ways: the Way of Being and the Way of Nonbeing. According to Parmenides, the Way of Being is the only way of true knowledge, while the Way of Nonbeing is utterly indiscernible.[53] Similarly, Ibn al-ʿArabī states that there is a Path of knowledge, the extreme limit of which is Being. The followers of this Path identify Being (*al-wujūd*) with the Real (*al-ḥaqq*). Then there is the Path of Nonbeing, which has no limit (no definition) and, consequently, it cannot be known.

The Path of Nonbeing is followed by those who divest God of his attributes (*muʿaṭṭila*). *Taʿṭīl* (divesting God of the attributes which pertain to the world) is the negative equivalent to *tanzīh* (declaring God dissimilar to the world).[54] The *muʿaṭṭila* strip God of his attributes, which pertain to his creation, rendering the knowledge of him ineffective. Those who identify the Real with Being have chosen the right Path. Among them are included not only the unitarians, but also those who associate other gods with God (*mushrikūn*). Ibn al-ʿArabī explains this rather peculiar statement by saying that the associators associate other gods with God not because they are totally ignorant of him, but because through association they seek to come closer to him.[55] That the unitarians and the associators are classified under the same category is peculiar, but even more peculiar is Ibn al-ʿArabī's insistence that although those who profess the oneness of God are correct, the associators have demonstrated in their own way more correctly the truth of the reports about God's oneness. He insists that there can be no escape from associating others with God, and that expressing the oneness of God (*tawḥīd*) is actually impossible.[56]

That associating others with God (*shirk*) is more correct an indicator of the truth about the unity of God than proclaiming his oneness must sound as outrageous as the idea that breaking the boat in the story of the encounter between Khaḍir and Moses was more correct than keeping it whole. However, it was the breaking of the boat that kept it safe for its owners. Had Khaḍir not scuttled the boat, he would have caused it to be lost to its owners, since a cruel king was seizing on every undamaged boat by force. Likewise, by expressing God's Unity, one actually inserts duality into it and, consequently, causes it to vanish. For one to preserve God's Unity, there seems to be no other way but to remain silent, that is, to desist from proclaiming God's Unity. Hence, the prophet Noah made a mistake when he called upon God to punish his "heedless contemporaries" for worshiping idols and for not worshiping him in his extreme transcendence. Ibn al-ʿArabī blames Noah for doing so, since by inviting his people to worship a transcendent God, he was unknowingly inviting them to worship something that is utterly unknown to them; he was inviting them to the Path of Nonbeing.[57]

Among the followers of the Path of Being, who identify Being with the Real, are the believers. In the following passage from the Thirteenth Discussion of *The Incoherence of the Incoherence*, Ibn Rushd, the philosopher-believer, expresses his explicit belief in the unity between Being and God: "And this is the meaning of the ancient philosophers, when they say that God is the totality of the existents which He bestows on us in His bounty and of which He is the agent. And therefore the chiefs of the Ṣūfīs say: *Not-He is but-He.* But all this is the knowledge of those who are steadfast in their knowledge, and this must not be written down and must not be an obligation of faith, and therefore it is not taught by the Divine Law. And one who mentions this truth where it should not be mentioned sins, and one who withholds it from those to whom it should be told sins too."[58]

One should not mention the notion of the identification of God with the totality of the existents, that is, the doctrine of the Unity of Being, where it should not be mentioned. Who are those to whom the doctrine that God is the totality of the existents should not be mentioned, and why does Ibn Rushd insist that this doctrine must not be written down? George Hourani brings Ibn

Rushd's answer to the first question. The reason has to do with the right, which Ibn Rushd reserves exclusively to the philosophers, to interpret allegorically (*ta'wīl*) scriptural texts that deal with the relationship between God and the world. This right has to be conditional on the person's competence in demonstrative reasoning, and his capacity for deciphering the inner meanings of scriptures.[59] Ibn Rushd insists that the inner meanings of scriptures, which are discerned only through the interpretive effort of demonstrative reasoning, should not be revealed to the dialectical (theological reasoning) and rhetorical classes of people. He provides two reasons for this prohibition. One reason is that teaching allegorical interpretation to those who are incompetent generates doubts about religion. The second reason is that allegorical interpretation, when employed by nonexperts, can give rise to dissension and strife in the Islamic community through the growth of sects, each with its interpreted doctrine.[60]

The question now is whether Ibn Rushd considers it forbidden to write down such doctrines in any book whatsoever, or whether he permits writing down these doctrines, but only under certain conditions. In the Sixth Discussion of *The Incoherence of the Incoherence*, entitled "On the Denial of Attributes," Ibn Rushd opts for the second possibility: "This problem indeed is reserved for the men versed in profound knowledge to whom God has permitted the sight of the true realities, and therefore they must not be mentioned in any books *except those that are composed according to a strictly rational pattern,* that is, such books as must be read in a rational order and after the acquisition of other sciences the study of which according to a demonstrative method is too difficult for most men, even those who possess by nature a sound understanding, although such men are very scarce."[61]

He provides further clarification for his meaning in the Twelfth Discussion: "The Holy Law ascribes hearing and seeing to God to remind us that God is not deprived of any kind of knowledge and understanding, and the masses cannot be made to grasp this meaning except by the use of the terms hearing and seeing, and for this reason this exegesis is limited to the learned, and therefore cannot be taken as one of the dogmas of the Holy Law common to the masses."[62]

Ibn Rushd thinks that by presenting God to the masses in extreme transcendental terms, one runs the risk of causing the meaning of the Divinity to become void.[63] From Ibn al-ʿArabī's perspective, Ibn Rushd seems to have shown more awareness of the problem of the nature of God's unity than the prophet Noah. For according to Ibn Rushd, the words of the Scripture, which attribute seeing and hearing to God, must be interpreted, but this interpretation must not be revealed to the masses, since this may endanger their simple belief. This is, however, not the end of the story. For on the one hand, Ibn Rushd is aware that we need to delimit God in order to perceive Him, otherwise the totally nondelimited God would be incomprehensible for us. On the other hand, however, it seems that Ibn Rushd's awareness is not complete. For he tends to interpret rationally the reports concerning God's manifestation in the delimited forms of his creatures. After all, Ibn Rushd's interpretation is not faithful to the reports themselves, which clearly confirm God's delimitation. Thinking in terms of either/or (God is either totally comparable or totally incomparable with the world) Ibn Rushd opted for extreme incomparability. He was aware that God's reports declare him both unlimited and limited but chose to interpret rationally the reports about God's limitation. By doing so, however, he was not aware that he was delimiting God. For if God is totally unlimited, he must not be limited by unlimitation: "God is absolutely incomparable with any declaration of incomparability which delimits."[64] Ibn Rushd followed the dictates of his rational faculty, and rational faculty "has come with one-half the knowledge of God, that is, the declaration of incomparability and the negation of multiple properties from Him. But the Lawgiver brought news of God by affirming what the rational faculty's proofs (*dalāla*) have negated from Him and established what the rational faculty has stripped from Him."[65]

Only those Realizers who have emerged from the Barzakhī Path and reentered the Path of Being are capable of perceiving God in both his identity with and difference from Being. From the Barzakhī Path they have acquired a form which appears on them in the waystation of the Being the Real, by which they know each other, and which is not recognized by the people of the other two Paths. This sign by which the Realizers are recognized is that they *are and are not*. The Realizers have become a State (*ḥāl*), a link between the Creator and creation. Even the most rooted in rational knowledge, those who have achieved some kind of dim awareness of the Right Path, such as Ibn Rushd, would not be able to recognize them: "[H]e was made to appear before me in an ecstasy (*fī l-waqiʿa*) in such a form (*sūrah*) that between him and me there was a fine veil (*ḥijāb raqīq*), so that I could see him but he could not perceive me nor know that I was present–so preoccupied was he with himself! I said to myself, 'Truly, he is not intended for that which we are!'"[66]

William Chittick describes the history of Islamic thought as a gradual unfolding of the religious teaching concerning God's Unity (*tawḥīd*).[67] In my opinion, Islamic thinkers understood the notion of the Unity of God in terms of the Unity of Being. This, I think, can be said not only about Islamic philosophers, but also about Islamic theologians. For despite their belief in the creation of the world ex nihilo, the theologians did not attempt to rationalize the notion of Nonbeing. Thus, both philosophers and theologians were laboring within the limits set by Parmenides to all metaphysics, the limits of Being. This does not mean, however, that they made no progress beyond Parmenides. On the contrary, their labor yielded notions that indicated a serious potential venture beyond the Being (the Ultimate Limit) of Parmenides. The Muʿtazilites came out with the notion of the nonexistent (*al-maʿdūm*) which is something; the

Ashʿarites came out with the notion of the States (*aḥwāl*), which are neither existent nor nonexistent; Ibn Sīnā came out with the notion of the possible-in-itself and necessary-by-the-other; and Ibn Rushd introduced the paradoxical notion of actualized actuality. In my view, these notions had a significant impact on Ibn al-ʿArabī's barzakh concept. I will introduce this concept in the following chapter.

CHAPTER 5

The Barzakh

The Intermediate State (Barzakh) in the Qur'ān and in the Canonical Tradition

Barzakh appears three times in the Qur'ān, in which it plays the role of a barrier between two things (bodies, situations). It is presented as a limit that separates two entities, preventing them from mixing with each other. In this respect, the barzakh shares with the common conception of the limit its main characteristic, namely, its being an extremity either in the form of absolute beginning or in the form of absolute end. With Ibn al-ʿArabī this absolute conception of the limit undergoes major modification to become the relative conception of the Limit characteristic of his barzakh concept. The three Qur'ānic verses in which the barzakh appreas are the following:

> In falsehood will they be until, when death comes to one of them, he says: "O my Lord! Send me back (to life)—in order that I may work righteousness in the things I neglected"—"By no means! It is but a word he says"—Before them is a partition [barzakh] till the day they are raised up. (Q 23: 99–100)

> It is He Who has let free the two bodies of flowing water,[1] one palpable and sweet, and the other salt and bitter. Yet has He made a barrier [barzakh] between them, a partition that is forbidden to be passed. (Q 25:53)

> He has let free the two bodies of flowing water, meeting together: Between them is a barrier [barzakh] which they do not transgress. (Q 55:19–20)[2]

In his commentary on Q 25:53, ʿAbdullah Yūsuf ʿAlī explains that by the two bodies of water are meant the salt ocean and the bodies of sweet water fed by rain. He considers it a wonderful sign that although the two bodies of water pass through each other, they remain distinct bodies. This, he says, is a sign that demonstrates God's power and wisdom.[3] And indeed, chapter 55, in which the barzakh is mentioned for the third and the last time in the Qur'ān, consists of verses that are followed immediately by the reminder: "Then which of the favors of your Lord will you deny?"[4] This reminder is repeated thirty-one times in chapter 55, as the sheer number of its reoccurrence implies that a certain message about God's omnipotence is delivered.

The Qur'ānic example of the separation of the two bodies of water had a significant impact on Ibn al-ʿArabī's mystical theory in general and on his barzakh concept in particular. Consider, for example, the following passage, in which he provides his own version of chapter 55:

> He has let free the Two Seas, meeting together: between them there is a barzakh, which they do not transgress. Then which of the favors of your Lord will you deny? Will you deny the Sea that He attached to Himself and concealed from the Entities (*aʿyān*), or the Sea that he detached from Himself and named Worlds (*akwān*), or the barzakh upon which the All-Merciful (*al-Raḥmān*) sat? Then which of the favors of your Lord will you deny? He extracts from the Sea of Eternity pearls and from the Ever-lasting Sea He extracts coral. Then which of the favors of your Lord will you deny? . . . Soon shall We settle your affairs, O you Two Worlds. Then which of the favors of your Lord will you deny? Were the Qur'ān to be consulted, no two would differ, no two adversaries would emerge with an argument.[5]

The fact that Ibn al-ʿArabī refers in many places of the *Futūḥāt* to the Qur'ānic mention of the barzakh that separates between the Two Seas throws some doubt on the opinions of scholars such as ʿAffīfī, who claims that Ibn al-ʿArabī had drawn the notion of the barzakh from Jewish and Christian philosophical sources, especially the notion of the Logos in the philosophy of Philo, rather than from the Qur'ān.[6] In this and the next chapters, I will emphasize the close similarity between Ibn al-ʿArabī's notion of the immutable entity, his main example of the barzakh, and the Platonic ideas. In my opinion the Platonic doctrine of the ideas had some influence on Ibn al-ʿArabī's barzakh concept. However, I do not think that it would be correct to claim, like ʿAffīfī does, that Ibn al-ʿArabī's notion of the barzakh was borrowed exclusively from the thought of this or that thinker. As Naṣr Ḥāmid Abū Zayd points out in correcting ʿAffīfī's view, Ibn al-ʿArabī's barzakh concept has Qur'ānic as well as philosophic roots.[7] Moreover, Abū Zayd is correct in his observation that Ibn al-ʿArabī supports his philosophical interpretation of the notion of the barzakh by reference to the Islamic canonical tradition (*ḥadīth*). In what follows, I will examine the influence of the Islamic canonical tradition—especially the traditions that deal with the grave as an intermediate state between death and resurrection—on Ibn al-ʿArabī's barzakh concept.[8]

In the canonical tradition the notion of the intermediate state between death and the final judgment, which is called "barzakh" in Q 23:100, is linked essentially with the grave and the punishment that occurs in it. The grave is the intermediate state in which the dead person lingers from the time of his death until the time of resurrection. Two angels interrogate the dead, inquiring about their religion and who they consider Muḥammad to be. The dead are asked also whether God can be seen, a question that was considered important in theological controversies. According to the traditions, the unbeliever answers with a laugh, while the believer answers by confessing, "There is no god but Allah."[9]

Another form of punishment that is mentioned in the traditions is the pressure of the grave (*ḍaghṭa*). In this, the sides of the grave approach each other while the dead occupant is subjected to great pressure. This occurs in the case of the unbeliever. In the case of the believer the grave is enlarged and lightened. Ragnar Eklund connects this tradition with another tradition attributed to Tirmidhī (d. 908), according to which the grave is a pleasure garden (*rawḍa*) of paradise for the believer and a cave of fire (*ḥufra*) for the unbeliever. He says that when judging the original meaning of Tirmidhī's tradition we must take into consideration other similar traditions, like the one according to which the Prophet says, "What is between my grave (*qabr*) and my pulpit (*minbar*) is one of the gardens of paradise."[10] He does not explain what original meaning he thinks Tirmidhī's tradition signifies, and why we should relate it to the saying of the Prophet. Hopefully, reference to Ibn al-ʿArabī may elucidate the connection. In the following I will cite and comment on two passages from the *Futūḥāt* which mention the Prophet's saying. Notice that in both passages there is reference to some sort of *third entity*, a locus of manifestation that appears in different or even opposite forms, as the form in which it appears hides its hidden essence from the eyes of the viewer. Such is the case with rivers like the Nile and the Euphrates that are said to be rivers of the Garden although in this world they have become manifest in a form different from that in which they appear in the last world. The first citation is from chapter 356, entitled "On the true knowledge of three secreted mysteries, of the Arabic mystery in the divine courtesy, and of the revelation through the self and nature."

> The cosmos never ceases undergoing transmutation perpetually. This is the *new creation* concerning which most people are *uncertain* (50:151) and doubtful. Those of the Folk of God who know this—those whom God has caused to witness it in entity in their secret hearts—know the

> transmutation of this world into the last world and the transmutation of parts of the last world into other parts, just as parts of it were transmuted into this world.[11] For example, a report has come that the Nile, the Euphrates, the Pyramus, and the Sarus are among the rivers of the Garden that have been transmuted, so in this world they have become manifest in a form different from the form that they have in the last world. Another example is the Prophet's words, "Between my grave and my pulpit is one of the garden plots of the Garden."[12]

The second passage is from chapter 302, entitled "On the true knowledge of the waystation of the disappearance of the higher world and the being (*wujūd* in Chittick) of the lower world":

> Know, my brother—may God take charge of you with His mercy—that the Garden that is reached in the last world by those who are its folk is witnessed by you today in respect of its locus, *not in respect of its form.*[13] Within it you undergo fluctuations in your states, but you do not know that you are within it, because the form within which it discloses itself to you veils you. . . . Most of the folk of unveiling see this at the beginning of the path. The Shariah has called attention to this with the Prophet's words, "Between my grave and my pulpit is one of the garden plots of the Garden." The folk of unveiling see it as a garden plot as he said. They see the Nile, the Euphrates, the Sarus, and the Pyramus as rivers of honey, water, wine, and milk, as they are in the Garden. After all, the Prophet reported that these rivers belong to the Garden.[14]

Chapters 356 and 302 mention the barzakh. They also contain a reference to Q 55:29, "Every day He is upon some novel activity," a verse that Ibn al-ʿArabī quotes frequently in support of an important theme in his mystical theory, namely, the doctrine of the perpetual renewal of creation (*al-khalq al-mutajaddid*).[15] The world, according to Ibn al-ʿArabī, is the locus of manifestation of the self-disclosures of God. God never discloses himself in the same form twice, since his self-disclosures are diverse and unlimited.[16] As William Chittick, points out, Ibn al-ʿArabī often quotes Abū Ṭālib al-Makkī's saying, "God never discloses Himself in a single form to two individuals, nor in a single form twice."[17] Ibn al-ʿArabī was also fascinated with another saying of another mystic, Abū Saʿīd al-Kharrāz: "I knew God by His gathering between the opposites."[18] He who possesses knowledge of the unlimited nature of God's self-disclosure, and understands that the meaning of this unlimitedness is that God can disclose himself in the same locus of manifestation (the world) in two opposite forms, knows the meaning of the Prophet's words, "What is between my grave and my pulpit is one of the gardens of paradise." What is between the grave and pulpit is a locus of manifestation, an intermediate state, which may take on opposite forms. In the same manner, the grave in Tirmidhī's tradition can become a pleasure garden of paradise for the believer or a cave of fire for the unbeliever. For the grave is the locus of manifestation for the deeds of the dead. If those are righteous the grave becomes a garden; if unrighteous the grave becomes a cave of fire. This can be related to the tradition about the pressure of the grave, according to which the grave may become very narrow, so narrow that its sides almost touch each other in the case of the unrighteous, or, if the deeds of the dead were perfectly righteous, the grave may become large, as large as the range of vision.[19]

All this is in agreement with Ibn al-ʿArabī's repeated statement that in the presence of the barzakh meanings are embodied and spiritual entities are manifested in corporeal forms. Thus, the dead person may see his deeds in a perfect form if in his lifetime he managed to perfect himself through obedience to the Law, whereas the opposite happens if the person neglects his duty as a believer.[20] Moreover, evidence from Ibn al-ʿArabī's works indicates that he was aware of the logical consequences that follow from the descriptions in traditions of the embodiment of spiritual states in corporeal forms. For example, according to the tradition about the pressure of the grave, the grave may become large or narrow according to the positive or negative value of the deeds of the person. Consequently, if a righteous person lies dead in the same grave to the side of an unrighteous person, the same grave would become both large and narrow. This is impossible according to rational principles. However, in the imaginal presence,[21] the presence of the barzakh, such occurrences are not impossible, as Ibn al-ʿArabī affirms in the following passage:

> I saw a tremendous place of witnessing, in sensory form—not in intelligible form—a form of the Real, not a meaning. In this self-disclosure there became manifest to me the manner in which the small expands in order for the large to enter into it, while it remains small and the large remains large, like the camel, which passes through the eye of the needle. That is contemplated in sensory, not imaginal, form, and the small embraces the large; you do not know how, but you do not deny what you see. So glory be to Him who is exalted high beyond a perception that satisfies rational faculties and who preferred the eyes over rational faculties! "There is no god but He, the inaccessible, the Wise." (Q 3:6)[22]

In the barzakh not only does a small body expand in order for a large body to enter into it, but a long period of time can enter into a short one. Ibn al-ʿArabī confirms this point in his answers to two questions posed by Tirmidhī al-Ḥakīm.[23] In his answer to the question, "How has His command become like the glance of the eye?" Ibn al-ʿArabī says that the activity in respect of God is one, while in respect of the receptivities (*qawābil*) of the world it is infinitely many.[24] In his answer to the question, "What is the meaning of His words: 'The affair of the Hour [the Hour of Resurrection] is like the glance of the eye or even closer than that?'" Ibn al-ʿArabī says that no one knows the reality of the proximity between the time of resurrection and the time of the death of a person in this life except he who knows God's capacity to manifest the Imaginal in the existence of the natural world.[25] He adds that he who knows this knows the meaning of the following visionary event:

> Al-Jawharī carried the dough from his home to the oven. He came to the bank of the Nile to perform the major ritual ablution, since on him there was a major ritual impurity. While in the water he saw, as in a dream, that he was in Baghdad and that he had wedded a woman and lived with her and her children (whose number I do not recall) for six years. Then he was brought back to himself while still in the water. He finished washing himself, left the water, and put on his clothes. He came to the oven, picked up the bread, and went home. There he told his people about what he had seen in his visionary event (*wāqiʿa*). And so it happened that months later the woman, whom he had married in the visionary event, arrived and asked about his dwelling place. When they gathered together, he recognized her and her children and did not deny them. She was asked concerning the time of their marriage, and she answered: "It was six years ago, and these are my children from him." And so what had taken place in Imagination materialized in sensory form.[26]

From the preceding examples we learn that the Islamic canonical traditions about the grave, being an intermediate state between death and resurrection, exerted a strong influence on Ibn al-ʿArabī's barzakh concept, especially on his relativistic conception of space and time most characteristic of his notion of the barzakh.

The Barzakh in the Exegesis of the Qur'ān and in Scholastic Theology

Barzakh was mentioned in the exegesis of the Qur'ān and in theology but not in the Islamic canonical tradition. Yet, as Eklund points out, the application of the term did not attain to the same value in the exegesis of the Qur'ān as the "life-hereafter." Neither Zamakhsharī nor Bayḍāwī, for example, provided any other interpretation of the barzakh than that of an obstacle to the return of the dead until the day of resurrection.[27] The same thing can be said about the application of the concept in theology. In the controversies between the Ashʿarites and the Muʿtazilites the barzakh did not play a significant part.[28] Eklund mentions an important development of the barzakh concept in the Islamic tradition. This is the development of the concept from its temporal designation in orthodoxy, signifying a period of time that extends between death and resurrection, to its spatial designation within mysticism. The latter development was associated with Tirmidhī al-Ḥakīm, who reported a tradition traced back to Salmān al-Fārisī, according to which the spirits of the believers after death move in an earthly barzakh (*barzakh min al-arḍ*) wherever they please from heaven to earth until God restores them to their bodies. Eklund emphasizes the significance of attributing this tradition to Salmān al-Fārisī, who was considered one of the founders of Ṣūfīsm.[29]

Tirmidhī al-Ḥakīm exerted a significant influence on Islamic mysticism in general and on Ibn al-ʿArabī in particular, as this must be evident from the several references to him in Ibn al-ʿArabī's works. Another theologian-mystic who exerted a strong influence on Ibn al-ʿArabī was Ghazālī. There can be no doubt that Ghazālī's *Revival of the Sciences of Religion* (*Iḥyā' ʿUlūm al-Dīn*) had a serious impact on Ibn al-ʿArabī's thought. Franz Rosenthal says that Ghazālī was Ibn al-ʿArabī's great immediate model, and that Ibn al-ʿArabī aspired to replace Ghazālī's *Revival* with his own renewal of religion in a purer, mystical language.[30] The term *barzakh* is found in Ghazālī's works, but Ghazālī's concern was mostly with the grave as the intermediate state between death and resurrection. In his discussion of the conditions after death in the grave, he emphasizes the difficulty about the rational interpretations of traditions describing occurrences such as the ninety-nine snakes that torment the dead in the grave. He insists, however, that we should not yield to one who judges rationally in reliance on the testimony of his senses that the described snakes do not exist in reality. He argues that the traditions depict real things, but that their reality is different from the reality of objects that are perceived by sense perception:

> [Even if a person] does not see them with his eyes, which is impossible in the case of *malakūtic* things . . . he can follow the example of the first disciples who believed in Gabriel's descent, which not they but only the Prophet witnessed. He who believes in angels and other things which the Prophet but not his *umma* has seen, ought also to believe in these things . . . especially as the snakes of the grave are of quite another kind than those known on earth, just as the angels are beings different in kind from human beings. You witness how a sleeper in his sleep sees a snake that bites him, at which you hear him cry, see the sweat break out on his forehead, and see him roll over from his place. . . . You, on the other hand, will find everything outwardly

> quiet, no snake wriggles round the man. The snake only exists within his imagination while punishment is going on, but there is nothing to be seen in your sphere. And with regard to the pain itself of the snake-bite there is no difference whether the snake exists according to an imagination or an observation.[31]

Ghazālī applies the example of sleep and the dreams that occur in it to point at the possibility of an experience that is related to the hereafter, and that is quite removed from our sensory reach. Dreams play a significant role in Ibn al-ʿArabī's thought as well. In the following passage, Ibn al-ʿArabī refers to the things that occur to the person after death (the "greater death"), comparing these to things that occur in the experience of sleep (the "lesser death"):

> Do you not see that, when he is transferred to the barzakh through the greater death or the lesser death, he sees in the lesser death affairs that he was considering rationally impossible in the state of wakefulness? Yet, in the barzakh, he perceives them as sensory things, just as, in the state of wakefulness, he perceives that to which his sensation is connected, so he does not deny it. Despite the fact that his rational faculty proves to him that a certain affair cannot have being [*wujūd* in Chittick], he sees it existent in the *barzakh*. There is no doubt that it is an affair of being [*wujūd* in Chittick] to which sensation becomes connected in the *barzakh*. After all, the homesteads of sensation are diverse, so the properties are diverse.[32]

Like Ghazālī, Ibn al-ʿArabī emphasizes the importance of dreams in realizing the possibility of the existence of another Presence (*ḥaḍra*) besides that of sense perception. He emphasizes the swiftness of the transmutation (*taḥawwul*) of the forms that appear in this Presence, which he calls "the Presence of Imagination." According to him, only Unveiling can catch up with this swiftness and reach to the root of the transmutation of forms that transpire in this Presence. In contrast to Unveiling, reflection, which is bound to the forms of sense perception, falls short of attaining to the Presence of Imagination.[33] Comparing the two passages from the *Iḥyā'* and the *Futūḥāt*, one must notice the technically, fully developed, mystical language of Ibn al-ʿArabī's *Futūḥāt* compared with the more sensually descriptive and concrete terminology of Ghazālī's *Iḥyā'*. With Ibn al-ʿArabī mystical terminology reached its full development, synthesizing views of mystics, theologians, and philosophers. Like Ghazālī, Ibn al-ʿArabī was critical of the philosophers. But while Ghazālī attacked philosophical thought from a theological point of view, Ibn al-ʿArabī directed his criticism to the rational thought of both philosophers and theologians. This allowed him to be opened to the possibility of learning from the (few) philosophers that he considered as possessors of true knowledge. One of the philosophers that Ibn al-ʿArabī had enormous respect for was Plato. In the following section, I will discuss the philosophical background to Ibn al-ʿArabī's barzakh concept in Plato's theory of the Forms.

Plato's Theory of the Forms

Plato's early (Socratic) dialogues revolved around the problem of definition.[34] Socrates asks his interlocutors to define the essence of a certain idea—holiness, for example. His assumption is that once the essence of the idea is defined, it then becomes a matter of a simple application of the obtained definition to the case under discussion and a thing or an action can be determined as holy or unholy. A curious process ensues in which each determination or actual exemplification of the essence of the idea is found lacking in precision. The interlocutor attempts another existential determination but the new determination is soon transcended, indicating the indeterminacy intrinsic to the idea. This interplay between determination and indetermination (the transcendence of a given determination) constitutes the heartbeat of the Socratic dialogues. The conclusion of the Socratic dialogues, which is not stated explicitly in the dialogues themselves, is that the essential nature of ideas is intrinsically indeterminate in the sense that the definition of the idea cannot be identified with this or that sensible exemplification of it.

In his later dialogues, Plato explains that the real aim of the Socratic dialogues was to establish the theory of Forms. According to him, objects are divided into sensible and intelligible objects. The sensible objects are the images that participate in the intelligible objects, their universal patterns. Plato states in *Phaedo*, "[W]hatever else is beautiful apart from absolute beauty is beautiful because it partakes of that absolute beauty, not for any other reason."[35] That is, he refuses to admit any kind of causal explanation to the being as such (beautiful, holy, and so on) of a certain object other than the causality that is characteristic of the participation of sensible objects in their universal Forms.

The first to attack the theory of Forms was Plato himself. In *Parmenides*, Plato presents Socrates as a young man facing the worst of difficulties in defending the theory of Forms against Parmenides' attacks. Huntington Cairns wonders why Plato should have made Parmenides follow such a curious procedure, which aimed at the refutation of his own theory.[36] He expresses the opinion that the reason behind Plato's attempt was his relentless adherence to a rather extreme rational methodology, which is exactly what makes him so different from mystical thinkers.[37] On the contrary, I think that by making Parmenides criticize and, in a sense, rationally refute the theory of Forms, Plato was doing a great service to the theory itself. For, according to Plato, an understanding of the theory of Forms depends on one's capacity to transcend the limitations of rational thinking: "Hardly after practicing detailed comparisons of names and definitions and visual and other sense perceptions, after scrutinizing them in benevolent disputation by the use of question and answer without jealousy, at last in a flash understanding of each blazes up, and the mind, as it exerts all its powers to the limit of human capacity, is flooded with light."[38]

Parmenides' attack on the theory of Forms is established on the basis of demonstrating that it is impossible to rationally relate the Forms to the sensible objects that participate in them. In Plato's *Parmenides* we read:

PARMENIDES:	Then each thing that partakes receives as its share either the form as a whole or a part of it? Or can there be any other way of partaking besides this?
SOCRATES:	No, how could there be?
PARMENIDES:	Do you hold, then, that the form as a whole, a single thing, is in each of the many, or how?
SOCRATES:	Why should it not be in each, Parmenides?
PARMENIDES:	If so, a form which is one and the same will be at the same time, as a whole, in a number of things which are separate, and consequently will be separate from itself.[39]

The absolute unity of the Forms, a unity that is characteristic of Parmenides' Being, is rent asunder upon their encounter with the multiplicity of things in the world of Becoming. A relation between the simple unity of the Forms and the complex nature of the things in the world requires a conception of the relation between Being and Becoming that forfeits the simplicity of Being, which was considered by Parmenides as the Absolute Limit of thought.[40] Plato's final solution to Parmenides's challenge emerges only in the *Timaeus* in the context of dealing with the problem of the creation of the world. I will discuss this solution in the next chapter in dealing with Ibn al-ʿArabī's doctrine of the Third Thing. First, however, attention must be given to Aristotle's criticism to Plato's theory of the Forms, since it is against the background of Aristotle's criticism that Ibn al-ʿArabī's barzakh concept will be introduced. Aristotle reasserted the points of criticism introduced by Plato against his own theory, insisting that speaking about Forms as both substances and causes of sensible things may involve us in many unsolvable difficulties. One of these difficulties is that in order to establish a relation of causality between a Form and a sensible thing that participates in it, we must place intermediate objects between them. But then where should we locate these intermediate objects? Are we to say that they exist in sensible objects? If so, the Forms themselves must exist in the sensible objects, for both Forms and the intermediate objects possess the same abstract nature and therefore they must come under the same argument.[41] As their title indicates, intermediate objects must be posited between the sensible objects and the Forms. But this opens the door for a serious difficulty, since positing intermediates between the Forms and sensible objects leads to an infinite regress. Ibn Rushd's elaboration on the difficulty in his commentary on *Metaphysics,* 991 b: 31–37 may be helpful in clarifying Aristotle's argument:

> [Let us assume that] the mathematical number is an Intermediate between the Forms and the sensible objects. Every Intermediate is made up either from simple principles (indivisible things) or from indivisible things in addition to intermediate objects that are made up of these indivisible things, or from the Forms themselves of the intermediate objects. The intermediate objects, which are made up of preceding intermediate objects, must be made up of these preceding intermediate objects not as the latter are intermediate objects as such, but in respect of their being the Forms of the generated intermediate objects, that is, in respect of their being Forms that are different from the intermediate objects as such. This is because, if the intermediate objects were made up of intermediate objects as such, the process would lead from one intermediate object to another *ad infinitum.*[42]

Due to their intermediatory nature, the intermediate objects cannot be made up either of indivisible things or from Forms of intermediate objects, since indivisible things and Forms are simple unities, while intermediate objects are dualities. The assumed intermediate objects must be made up of other intermediate objects, which must also be made up of other intermediate objects ad infinitum. The positing of Forms necessitates the positing of an infinite number of intermediate objects each providing a definition for that which precedes it, which is absurd. All this is in agreement with Aristotle's theory of definitions and his belief in the impossibility of the existence of the actual infinite. Aristotle says that a definition cannot always be reduced to another definition longer than the preceding one ad infinitum. For if there is no final definition that is first, neither will any of the other definitions be such as stated. Aristotle insists that those who speak in this manner eliminate knowledge, for it is not possible for us to understand unless we come to things that function as limits.[43]

It should be clear, however, that Aristotle's argument against the existence of intermediate objects is won the moment these objects are defined as dualities exclusive to unities. From here, the way is very short to showing that demanding a definition for what is defined exclusively as a duality involves one necessarily in an infinite regress. The intermediate objects are defined as possessing no definition, that is, as possessing no limit that could render them unities. How can they then function as limits that endow the objects, between which they mediate, with definition? The intermediate objects cannot set limits to things because they are defined as lacking a limit of their own, which renders them essenceless. This becomes clear from Aristotle's definition of the limit: "'Limit' means (1) the ultimate part of each thing, or the first part outside of which no part can be found, or the first part inside of which all parts exist; (2) the form of a magnitude or of that which has magnitude; (3) the end of each thing, such being that toward which, but not that from which, a motion or an *action* is directed, although sometimes it is both that from which and that toward which; (4) the final cause; (5) the *substance* of each thing, or the essence of each thing, for this is said to be the limit of knowledge; and if of knowledge then of the thing also."[44]

It is in contrast to Aristotle's definition that Ibn al-ʿArabī's conception of the limit will be introduced. Like Aristotle, he says that limit is the essence of everything, but his limit is the essence of every thing not in the Aristotelian but in the Platonic sense, that is, in the sense that things participate in the limit not that the limit constitutes the final part of a thing.

Ibn al-ʿArabī's Definition of the Barzakh

In the following Ibn al-ʿArabī introduces one of his most elaborated characterizations of the concept of the Limit (barzakh). He begins by connecting his concept to Q 25:53, which mentions the Two Seas between which there is a barrier that they do not overpass. He proceeds by introducing what he believes to be the false concept of the Limit, a concept that depicts it as a duality instead of a unity. He explains that this false depiction of the Limit precludes it from fulfilling the very function for the sake of which it is introduced and that is providing unity to a given duality:

> You should know that this waystation is the waystation of the true barzakh. People think widely about the barzakh, but it is not what they think. It is rather as God identified it to us in His words concerning the Two Seas between which there is a barzakh, which they do not overpass. The truth about the barzakh is that there can be no barzakh in it. The barzakh is what meets the two [sides which it separates] with its [undivided] essence. If it were to meet the one side with a face that is other than the face with which it meets the other side, there would have to be between the two faces a barzakh to separate them so that they do not meet. In that case it [that which meets one of the things with a face which is other than the face with which it meets the other] is not a barzakh. The true barzakh is that which meets one

> of the things between which it separates with the very face with which it meets the other.
>
> It is in its essence identical to everything that it meets. *Hence the separation between the things and the separating factor become manifest as one in entity*. . . . Its likeness is the whiteness of every white thing through its very essence. *It is not in one white thing through one of its faces, and in another through another face. On the contrary, through its own entity it is in every white thing*. The two white things may be distinct from each other, but whiteness is their counterpart only through its essence. . . . Hence the "one" is the true *barzakh*. Anything that can be divided is not one. *The one divides but it is not divided, which is to say that it is not divisible in itself*. After all, if it receives division in its entity, then it is not one. If it is not one, then it is not the counterpart of each of the two things between which it stands through its essence. But in such a situation the one is known to be one, without doubt. The *barzakh* is known but not perceived, rationally understood but not witnessed. . . . Do not you see the forms that are in the Market of the Garden? All of them are *barzakhs*. The folk of the Garden come to this Market because of these forms. . . . When they enter this Market, everyone who has the appetite for a form enters into it and goes back with it to his family, just as he would go back with the needed thing that he had bought from the market. . . . No one knows the reality of this affair . . . save him who knows the *configuration of the last world, the reality of the barzakh, and the self-disclosure of the Real in numerous forms*. He transmutes Himself within them from form to form, but the Entity is one.[45]

The definition that Ibn al-ʿArabī provides here for the barzakh can only be tentative. For the barzakh is the very thing that makes the activity of defining possible. This is the meaning of his words that the separation between the things (defining) and the separating factor (that which defines) become manifest as one in entity. Understanding the definition of the barzakh is identical to understanding the essence of the activity of defining, which consists of differentiating between things. Ibn al-ʿArabī says that differentiation (*tafriqa*) is the root of all things.[46] This is because through the process of differentiation limits (*ḥudūd*) are set between things, and except for the limits knowledge would be impossible.[47] There is a paradoxical aspect intrinsic to the activity of defining that consists of differentiating one thing from another. Something is defined through a process in which it is separated from all relations with Other. But difference itself is a relation, indeed, the most unifying of relations, "The closest, most affectionate, and most unifying of relations is one between

Other (*khilāf*) and its other, from which it is differentiated. . . . Affection (*mawadda*) between differentiated things prevents each of them from wanting the disappearance of its other from existence. Each desires and wishes that it could become one with its other for the sake of avoiding any difference between itself and Other, so that witnessing becomes only for the one and that the other disappears in it."[48]

The argument that leads Ibn al-ʿArabī to the conclusion that "the closest, most affectionate and most unifying of relations is one between Other (*khilāf*) and its other, from which it is differentiated," can be reconstructed from the passage cited above as follows: Something defines itself through a process of differentiating itself from all relation to Other. But differentiating is a sort of relation. By differentiating itself from Other, Something relates itself to Other. To avoid this paradoxical situation, Something seeks to differentiate itself from all relations to Other, *including the relation of difference from Other*. But the only way Something can differentiate itself from difference to Other is by making Other disappear in it, that is, by uniting with Other. Hence, by completely differentiating itself from Other, Something completely unites with Other.

The argument yields the paradoxical conclusion that by identifying themselves things lose their very identity, since they become other than themselves. This means that things cease to be when they come to be, or that the existence of things is the same as their nonexistence. This is certainly not the conclusion that a rational thinker would approve of, and when confronted with it, "the philosopher tosses it away, as do all the companions of rational proofs."[49] According to Ibn al-ʿArabī, only the sophists come close to the realization that the moment of the coming to be of things is the same as the moment of their annihilation.[50] Nevertheless, he insists that the sophists make a mistake when they draw the conclusion that things do not possess any reality whatsoever.[51] But how can Ibn al-ʿArabī maintain that things have a reality when the moment of their coming-to-be is the same as the moment of their ceasing-to-be, that is, when things do not possess any unity specific to them? His position seems to be paradoxical through and through, and unless we understand the nature of the paradox that is involved in his position, we may not fully appreciate his way of thinking.

We started our inquiry about definitions, or what is involved in the practice of defining, with the assumption that in our common experience we do perceive things as possessing definitions, or, as possessing specific unities. With this assumption as our starting point we have arrived at the conclusion that the coming-to-be of the things is the same as their ceasing-to-be, which means that things do not really have unities or realities specific to them. We may adhere to the assumption (that things have realities specific to them) but then we will be ignoring the conclusion to which this assumption has led us; or we may accept the conclusion, but then we will be ignoring the fact that in reality we do perceive things as possessing realities specific to them. Ibn al-ʿArabī's choice was to accept both the assumption and the conclusion of the argument. Things are both real and not real, and in this paradoxical notion is to be found their very reality. More important, he thinks that the paradoxical reality of things comes to them by virtue of their being images of their immutable or fixed entities (*aʿyān thābita*), which are barzakhs between them and the Real. Things in the cosmos possess only a relational existence. Their existence resembles that of an image in the mirror:

> If you possess the power of reasoning and you perceive the image you realize that you have perceived an affair of being (*wujūd*) on which your sight has fallen, but you immediately know, with manifest certainty, that originally there was nothing there to be witnessed. Then what is the thing for which you had affirmed an entified being, and that you negated even in the very state of your affirming it? Imagination is neither existent (*mawjūd*) nor nonexistent (*maʿdūm*) neither known nor unknown neither affirmed nor negated. A person who sees his image in the mirror knows decisively that he has perceived his form in some respect and that he has not perceived his form in some other respect. Since he has perceived minuteness in the image, which is due to the small size of the mirror, he realizes that his form is bigger than the one he has seen, which rules out any possibility of identifying between the two forms. . . . Then if he says: "I saw my form, I did not see my form," he will be neither a truth-teller nor a liar.[52]

One way to state the ontological status of images is to say that they are both existent and nonexistent. Another way to express the truth about their reality is to say that they are neither existent nor nonexistent. Consequently, one can neither affirm nor negate their existence. Rational thinkers, who establish their judgment on the basis of the inputs of their senses, take the existence of the images for granted. For them, things are not images but "solid" entities that possess essential existence. Rational thinkers fall victim, therefore, to the illusion, which is illustrated in the following observation: "Look at the form manifest to the eye in a polished surface and verify your vision. You will find that the form has come between you and your perception of the polished surface, which is the locus of disclosure. So you will never see the surface."[53]

The surface of the mirror signifies the fixed entity (*ʿayn thābita*), which is Ibn al-ʿArabī's main example for the barzakh concept, and which is similar in meaning to Plato's Form. The forms which appear in the mirror prevent the perceiver from seeing the mirror's surface (the Form). The forms in the mirror, therefore, prevent the perceiver from seeing their realities, or what relates them to the Real, Who is the root of their existence. As a matter of fact, this observation was originally Ghazālī's:

> It is not unlikely that a person could look into a mirror in an unexpected place and not see the mirror at all. He supposes that the form he sees is the mirror's form and that it is united with the mirror. Likewise he could see wine in a glass and suppose that the wine is the glass's color. When the situation becomes familiar to him and his foot becomes firmly established within it, he asks for forgiveness from God and says:
>
> "The glass is clear, the wine is clear, the two are similar, the affair confused. As if there is wine and no glass, or glass and no wine. There is a difference between saying 'The wine is the cup' and 'It is as *if* the wine is the cup.'"[54]

What happens when the surface of the mirror is not carefully polished? What happens is that it fails to reflect the exact form of the viewer in the mirror, that is, it fails to provide perfect representation of the viewer through his reflected image. When the surface of the mirror is thoroughly polished, a perfect representation of the viewer through his form in the mirror is obtained. But in that case the surface of the mirror itself disappears (ceases to exist). It seems that we have a dilemma here, which is about the same difficulty that was raised by Aristotle in relation to the intermediate objects that we posit between sensible things and the Forms in order to account for the participation of the former in the latter. According to the difficulty, positing the Forms to account for the reality of sensible things leads to an infinite regress.[55] The only way to escape this infinite regress, that is, the only way to recover the reality of things, is to make the intermediate objects vanish. The process that we started and that was supposed to provide for a link between the sensible objects and their realities terminated in canceling the link and identifying these realities with the sensible things themselves.

As it is obvious, the whole dilemma stems from the assumption that a duality is what constitutes the essence of intermediate objects, a duality that once posited must engender an infinite regress. For the two faces of the duality require another relation to provide for their unity. Again, by definition, this new relation requires another relation to unify its dual faces ad infinitum. Ibn al-ʿArabī insists, however, that the intermediate object must meet each of the two things between which it separates by its very essence. "If it were to meet the one side with a face that is other than the face with which it meets the other side, there must be between the two faces a barzakh to separate between them so that they do not meet."[56] If the barzakh meets the two things between which it separates with the one and the same face, it must be an undivided unity. But then it cannot exist in its entirety in many objects, since in that case it will be separated from itself. Ibn al-ʿArabī refuses to admit this conclusion, insisting that whiteness, for example, "is in every white thing through its very essence. It is not in one white thing through one of its faces, and in another through another face, on the contrary, through its own entity it is in every white thing." [57] But how can this be possible? The young Socrates in Plato's *Parmenides* suggested that it was something like the one and the same day being in many places at the same time. But then we may object, with Parmenides, that only a part of the day would be in each place but not the day in its entirety, and so Forms will be divisible necessarily.[58] Ibn al-ʿArabī insists, however, that the barzakh divides but is not divided in itself. How can this be the case? How can the one barzakh set limits to things (divide between things), and yet remain limitless (undivided)?

According to Ibn al-ʿArabī, no one knows the reality of the barzakh except he who knows the reality of the self-disclosures of the infinite Real in the finite forms of the cosmos. This is because the Real is a barzakh between his two faces, the face that is the nonmanifest (*bāṭin*) and the face that is the manifest (*ẓāhir*). The barzakh is the essence of the two things between which it differentiates, so that the Real becomes the Essence of the manifest and the nonmanifest. Ibn al-ʿArabī brings Abū Saʿīd al-Kharrāz's words, "I knew God by His gathering between the opposites," and comments on them, "Upon hearing this from us, our companion Tāj al-Dīn al-Akhlāī said: Rather He is the (very) opposites, telling the truth, since the saying of Kharrāz makes you think that there is an entity which is added to the opposites and which accepts both. The affair in itself is not like that. For He is the (very) opposites and no entity is added to that. The Manifest is the same entity as the Nonmanifest, the First and the Last; the First is the same entity as the Last, the Manifest and the Nonmanifest."[59]

This one reality, which brings the manifest and the nonmanifest together while keeping them apart, is the reality of the barzakh. One who knows the reality of the barzakh knows how impossible things (*muḥāl*) are made possible: "In this waystation you know in what manner . . . the large enters into the narrow, while the narrow remains narrow and the large remains large. The narrow and the large remain in the same state but not in the manner described by the possessors of demonstration such as the theologians and the philosophers, as they believe that the large and the narrow become one in definition but not in corporeal form."[60]

That a large thing enters into a small thing while the large remains large and the small remains small, or that a thing can be at two places at the same time is considered a break in the natural law. For Ibn al-ʿArabī, however, this is not more impossible than the self-disclosure of the Real in cosmic forms. For how can the infinite (Real) enter into the finite (creation)? Or how can that which is finite encompass that which is infinite? To know how the infinite enters into the finite, a special knowledge is needed,[61] and this knowledge is none other than the knowledge of the reality of the barzakh, without which no correct knowledge is possible.[62] The knowledge of the barzakh and the knowledge of the self-disclosure of the infinite Real in the finite forms of the cosmos are identical. It turns out that both sorts of knowledge are based on a special understanding of the conception of *relation*, whether it is the relation between things in the world and their fixed entities or the relation between the world as a whole and the Real.

Ibn al-ʿArabī versus Ibn Sīnā: Two Conceptions of the Relative

In what follows I will provide an examination of Ibn al-ʿArabī's conception of relation, comparing it with that of Ibn Sīnā. In introducing Ibn Sīnā's conception of relation, I will rely on Michael E. Marmura's "Avicenna's Chapter, 'On the Relative' in the *Metaphysics* of the *Shifā'*."[63] According to Ibn Sīnā's definition of relation, whatever relates to another thing relates in itself, not through something else that is relation:

> Each of the two related things has in itself an idea with respect to the other, which is not the idea the other has in itself with respect to [the first]. This is evident in the things whose related terms differ, as in the case of the father. Its relation to fatherhood, which is a description of its existence, is in the father alone. But it belongs to the father with respect to something else [only as something] in the father. Its being with respect to the other does not make it exist in the other. *Fatherhood does not exist in the son. . . .* Rather, fatherhood belongs to the father. The same applies to the state of the son with respect to the father. There is nothing here at all which is in both of them. Here there is nothing but fatherhood and sonship. *As for a state posited for both fatherhood and sonship, this is something unknown to us and has no name. . . .* This is similar to the state of the swan and snow, each of which is white. Nor is [this state] rendered identical by the fact that [it stands] with respect to the other; for whatever belongs to each individual with respect to the other, belongs to that individual and not the other; but it [possesses] it with respect to the other.[64]

Ibn Sīnā's definition of relations is based on the same logic underlying his distinction between the essence of a thing and its existence, according to which the modes of the existence of a thing may vary, but *in itself* the thing remains one and the same entity. In reality things exist necessarily, but in our minds we can subtract the essence of things from their existence. Following the same logic, Ibn Sīnā argues that although the relation of fatherhood, for example, must exist always in its concrete instances, the relation *in itself* exists absolutely.

Ibn Sīnā applies this absolute definition of relation to the solution of a serious objection to the existence of universals outside the mind, which was raised by Islamic theologians. According to the argument, if relations exist in things, that is, outside the mind, then an infinite regress ensues. Take for example the relation between father and son. Under the assumption that relations exist outside the mind, that is, in their concrete instances, we will have fatherhood related to the father, the subject of its occurrence, and sonship related to the son, the subject of its occurrence. Thus we will have a relation between fatherhood and the father in the father, and a relation between sonship and the son in the son. These two relations require an additional relation to bring them together. Again this relation must exist also in the father, also in the son, and the process goes on ad infinitum.[65]

In his response to the argument, Ibn Sīnā applies his "absolute" definition of relation; according to which whatever is related to another thing is related in itself and not through something else, which is relation. This definition enjoins that relation should be an accident and not a self-subsisting thing, one in number, connecting two things. Applying this absolute definition of relation, we can say that the relation of fatherhood, which is a relation between father and son, and the relation of fatherhood *in itself* are related in themselves, not through something that is relation. Thus relations become finite, and an infinite regress does not follow.[66]

In his absolute definition of relation, Ibn Sīnā says that each of the two related things is related to the other in itself, that is, through an idea, which is not the idea that the other has in itself with respect to it. This seems exactly the opposite of what Ibn al-ʿArabī says. For he insists that the likeness of the idea that relates between two white things, for example, is "the whiteness of every white thing through its very essence. It is not in one white thing through one of its faces, and in another through another face. On the contrary, through its own entity it is in every white thing."[67] The relation that Ibn al-ʿArabī is thinking about is *in* the related things; it is an essential relation that includes the related things. In contrast to the accidentiality that Ibn Sīnā characterizes relations with, Ibn al-ʿArabī characterizes relations as most substantial, especially regarding knowledge of things: "He who knows relations (*nisab*) knows God (Allah) and he who is ignorant of relations is ignorant of God. He who knows that the possible existents demand relations knows the world and he who knows the lifting (*irtifāʿ*) of relations knows the Essence of the Real (*al-ḥaqq*) *via negativa*."[68]

In what follows, Ibn al-ʿArabī provides further explanation of the significance of the knowledge of relations. Notice the manner in which he connects this to the discussion of the problem of the relationship between God and the world:

> Thus if you say "Zayd is ʿAmr's son," or "ʿAmr's slave," then there can be no doubt that the designation *sonship* newly arrived to Zayd in virtue of being ʿAmr's son, and that the designation *fatherhood* newly arrived to ʿAmr in virtue of being Zayd's father. The sonship of Zayd gave fatherhood to ʿAmr and the fatherhood of ʿAmr gave sonship to Zayd. Each one of the related persons made a meaning newly arrive to the other to whom he is related, a meaning that was not attributed to the other prior to the occurrence of the relation. . . . By saying that a human being, or, human beings are Allah's slaves, you are saying that Allah is their Owner; there is no escape from that. If you think it possible in your mind that the world on the whole can disappear in respect of its being owned, then that will not make the Being of the Real disappear, following the disappearance of the world. But the disappearance of the world will make the meaning of Owner disappear from the Real necessarily. For, the being of the world is tied to the Being of the Real in act, as it is also dependent on it in [bestowing] goodness. It follows that the Name Owner is Allah's, exalted be He, from eternity. Even as the entity of the world is nonexistent in itself, its comprehensibility exists as it is tied to the Name Owner necessarily, since it is owned by Allah, exalted be He, in respect of existing, acting, and ordaining. Thus, if you have understood this, be intelligent and know that there is not between the Real and the world a reasonable difference originally, except through differentiation in meanings *(al-tamyīz bi'l ḥaqā'iq)*.[69]

The Owner is one of God's Most Beautiful Names (*asmā' ḥusnā*). The Names designate predicates (*aḥkām*) that connect the Real to the world. We can assume that the world should cease to exist and this will not affect the existence of the Real, since the Real in respect of his Essence exists independently of the world. However, in respect of his properties (*aḥkām*) the Real is dependent on the world. This paradoxical dependence of the Independent on the dependent renders the Real entirely unknown apart from the world. Ibn al-ʿArabī blames thinkers like Ibn Sīnā and Ghazālī for contemplating the possibility of knowing the Real apart from the world: "Certain sages, among them Abū Ḥāmid al-Ghazālī,[70] have asserted that God can be known without any reference to the created Cosmos, but this is mistaken. It is true that a primordial eternal essence can be known, but it cannot be known as a Divinity unless knowledge of that to which it can be related is assumed, for it is the dependent who confirms the independence of the Independent."[71]

In virtue of possessing a certain property that relates him to the world, the Real is a Lord (*rabb*). The Real as Lord requires the existence of his vassal (*marbūb*). Ibn al-ʿArabī explains that the relation between the Real as Lord and His vassal is a relation between correlatives (*mutaḍayiffūn*). He mentions Zayd's fatherhood and ʿAmr's sonship as examples for correlative terms. Interestingly, he designates Time as the ruling property over correlatives: "Hence the time of Zayd's fatherhood is ʿAmr's sonship and the time of ʿAmr's sonship is the time of Zayd's fatherhood. Thus the son is the father's time, and the father is the son's time."[72] Following the same logic, he assigns to Time the ruling property over both Lord and vassal: "So the Lord's time is the vassal, and the vassal's time is the Lord, since the property through which the ruling properties of either is determined is not affirmed without the other."[73]

Ibn al-ʿArabī states that Time is the Limit that defines the kind of correlation that holds between the Real and the world. Under the ruling property of this correlating Limit or Liminal correlation, the Real as Lord and his vassal become entirely dependent on each other. He says that because of this correlation, God named himself "Aeon" (*dahr*). *Dahr* means "time." God applied the word *dahr* and not *zamān* (time) in order to distinguish His ruling property from the ruling property of the time that is imagined as a straight line with beginning and end.[74] Instead, God's Time is the Limit, which resembles any point that we suppose on the circumference of the circle. This point can be considered both the beginning and the end of the circle:

> In respect to newly arrived things, this is "time," but in respect to the Eternal, it is "eternity without beginning." What the rational faculty understands from time is something imagined, extended, and lacking the two sides. We judge that what has passed away within it is "the past," we judge that what will come in it is "the future," and we judge that what is within it is "the [present] state" [*ḥāl*]. This last is called "the instant" [*al-ān*]. Although the instant is a time, it is a limit for what is past in time and what is future. It is like a point that we suppose on the circumference of a circle. Wherever we suppose the point to be origin and end are designated for the circumference. "Eternity without beginning" and "eternity without end" are the nonexistence of time's two sides, for it has no first and no last. Rather, it has perpetuity [*dawām*], and perpetuity is the time of the [present] state, while the state possesses perpetuity. Hence the cosmos never ceases to be under the ruling property of the time of the [present] state, and God's ruling property in the cosmos never ceases to be in the ruling property of time.[75]

The present state is the Limit between the past time, which is nonexistent, and the future time, which is also nonexistent. Likewise, God as the Limit is between the world, which is nonexistent in itself, and the Essence of the Real, which also cannot enter (entirely) in existence. However, the nonexistence in question is not the simple negation of existence, but the nonexistence that transcends existence, and includes it as a transcended moment, exactly as the moment of the present is present in the past moment and includes it as a transcendent moment:

> If you have fully understood the fruits of time, time is clearly recognized, known to be the child of imagination.
> Similar to the natural world, its power lies in its effect;[76] in itself, however, time, just as nature, is a non-entity.
> All things receive their particularity through time although it itself has not being (*'ayn*) through which to rule.
> Human intelligence cannot grasp its form, wherefore we say, time (*dahr*) is imaginary.
> Had it not honored His transcendence, God would not have called His existence by time's name; thus in man's heart it is glorified.
> Strictly speaking, time takes its origin from eternity (*azal*), even while ruled over, its own rule is eternal.
> Like the depths of space it is a limitless extension, possessed of no physical shape; imagination alone gives it body.[77]

The Real's Existence, like Time's existence, is characterized by nonexistence, not the simple negation of existence, but something that signifies a "thingness" that transcends both existence and its negation. "This is what we meant in the first sentence of this book by our words, 'Praise belongs to God who brought the things into existence from a nonexistence and from its nonexistence.'"[78] The reality of the nonexistence that transcends existence is the reality of the Third Thing (*al-shay' al-thālith*), which stands as a Supreme Barzakh between the Real as the Manifest (the world) and the Real as the Nonmanifest (the Essence). The Third Thing is one thing but it can be seen from two different aspects: the ontological and the epistemological. The ontological aspect of the Third Thing will be the subject matter of the next chapter.

CHAPTER 6

The Third Entity: The Supreme Barzakh

Plato's Form, The Muʿtazilites' Nonexistent, and Ibn al-ʿArabī's Fixed Entity

In chapter 2 I discussed the controversy between the Ashʿarites and the Muʿtazilites over the question of whether the world was created from absolute nothingness or from a preexistent matter. I mentioned Wolfson's view that the Muʿtazilites' belief in the world's creation from a preexistent matter was due to their acquaintance with Plato's theory of the creation of the world out of a preexistent matter, as the theory is introduced in *Timaeus*, and with Aristotle's theory of the eternity of the world.[1] As scholars attest,[2] the Muʿtazilites' notion of the nonexistent (*al-maʿdūm*) was a major influence on Ibn al-ʿArabī's thought. This should become clear from the several occasions in which Ibn al-ʿArabī supports the Muʿtazilites' position regarding the problem of the nonexistent and criticizes that of the Ashʿarites. In the following passage, for example, he identifies his barzakh concept with the notion of the nonexistent: "The Barzakh is like the dividing line between existence and nonexistence. It is neither existent nor nonexistent. If you attribute it to existence, you will find a whiff of existence within it, since it is immutable. But if you attribute it to nonexistence, you will speak the truth, since it has no existence. I wonder at the Ashʿarites![3] How could they reject him who says that the nonexistent is a thing in the state of its nonexistence and that first it possesses an immutable entity, then existence is added to the entity?"[4]

In the previous chapter I pointed out the similarity between Ibn al-ʿArabī's immutable or fixed entity (*ʿayn thābita*), his main example for the barzakh, and the Platonic Form. I do think, therefore, that the Muʿtazilites' "nonexistent,"

Ibn al-ʿArabī's fixed entity, and Plato's Form are three concepts that have similar meanings. Here, however, Wolfsons' reservation against identifying the Muʿtazilites' "nonexistent" with the Platonic Form, and Chittick's reservation against identifying the Platonic Form with Ibn al-ʿArabī's fixed entity must not be overlooked. Wolfson writes, "Now, to say that the 'nonexistent' in the *Kalām* controversy refers to Platonic ideas, and that these ideas are called non-existent because they have not yet acquired the accidental or temporal existence characteristic of sensible things, is an assumption which cannot be sustained. Plato himself never describes the ideas as nonexistent. On the contrary, the ideas in their totality are described by him as 'true substance,' as 'existing in reality,' as 'existing absolutely,' and as 'existing eternally.' How then could these Platonic ideas come to be described as "nonexistent'?"[5] Wolfson's argument is inconsistent with what he states elsewhere.[6] The Muʿtazilites did not conceive of the nonexistent as the simple negation of existence, but only as something whose existence is to be distinguished from the mode of existence of things in the sensible world. Following the example of Plato's "eternal matter," the nonexistent can be considered as even more substantial than ordinary existents.

Chittick criticizes the view that identifies Ibn al-ʿArabī 's fixed entity (*ʿayn thābita*) with Plato's Form:

> If many translators have rendered *ʿayn* as "archetype," this is because God creates the cosmos in accordance with his eternal knowledge of it. Thereby He gives each thing known by Him—each entity "immutably fixed" (*thābit*) within His knowledge—existence in the universe. However, the term "archetype" may suggest that what is being discussed becomes the model for many individuals in the manner of a Platonic idea. In fact what corresponds to the Platonic ideas in Ibn al-ʿArabī's teachings is the divine names, while the immutable entities are the things themselves "before" they are given existence in the world.[7]

It is not decisively clear, however, what Plato means by the notion of the participation of things in their Forms, or by the idea that the Forms are the models of things. Indeed, a great deal of Plato's reconsideration of his theory of Forms in *Parmenides* is based on a reexamination of the whole subject of the manner of the participation of things in their Forms. The sort of relation that holds between the Forms and things, which determines the mode of the participation of the former in the latter, seems to be an open question in Plato.[8] Moreover, examples that Plato introduces for Forms and examples that Ibn al-ʿArabī introduces for the fixed entities make the author of this work convinced that the two thinkers are talking about something similar in meaning.

In the second chapter I presented Wolfson's suggestion that in order to properly understand the dispute between the Ashʿarites and the Muʿtazilites over the question of whether the nonexistent is something or nothing, we have to situate the problem in its real context, which has to do with the problem of the creation of the world.[9] Likewise, I think that Plato's distinction between the sensible things and the Forms, and the manner of the participation of the former in the latter, can be properly understood in the context of Plato's philosophical discussion of the problem of creation. In *Timaeus*, Plato introduces the distinction between Forms and sensible things in the context of discussing this problem. The distinction that he introduces between sensible objects and Forms proves, however, to be insufficient due to the strong demands of a more consistent theory of creation. Plato finds himself compelled to improve his ontological division by introducing a third ontological entity—the Receptacle. In my view, examining the reasoning that led Plato to introduce the Receptacle can be helpful in reconstructing the reasoning that led Ibn al-ʿArabī to introduce an important notion in his ontological theory, the notion of the Third Thing *(al-shay' al-thālith)*. I will dedicate the discussion of the next section to Plato's introduction of the Receptacle and the section that follows it to Ibn al-ʿArabī's introduction of the Third Thing.

Plato's Introduction of the Receptacle

Naomi Reshotko sees a connection between Plato's argument for the introduction of the Forms, which Aristotle named "The Argument From The Sciences," and his argument for the introduction of the Receptacle in *Timaeus*.[10] According to Reshotko, the reasoning that led Plato to introduce the Receptacle, described by him as a "bastard" kind of reasoning, is based on the same kind of reasoning that is involved in his argument for the existence of the Forms. Reshotko presents the following contemporary summation of the Argument From The Sciences:

(1) There exists a scientific practice.
(2) Central to the scientific practice is the making of hypotheses.
(3) Scientific hypotheses are inductive generalizations where we make a prediction about the future behavior of an unobserved sample by extending our observations from an observed sample.
(4) Such inductive generalizations are only rationally justified if we assume that the observed sample and the unobserved sample have some one thing in common.
(5) This one thing that the observed and unobserved samples have in common must not exist in space and time, since the samples occupy different areas of space/time and a single physical thing cannot exist in two places at the same time.

> Therefore, (6) We are committed to the existence of some one thing that the two physical things have in common and this thing must not itself be physical.[11]

Reshotko explains that on the Argument From The Sciences we start with what is given to us by our senses, and we draw conclusions as to what additions we need to make in order to increase our ontology. On the basis of our empirical observations, we conclude that in order to enlarge our scientific practice we have to admit the existence of the abstract entities that we call Forms.[12]

As a matter of fact, Plato's Argument From The Sciences is not stated explicitly in the *Timaeus*. The *Timaeus*'s main concern is with the problem of the world's origination, and it is in the context of discussing this problem that the division of objects into sensibles and intelligibles is advanced. In 28b7, Timaeus asks whether the world was always in existence and without beginning, or whether it was created. "Created," was his answer, and "being visible and tangible and having a body and therefore sensible, and all sensible things are apprehended by opinion and sense, and are in a process of creation and created."[13] Timaeus then states that a Maker created the world, but that he is past *finding out*, and even if he could be found,[14] it would be impossible for us to communicate this finding to others. In creating the world, the Maker looked to the realm of the eternal Forms, and made the world a sensible copy of that intelligible original.[15] Timaeus explains that this process took place through the combined work of necessity and mind. In 48 a6, however, he stipulates that in order to truly tell of the way in which the work was accomplished, one should include in addition to necessity and mind the *variable cause* as well. And in order to do that, he suggests a consideration of the nature of fire, water, air, and earth and the form in which they existed prior to the creation of the world. Timaeus considers this as a new beginning in the discussion of the ontological status of the universe, which demands the introduction of a fuller division than that between the eternal intelligible patterns and their copies or imitations, since this division seemed to be rather insufficient for comprehending the world in its present state. He states that in addition to the sensible and the intelligible things there is a third kind of thing, the Receptacle, "which is difficult of explanation and dimly seen," and which is the "nurse of all generation."[16]

The reasoning that led Plato to the introduction of the Receptacle is the following: From experience we learn that water becomes solid by condensation, and this if melted passes into vapor and air. Air becomes fire when inflamed and fire passes into a form of air when dispersed, which becomes cloud and mist, and from this comes water. Thus, it seems that generation is transmitted from one element to another in a circle. Moreover, things seem to change even while one is making assertions about them, and one cannot be assured anymore if any element can be called by the name given to it. Consequently,

Timaeus determines that we should not describe things as *this* or *that* but only as *of such a nature*. Since things, which are assumed to be *thises*, turn out to be *suches* we are compelled to posit a unifying principle, circulating in all the elements, a principle that accounts for the identification of the *suches* in terms of *thises*.[17] This unifying principle "must be always called the same, for, inasmuch as she always receives all things, she never departs at all from her own nature and never, in any way or at any time, assume a form like that of any of the things which enter into her; she is the natural recipient of all impressions, and is stirred and informed by them, and appears different from time to time by reason of them. But the forms which enter into and go out of her are the likenesses of eternal realities modeled after their patterns in a wonderful and mysterious manner."[18]

Timaeus says that this unifying principle is eternal and indestructible and provides a home for all created things. But he adds that it "is apprehended, when all sense is absent, by a kind of spurious reason, and is hardly real."[19] Hence, I think that by introducing the notion of the Receptacle, which is conceived by a "kind of spurious reason," Plato attempts to transcend the rational and the reality that is represented by it to a reality that is more of the imaginal. This imaginal reality, which is the reality of the Receptacle, is "hardly real." But this does not mean that it is not real, as the phrase "spurious reason" might create the impression that we are dealing here with some kind of illusion. It is important to keep in mind here that the use that Plato is making of phrases like "spurious reason" and "hardly real" represents the reflection of the rational agent about the notion of the Receptacle rather than the maturer reflection from the level of the reality of the Receptacle itself. I will elaborate on this point in the following. But first I will summarize Plato's argument for the existence of the Receptacle as Plato relates between it and his argument for the existence of Forms.

We begin the process of reasoning by asking the question as to what accounts for our identification for things that we observe or come across as *this* or *that* thing, and what validates our continuing to characterize objects as such. We answer by saying that things receive their specific identity by participating in certain types of things, which we call Forms. The fact that in reality we do identify (physical) objects as *this* or *that* object, necessitates the positing of metaphysical universal patterns to account for the act of identification. A deeper reflection, however, reveals to us that things cannot really be identified as *this* or *that* thing, and that they seem to change even as we make judgments about them. Yet, that things can be identified as *this* or *that* was the assumption on the basis of which we arrived at the conclusion that Forms must exist. The existence of the Forms, which is posited to explain the manner in which things are identified, seems now to rest on an assumption that is no longer valid. Again, we are compelled to assume the existence of a third kind of thing to account for the identification in question. This thing is the Receptacle, the unifying principle that accounts for the stability of the variability in a universe that does not only consist of fixed universal patterns and copies of them, coexisting in a motionless reality, but rather one that is in a constant process of actualization.

One might wonder why Plato insists on characterizing the reasoning that leads to the introduction of the Receptacle as a "bastard" kind of reasoning. The reason for this rather strange characterization, as Reshotko alludes to it, is the following. In the argument for the Forms, reasoning starts from the level of common sense experience and, by reflecting on its activity of defining things, it arrives at the existence of Forms. In introducing the Receptacle, reason is compelled to lift itself to a yet higher level of abstraction. The fact that reason is compelled twice and not only once, as was the case in the argument for the Forms, to lift itself to a higher level of abstraction, creates the impression that it is becoming a kind of "bastard" reason, alienated from the sense-perceptual reality from which it made its initial move.[20]

Ibn al-ʿArabī's Introduction of the Third Thing

In the previous chapter I began the discussion of the Qur'ānic roots of the barzakh concept by citing Q 25:53 as one of the three verses in which the term barzakh is mentioned:

> It is He Who has
> Let free the two bodies
> Of flowing water:
> One palpable and sweet,
> And the other salt and bitter;
> Yet Has He
> Made a barrier (barzakh) between them,
> A partition that is forbidden
> To be passed.

Upon observing the behavior of the two bodies of water and noticing that their identity is preserved despite their coming together, we conclude that a Limit (barzakh) must exist between them to account for the objects' differentiation through their unification. We are compelled, furthermore, to ascribe an abstract nature to this Limit. This is because a limit that has a complex nature calls for another limit to unify its parts, and if this latter has also a complex nature another limit will be needed, and so an infinite regress will be unavoidable. Hence, the Limit that we need must be an undivided unity. Ibn al-ʿArabī calls this Limit "barzakh." His main example of the barzakh is what he calls "fixed entity" (*ʿayn thābita*), such as whiteness and humanity. The barzakhs are the "essential limits of limited things, without which limited things cannot be rationally conceived, and which upon their disappearance, the known things become nonexistent."[21] Hence, the barzakhs or essential limits are, like the Platonic Forms, responsible epistemologically and ontologically for the existence of the objects that are their existential copies: "And it is a being running (*sārī*) in all beings but it is not felt due to its subtlety, like the line that divides the shade from the sun, and is rationally recognized but not perceived with the senses. These are the limits (*ḥudūd*) between things with a specific face to each of the two things between which they lie, and that is despite the fact that they are not divided in themselves. And so they are in themselves in every limited thing (*maḥdūd*), and this is why it is hard to find the self-acting (*dhātiyya*) limits, unlike the formal and verbal limits that are with the rational thinkers."[22]

The question is, how are we to account for the paradoxical nature of the essential limits, being unities related to dualities? In order to understand the manner of the participation of limited objects in their essential limits, we are compelled to reassess our commitment to the ontological order of the relation between limited objects and their essential limits. This reassessment results in the limits becoming prior ontologically to the limited objects. Consequently, the limited objects lose their independent or essential ontological status. They become not *thises* but *suches*, relations, or, States (*aḥwāl*): "The forms in the cosmos are all relations and states that are neither existent nor nonexistent. Although they are witnessed in one respect, they are not witnessed in another respect. The time of the annihilation of the forms is identical with the time of the being [*wujūd* in Chittick] of the forms."[23]

The forms that are the things in the world are *states*. States are neither existent nor nonexistent. They are relations and, as such, they seem to be completely devoid of identity. Their presumed identity depends totally on their fixed entities. Things in the cosmos have lost their identity to their essential limits, their fixed entities. This must be a sad conclusion for those who hold that things in the cosmos must possess essences specific to them. But even more shocking must be Ibn al-ʿArabī's next discovery that the essential limits of things are not *thises* but rather, like the things they provide with definition, relations or *suches*. Things in the cosmos are the existential individuations of their fixed entities. But these individuations, the specific formulations of the fixed entities, are not fixed as we have perhaps inadequately assumed. The element of variability has become essential to the definition of things and, consequently, it must be essential to their essential limits, since things are but existential individuations of their essential limits. Hence, the essential limits must be, like the things they define, relations related to other relations ad infinitum.[24]

Indeed the essential limits, which Ibn al-ʿArabī calls "realities" (*ḥaqā'iq*), are portrayed by him as consisting of combinations of more general realities, which consist of combinations of other realities ad infinitum. Each reality has become a relation related to an infinite number of relations.[25] This must be an absurd description of reality, since it designates a reality that is devoid of the crucial element of definability, or limitedness. Nevertheless, Ibn al-ʿArabī insists that no absurd consequences follow from assuming infinitude of relations.[26] The world that is being described here is certainly a different world from that of Ibn Sīnā, which consists of particular essences related to each other through accidental relations. At this stage, Ibn al-ʿArabī's world seems to be consisting of relations related to other relations ad infinitum. The element of limitation that characterizes entified existence, that is, the element of unity, seems to be completely lacking in a reality characterized as such.

This reality, which is characterized as consisting of relations related to other relations ad infinitum, is the reality of the unlimited god, the god that has not come to be limited by the world. It is the reality of the god that has not yet created, that is, has not yet entified himself. This god can hardly be the Real of Ibn al-ʿArabī, since the Real is not limited by the negation of limitation. The Real is neither limited nor unlimited. His reality can be referred to as a Third Thing, a unifying principle of the totality of both the limited and the unlimited aspects of existence. In the following passage, Ibn al-ʿArabī provides an elaborated characterization of the Third Thing. Notice how, by making the Third Thing a place for the gathering of the opposites (existence/nonexistence, temporal/eternal), Ibn al-ʿArabī seeks to find an answer for the problem of the creation of the world or the relationship between the Real and the world:

> The Universal Reality belongs to both the Real and the cosmos. It is described neither by existence nor by nonexistence, neither by temporal origination nor by eternity. If the Eternal is described by it, it is eternal; if the temporally originated is described by it, it is temporally originated. . . . If something exists without a precedent nonexistence, like the Real and His attributes, one says that this reality is an eternal existent, since the Real is described by it. If something exists after nonexistence, as it is the case with the existence of everything other than God, then this reality is temporally originated and existent through something other than itself; and one says concerning it that it is temporally originated. . . . In the same order of things, you should know that this Reality is not described as prior to the cosmos, and the cosmos described as posterior to it. But it is the root of all existent things. It is the root of substance, the Sphere of Life (*falak al-ḥayāt*), the Real Through Whom Creation Takes Place, and so forth. It is the all-encompassing intelligible sphere.[27]

In *The Book of the Description of the Encompassing Circles* (*Kitāb Inshā' al Dawā'ir*), Ibn al-ʿArabī divides things according to three principle modes of existence: (1) That which is qualified by existence in itself. This is God the unlimited absolute Being, to whom nothing is similar but who, at the same time, is limited by all limitations. (2) That which is identified with limited being. This limited being is not existent in itself but only through God. This is the world, whose nonexistence is not located in time since it is Time itself. (3) That which is neither existent nor nonexistent. This is the Third Thing (*al-shay' al-thālith*), the Reality of Realities (*ḥaqīqat al-ḥaqā'iq*). The world in relation to it is not posterior, nor is it located in relation to it in place, since the Reality of Realities is the origin of the notion of place. The Third Entity includes the temporal and the eternal. It is the Supreme Barzakh, the Supreme Essential Limit, which increases by the multiplicity of existents without suffering any division in its unity. Thus, it is/not the world, it is/not God. It encompasses the perfection of all realities and can be called "the root of the universe" and "the atom (*jawhar fard*)," and "Primordial Matter" (*mādda ūlā*).[28]

It is also the root of the Sphere of Life (*falak al-ḥayāt*) and the Real Through Whom Creation Takes Place (*al-ḥaqq al-makhlūq bihi*). The Sphere of Life is the Divinity (*ulūha*), the level of existence of the Name Allah, which comprises the Most Beautiful Names of God. It is the level of Oneness (*waḥidiyya*), the level in which the Absolute Totality is determined in itself with a determination that encompasses all its actual determinations.[29] The Real Through Whom Creation Takes Place is the Cloud (*ʿamā'*), which is the level of the first determination of the Divinity (*ulūha*). This is the level of the fixed entities in which the things in the universe participate.[30]

To say that the level of the Third Thing is above the level of the Names of God and the level of the fixed entities does not mean that these levels are separated in reality. Rather, the Third Thing is what provides unity to all levels of existence. This is why it must be located in the level of Unity or Uniqueness (*aḥadiyya*), which is the level of the realities of the Divinity and the Real Through Whom Creation Takes Place. Kāshānī, the commentator on Ibn al-ʿArabī's *Fuṣūṣ al-Ḥikam*, describes the Third Thing, or the Reality of Realities, in the following words: "[It is] the Unity (*aḥadiyya*) that is the Essence, through which manifestation all realities are realized. It is the Reality (*ḥaqīqa*) of Existence (*wujūd*) in Itself (*min ḥaythu huwa huwa*). Through the Reality of Realities are realized all the realities of the lower and upper Worlds, and that is why he situated it between the spiritual and the corporeal World."[31]

Kāshānī's identification between the Third Thing and the level of the Unity (*aḥadiyya),* which is the level of the Divine Essence, might seem confusing. For according to Ibn al-ʿArabī, there can be no correlation (*munāsaba*) between the Real, as he exists in his Essence, and creation, as nothing comes from the

Real in respect of his being an Essence.[32] How then can the Third Thing, which is characterized as the Root of the universe and the atom, be identified with the Essence of the Real? In order to answer this question, we have to reexamine Ibn al-ʿArabī's definition of the mode of existence of the Real. He characterizes this mode of existence as follows: "That which is qualified by existence in itself, i.e. existence *per se* in its concrete reality and whose existence cannot proceed from nonbeing; it is absolute underived existence, which no thing pre-exists. Moreover, it existentiates all things, creates them, determines them, distinguishes them and rules them. It is *unlimited*, absolute Being. Such is God, the Living, the Everlasting, the Omniscient, the Willing, the Omnipotent, to Whom "no thing is similar, though He is the *Hearing and Seeing*" (Q 15:11)."[33]

The Real is characterized in this statement by incomparability and comparability, which seems self-contradictory. However, what seems to be a self-contradictory statement becomes, on second reflection, the closest indication of the definition of the Real's Essence, for the Essence of the Real is not limited by limitation or unlimitation. The Essence of the Real is limited neither by a divinity that is absolutely beyond creation, nor by a divinity that is fixed by creation. Its reality is that of a third kind of reality that is a midway between (limited) existence and (unlimited) nonexistence, being the Essence of both.

The Problem of the Creation of the World Revisited

The controversy that took place between the philosophers and the theologians over the world's origination revolved around the question of whether the relation between God and the world should be reflected upon in terms of continuity or discontinuity. Depicting the relation in terms of discontinuity brought Islamic thinkers face to face with the challenge that Parmenides posited to metaphysical thought. For discontinuity means separation and separation implies the notion of nonbeing, a notion that philosophers wanted to avoid by all means. Following their manner of absolutely identifying God with being, the philosophers sought to account for the world's creation in terms of continuity, and as a process that takes place within the limits of being. Nevertheless, the philosophers were driven by the force of argument to struggle with the logical consequences of their view. Reflecting on the relation between God and the world in terms of continuity yielded a conception of the world that was infinite. Thinking about the coming into existence of an infinite world turned out to be as irrational as positing a nonbeing between God and the world.

Ibn Sīnā sought a way out of the difficulty by invoking Aristotle's famous distinction between potential and actual infinites. This solution proved, however, to be insufficient. The distinction, as Ghazālī attempted to show on the basis of theological arguments, was not capable of explaining how the actually finite is related to the potentially infinite.

Ibn Rushd seemed to have found a way to ascribing both finitude and infinitude to the world without falling into contradiction. He detected the source of the difficulty about the infinite conception of the world in the adherence of theologians and philosophers alike to a linear conception of time. The time of the world, however, and the world itself, as time is inseparable from it, resembles a cyclical continuum. Any point at the circle can be regarded as finite, but the circle itself is infinite. Ibn Rushd was able to claim now that despite their contradictory views, both the theologians, who claimed that the world was finite, and the philosophers, who claimed that the world was infinite, could be correct.

Ibn Rushd's approach has been characterized as a *complementarity approach*: different theses or accounts of the same substance-matter may both be true even if their logical conjunction leads to a flat contradiction.[34] This approach proved to be effective as a successful model of separation between contradictory views of the same substance matter. The question, however, was whether Ibn Rushd was ready to say, as Ibn al-ʿArabī had, that the same substance matter could be both finite and infinite, not from two different respects but absolutely. For our aim is not to find out how a world which is characterized by infinitude in one respect, can be characterized by finitude from another respect. Our aim is to find out how the conception of an infinite world can be related to the conception of the same finite world. The relational factor was still not fully developed in Ibn Rushd's complementarity approach, as the notion of paradoxicality inherent in the conception of relation had not been thoroughly envisaged by him or, for that matter, by any Islamic thinker prior to Ibn al-ʿArabī.

In my opinion, Ibn al-ʿArabī's greatest achievement toward a solution of the problem of the relation between God and the world lies in his qualified identification of God with Being. Like all Muslim thinkers, Ibn al-ʿArabī identified God with Being, but he did not render this identification in terms of finality. Failing to understand this point has caused much misunderstanding regarding Ibn al-ʿArabī's celebrated doctrine of the Unity of Being (*waḥdat al-wujūd*).[35] By saying that Ibn al-ʿArabī does not render the identification of God with Being in terms of finality, I mean that he incorporated the element of *finding* (actuality) in his understanding of the conception of Being. The conception of Being understood as finding designates a dynamic process, rather than a static reality. This allowed Ibn al-ʿArabī to provide a transcendental (in contrast to a given) representation to the (infinite) Essence of God, which is found (actualized) only in an infinite or continuous process of finding.

God's Essence must not be limited by any limitation, not even by the limitation of an absolute or unlimited Being. This implies that in order to truly become infinite, God must transcend his own infinitude, and become finite. This conclusion must be absurd when considered from the level at which God is unqualifiedly identified with Being. Hence, a higher level of existence must be posited, which renders the synthesis between infinite and finite existence possible. At this level, the unlimited God can be characterized by extreme opposites, being, at the same time, also transcendent to the world and also immanent in it. This is the level of existence of the Third Thing, which synthesizes the unlimited and the limited aspects of Reality while preserving the unlimitation of the unlimited and the limitation of the limited.

Why should God become finite in order to become what he already is, that is, infinite? The answer to the question is that at the level of the Supreme Barzakh God does not become finite, God is already finite. This is impossible when considered from the level at which God is unqualifiedly identified with infinitude (when God is qualified by independence from creation) or with finitude (when God is qualified in relation to creation). But it is not impossible at the level of the Supreme Barzakh in which God is both absolutely limited and absolutely unlimited.

Without positing a higher level of existence it becomes impossible to make sense of what appears as the many contradictions in Ibn al-ʿArabī's writings. For example, in *The Book of the Description of the Encompassing Circles* he gives some examples of things whose existence is impossible, such as the existence of an associate for God, and the passing of the camel through the eye of a needle. In the *Futūḥāt*, however, he states that not only is association (*shirk*) possible, but that it is a universal reality and that it is an even better indication of the unity of God than declaring God's Unity.[36] He also describes an accident in which he himself was involved and in which he saw an occurrence which was as impossible as the passage of the camel through the eye of the needle.[37]

These impossibilities become possibilities due to the existence of the level of the Supreme Barzakh. This level is the level of the Reality of the Realities. The Reality of the Realities is, according to Kāshānī, the Essence through which manifestation of all realities is realized. It is the Reality of Existence in Itself (*min ḥaythu huwa huwa*).[38] Existence in Itself is identified by Ibn al-ʿArabī in *The Book of the Description of the Encompassing Circles* with God, to whom nothing is similar but who is at the same time the Hearing and the Seeing, that is, with God who is both limited and unlimited. But the Reality of the Realities is neither qualified by existence nor by nonexistence, how can it then be the reality of Existence in Itself? The answer is that it is in the nature of the reality of Existence in Itself to be qualified by neither existence nor nonexistence. The Reality of Existence is beyond existence (finitude) and nonexistence (infinitude). This is precisely the Reality of the infinitude of existence.

This Reality cannot be conceived by reason, since it is the root of the reality of the rational. That is why reason, according to Ibn al-ʿArabī, is forbidden from contemplating the Reality of the Unity of existence and nonexistence. In a sense Ibn al-ʿArabī would agree with Parmenides' warning against entertaining the notion of nonbeing. But he would qualify this warning, as it applies only to what is represented by means of rational deliberation, which adheres to the unqualified identification between God and Being. The limited rational faculty cannot comprehend the Reality or the Essence, since the Essence is not subject to limitation, not even to the limitation of an unlimited existence.

Ibn al-ʿArabī often repeats the statement that the Essence of God is unknowable and that rational thinkers err when they claim that they possess knowledge of It. Here Chittick's comment that Ibn al-ʿArabī's repeated warnings against thinking about the Essence of God does not mean that we should not say anything about it, is appropriate. As he points out, if that was Ibn al-ʿArabī's meaning he would be contradicting himself constantly.[39] He adds that Ibn al-ʿArabī's meaning is that we should not think it is possible to make a positive statement about the Essence of God through the use of reasoning, since reasoning is attached to relations while the Essence of God does not bear reference to any relationship with creation: "As for the unity of the Essence in Itself, no whatness (*māhiyya*) is known for it, so properties cannot be ascribed to It, for It is not similar to anything in the cosmos, and nothing is similar to It. No intelligent person undertakes to speak about His Essence except through a report from Him. And despite the coming of the report, we are ignorant of the relation of the property to Him because we are ignorant of Him."[40]

It is possible for us to say that the Essence of God cannot be known because it is beyond all relations or limitations. But it is also possible to say that the Essence of God cannot be known because it is limited by all limitations. This second interpretation is confirmed by Kāshānī, who explains that God's Essential Limit is not known because his Limit encompasses all limits of exterior and interior phenomena (objective and subjective modes of existence). The limits of exterior and interior phenomena are infinite. Hence, the Limit that comprises all of these limits must extend infinitely. That is why it can never be known.[41] Hence, Ibn al-ʿArabī does not think that God's Essence cannot be known altogether, only that it cannot be known in a rationally or conceptually finalized manner. The light of reason is not sufficient for discerning God's Essence. "However," writes Chittick, "there are also those who declare Unity through the light of faith over and above the light of reason. The light of faith bestows felicity, and in no way can it be gained through proofs."[42] The truth about the Unity of God, which is the unity of all existents, cannot be known through the light of reason, since reason delimits whereas the Unity of the totality of existence is unlimited. Nevertheless, this unlimited Unity can be witnessed with a second light:

> It is this second light that unveils to people their own unity and the unity of each existent thing through which it becomes distinct from others, whether or not there is an attribute that is shared. *There is no*

> *escape from a unity, specific to each thing, through which it is distinct from others.* When this light unveils the unity of the existent things to the servant, through it he knows for certain that God has a unity that is specific to Him. This unity must either be His own Entity—so that the Unitary in Essence is the Unitary in Level, such that they are identical—or it must be the unity of the Level. Hence unveiling conforms to the considerative proof, and the servant knows for certain that the Essence has a unity that is specific to It and is identical with It. This is the meaning of the words of Abū 'l-ʿAtāhiyya: "In each thing He has a sign signifying that He is one." That "sign" is the *unity of every object of knowledge*, whether it is many or not many. After all, to manyness belongs the unity of manyness, and to nothing else, of course.[43]

In a sense these words bring us back to Ibn Sīnā's specific unity of things. But there is a significant difference between Ibn Sīnā's specific unity and the specific unity that Ibn al-ʿArabī is talking about here. Ibn al-ʿArabī's specific unity cannot be revealed through rational or conceptual analysis, as it cannot be separated from the creative synthesis of which it is made, that is, the synthesis (correlation) of entified existence (finite existence) and relational existence (infinite existence). Not only is rational analysis incapable of knowing the Unity of the Essence, it is also incapable of properly comprehending the unity of anything in the cosmos, no matter how small or insignificant it may seem to be. Ibn al-ʿArabī challenges rational thinkers to attempt a definition of any such unity in the cosmos before attempting to capture the Unity of the Essence: "One of [the rational thinkers] says that He is a corporeal body and another says that He is not. One of them says that He is a substance and another says that He is not. One of them says that He is located toward some direction and another says that He is not. . . . If these thinkers were asked to demonstrate their knowledge of one essence in the world, they would not know it."[44]

The reason behind this inevitable failure to rationally define essential unities is stated in the following passage:

> The Folk of the Path of God have seen that when Oneness is demonstrated it becomes the same as association, since the One in Himself does not become One through your demonstration of His Oneness. Therefore, it is not the case that you have established the Oneness of the One. Rather, the One is established from within Himself. After all, you have realized that He is One not because you have demonstrated that this is the case. That is why some of our companions expressed themselves in the way they had. Therefore, he who unifies Him is a denier (*jāḥid*). The One cannot be unified for He does not accept that.

> If He accepted that, He would become a duality, a duality that embraces His Oneness as It is in Itself and His Oneness as demonstrated by the unifier. The One becomes, therefore, One in Himself and One by means of the demonstration of other. The One becomes a duality; His Oneness is negated. Whatever is demonstrated only through its own negation, its demonstration must be self-defeating. Unification abides in silence especially, whether in a manifested, or, otherwise, in a nonmanifested form. Once Unity has spoken, thereupon it has given birth to existence, and once it has given birth to existence, it has invoked association.[45] Silence is but a nonexistent attribute. Therefore only the Unity of His Being remains, while association does not enter into His Unity *except due to the giving of existence to creation.* Creation with its realities demands a multiplicity of relations, a fact that necessitates the existence of multiplicity in the properties, even though the Entity is one. Therefore, the harm has not been inflicted upon the Unity except through existence giving. Unification (*tawḥīd*) inflicted the harm upon itself, no existent thing has inflicted any harm upon it.[46]

Rational analysis can never lead to unification (*tawḥīd*), that is, to knowledge of Unity, because analysis starts necessarily with a given duality. A thought that makes analysis of duality its starting point can only reach farther and farther from Unity. What is needed is a knowledge that properly represents the infinite nature of Reality. This knowledge is liminal or barzakhī. Barzakhī knowledge is perfect knowledge, as perfect as its possessor, the Perfect Man, can be. The Perfect Man is a microcosmic epitome of the Infinity of Reality. By learning how the Perfect Man thinks, we can learn how Reality exists.[47]

CHAPTER 7

The Perfect Man: The Epistemological Aspect of the Third Thing

The notion of the Perfect Man will be presented in this chapter as the conclusion of divine love and divine knowledge. Between reason (*ʿaql*), which is delimiting, and the heart (*qalp*), which is fluctuating; between the unity (*waḥda*), which is binding, and difference (*tafriqa*), which is separating, and between stability (*tamkīn*), which is remaining in one state, and variegation (*talwīn*), which is alternating from one state to another, the Perfect Man strikes a careful Limit, and establishes a perfect state of unity through difference, and stability in variegation. As Chittick points out, in contrast to most Ṣūfīs who held that variegation is an imperfection, as the accomplished realizer strives to establish himself in stability, Ibn al-ʿArabī held that true realization consists of stability in variegation.[1] The stress in "stability in variegation" is on the careful balance that should be observed between stability, or unity, and variegation, or difference. As we are going to see in the following discussion, Ibn al-ʿArabī stresses the difficulty of keeping this balance, maintaining that only the Perfect Man is capable of observing it.

The Perfect Man as the Conclusion of Divine Love

Ibn al-ʿArabī often refers to the famous prophetic tradition, "I was a Treasure but was not known, so I loved to be known; I created the creatures and made Myself known to them, so they came to know me," to explain the reason behind God's bringing the cosmos into existence.[2] God created the cosmos out of His desire to be known. The cosmos is necessary for God since, "although the existence of the servant . . . . becomes manifest only through the existence of the Real and His existence—giving, no knowledge of the Real would be manifest except through the knowledge of the cosmos."[3] Ibn al-ʿArabī maintains that in supporting our existence (the existence of creation) the Real indicates his dependence on us and also his independence from us.[4] The Real is dependent on us, since he can be known only through our knowledge of him. Thus, his love to be known indicates his dependence on the creature through which the object of his love (to be known) is obtained. On the other hand, the Real's "love to be known is an indication that He is not known . . . since if He were to be known, He would be manifest, but He is the nonmanifest that does not become [fully] manifest."[5]

What is the meaning of Ibn al-ʿArabī's words, "His love to be known is an indication that He is not known"? The answer to this question can be found in the definition that Ibn al-ʿArabī provides for love,[6] according to which love is not to be identified with its actualization (*ḥāṣil*) but only with the permanence (*dawām*) and continuity (*istimrār*) of this actualization.[7] The continuity of love's actualization cannot, however, enter into existence in its entirety, since it is infinite. Ibn al-ʿArabī brings a possible objection to this statement and provides an answer for it:

> You may object and say: We loved sitting with a person, or kissing, or embracing, or intimacy, or conversation. Then we saw that it was achieved, but love did not disappear, even though there was embracing and mutual arrival. Hence, the object of love does not have to be nonexistent. We would reply: you are mistaken. When you embrace the person, and when the object of your love had been embracing, or sitting together, or intimacy, you have not achieved the object of your love through this situation. For the object is now the continuance and permanence of what you have achieved. This continuance is nonexistent. It has not entered into being [*wujūd* in Chittick], and its period has no end. Hence, in the state of arrival, love attaches itself only to a nonexistent thing, and that is its permanence.[8]

The object of love is not merely the act of embracing, kissing, or conversing with a person, but the continuity of these acts, a continuity that does not come to an end. Likewise, the continuity of the manifestation of the Real's Essence, which is the true object of the Real's love, has no end, since the Essence of the Real is infinite. Once the infinite Essence of the Real is brought into existence in a finite form of creation it is no longer his Essence. Thus, the Real's love to be known indicates, on the one hand, his dependence on creation, since it is only through creation that the Real becomes known and, on the other hand, it indicates his independence from creation, since the limitation of the Real's Essence in the limited form of creation implies his unlimitedness.

Ibn al-ʿArabī states that it is a main characteristic of the lover to gather between opposites in his love. For example, the lover desires to be always with his beloved, and he also desires whatever his beloved desires. And so, if the beloved desires separation, the lover must desire separation as well. In this case, the lover desires *to be and not to be* with his beloved.[9] According to Ibn al-ʿArabī, only the Perfect Man among all creatures joins opposites in his love. Man combines natural love (*ḥubb ṭabīʿī*), which is love for the manifest, and spiritual love (*ḥubb rūḥānī*), which is love for the nonmanifest.

Spiritual love aims at nothing other than fulfilling the desires of the beloved, whereas natural love aims at satisfying some personal desire, regardless of whether or not this pleases the beloved.[10] Ibn al-ʿArabī says that in his divine love for God (*ḥubb 'ilāhī*), Man combines the two kinds of love, the natural and the spiritual.[11] He emphasizes, however, that this manner of combining the two kinds of love "is a matter that is very hard to comprehend, since not every soul is given knowledge of things as they are in themselves, and sound belief in accordance with God's reports about Himself."[12] The manner in which the Perfect Man combines natural and spiritual love is described by Ibn al-ʿArabī as a process in which the human soul journeys from the state of animality to divine perfection.[13]

The journey of the soul starts from the moment when she finds herself in charge of her corporeal body. The soul conducts her affairs in a manner that accords with her natural needs. In occupying herself with the fulfillment of her natural needs, the soul forgets about her covenant with her Lord, according to which covenant she belongs in her entirety to him.[14] Then the rational faculty comes to the scene, drawing the attention of the soul to the truth about the contingency of her existence. The rational faculty leads the soul through a thinking process at the end of which she admits that she possesses only contingent being, and that there must exist a Maker that is necessary of being and that provides for her existence. Next a person appears, claiming that he is a messenger sent by him who made her. Her immediate response is to ask the messenger for a rational proof to the effect that he is a truth teller. He introduces his proof; the soul is convinced and starts to believe in her Maker. Then the messenger reminds the soul of her Covenant with her Lord; the soul fails to remember but promises to follow the prescriptions of the Lawgiver. She believes sincerely in her Maker, but her belief is still mixed with love for him, desire for her natural needs and fear that her needs may interfere with her obedience to him:

> She joined in her worship between two affairs, her worship *for* Him and her worship that is based on fear and desire. She loved Him for Himself in respect of her spiritual configuration, and she loved Him for her own self in respect of her natural configuration. Her fear and

> desire pertained to her natural configuration, while her worship for Him, which was based on love, pertained to her spiritual configuration. When she came to love a certain entity other than Him, she loved that entity out of her spiritual inclination to Him, and also out of her natural desire to meet a certain [selfish] concern. The Real saw her condition and knew that she was divided in her self, and in her joining between two kinds of love. The Real has described Himself by jealousy and disliked to be associated with. He wanted her to be devoted to Him entirely and to love none other than Him. Hence, He revealed Himself to her in a natural form and gave her a mark that she could not deny. This mark bestowed on her necessary knowledge. Thus she came to know that He is identical with the natural form in which He disclosed Himself. This [recognition] made her incline to Him both naturally and spiritually. Then, once He gained full possession of her and knew that, due to her natural configuration, she could be affected by certain affairs (*asbāb*), He gave her a sign by which she would recognize Him in all matters. Hence, she knew Him, and loved the affairs for His sake and not for her own. Then she became His in her entirety, not due to some natural inclination or for any other reason apart from Him. She saw Him in all things and she shone and rejoiced and realized that she was privileged over other souls with the possession of this truth. Then He revealed Himself to her through her very natural and spiritual configurations with that same mark, and she came to realize that she had seen Him only through Himself not through herself and that she loved Him only through Him, not through herself, since in reality He was the one who loved Himself. Then she looked at Him in every existent entity with that same "eye of recognition," and knew that no other loved Him but Himself, since He is the lover and the beloved, the seeker and the object sought.[15]

The Perfect Man begins his journey from a state of animality, in which state the fulfilling of his natural needs constitutes the sole object of his love. Rational reflection, combined with religious belief, prepares the soul of Man for a state of spirituality. Man begins to worship God. His worship, however, is mixed with love, fear, and desire. He cannot rid himself of the elements of fear and desire in his worship until he attains a stage in which he sees God manifested in both the natural and the spiritual aspects of reality. Once Man has arrived at this stage, he becomes a synthesis of the natural (manifest) and the spiritual (nonmanifest) aspects of reality. As such, he will have attained a state of perfection and become a barzakh between the Real (God as the nonmanifest) and His creation (God as the manifest): "The perfect human being brings together the form of the Real and the form of the cosmos. He is a barzakh between the Real and the cosmos, a raised-up mirror. The Real sees His form in the mirror of the human being, and creation also sees its form in him. He who gains this level has gained a level of perfection more perfect than which nothing is found in possibility."[16]

The Perfect Man is the creature whose spiritual and natural configurations have been penetrated or permeated by the Real, so much so that he has become a polished mirror, reflecting the whole of the reality of the Real, and giving expression to the Real's Most Beautiful Names, especially the Name Manifest, which pertains to the Real's creation, and the Name Nonmanifest, which pertains to his Essence.[17] As Toshihiko Izutsu has put it, the Perfect Man is the person who is fully aware of the permeation (*sarayān*) of the Real in all aspects of reality, since only in him the permeation of the Real in all reality reaches its highest degree of intensity.[18] Ibn al-ʿArabī finds in the title of honor of the prophet Abraham, Friend of God (*khalīl Allah*), a most adequate symbolization of the permeation of the Real in all aspects of reality. As Corbin explains, the title of honor of Abraham is used by Ibn al-ʿArabī as a symbol of the Perfect Man, "not simply because of the idea of *khulla* (sincere friendship, *ṣadāqa*), as is traditionally believed, but because of the idea connoted by the fifth form of the verb (*takhallala*), to mix, mingle, interpenetrate." The permeation (*takhallul*), Corbin adds, "is a pure symbol of the relationship between *Ḥaqq* and *khalq*, whose duality is necessary but comports no *alterity*, two aspects of the same absolute *ḥaqīqa*, coexisting the one through the other."[19] The title of honor of Abraham, *khalīl Allah*, is used as a symbol for the Perfect Man because of the idea of the permeation or the interpenetration of the Real (*Ḥaqq*) and creation (*khalq*). To understand the manner of this interpenetration, a special kind of divine knowledge is needed, which is possessed by the Perfect Man alone.

The Perfect Man as the Possessor of Divine Knowledge

> So also We show Abraham the power and the laws of the heavens and the earth that he might with understanding have certitude. (Q 6:75)
>
> When the night covered him over, he saw a star. He said: "This is my Lord." But when it set, he said: "I love not those that set." (Q 6: 76)
>
> When he saw the moon rising in splendour, he said: "This is my Lord." But when the moon set, he said: "Unless my Lord guide me, I shall surely be among those who go astray." (Q 6: 77)
>
> When he saw the sun rising in splendour, he said: "This is my Lord: This is the greatest (of all)." But when the sun set, he said: "O my people I am indeed free from your (guilt) of giving partners to Allah."(Q 6:78)[20]

ʿAbdullah Yūsuf ʿAlī brings the view of some commentators that the whole thrust of Abraham's reasoning in the cited verses is directed against the false beliefs of his people and provided as a demonstration of the folly of worshipping stars and other heavenly bodies. He thinks, therefore, that as such his statements may be seen as premises of his arguments against polytheism rather than as stages in his spiritual enlightenment.[21] For Ibn al-ʿArabī, however, such an interpretation misses the whole thrust of Abraham's reasoning. In his allusion to the cited verses Ibn al-ʿArabī says, "When the Follower asked him concerning the three lights, he said: 'It is my argument against my people. God had mercy on me and gave it to me. I did not say what I said as an associator, but rather used it as a hunter's net for snaring the minds of my people that have gone astray.'"[22] These words might persuade us that the view that Abraham's statements are premises of his argument against polytheism, rather than stages in his spiritual enlightenment, is correct. However, what Ibn al-ʿArabī says next makes it clear that such a view is shortsighted: "[Abraham said to the Follower]: 'Make your heart like this *Kaʿba* and be present with the Real in all your states, and know that of all the things that you have seen, nothing encompasses the Real like the heart of the believer, which is you.' When the possessor of consideration (*ṣāḥib al-naẓar*) heard these words, he said: '. . . I wish I had not made my reason (*ʿaqlī*) my guide, or that I did not enter with it into the path of reflection (*fikr*).'"[23]

Ibn al-ʿArabī's words cast serious doubt on the view that Abraham's words are meant to be merely premises in a rational argument against polytheism. For his words seem to be critical of reason or, strictly speaking, following reason into the path of reflection. But are not Ibn al-ʿArabī's words (the words uttered by Abraham's Follower in condemnation of rational reflection) rather incompatible with Q 6:75: "So also We show Abraham the power and the laws of the heavens and the earth, that he might with understanding have certitude"? The answer to this question is that Ibn al-ʿArabī does not condemn the rational faculty itself, but only its uncritical adherence to reflection (*fikr*). He provides rather unenthusiastic characterization to the latter by stating that reason (*ʿaql*) errs when it follows reflection uncritically. He says that reflection is a misfortune (*ibtilāʾ*) inflicted upon reason by God. God compelled reason to take from whatever reflection provides to it, despite its presumed dominance over reflection.[24] God endowed reflection with the power of determination over the forms of sense perception, which are provided to it by the faculty of imagination.[25] Reflection examines only what is given to it by this faculty. Hence sometimes it comes out with sound proofs and at other times it furnishes only specious arguments. Reason accepts these arguments and judges according to them. The result is that instead of amplifying its knowledge it only adds to its ignorance.[26]

Thus Ibn al-ʿArabī does not condemn reason itself but only its exclusive reliance on the categories of reflection and on its own proofs that may or may not hit the mark. God commanded reason to reflect (Q 39:9) and to come back to him for knowledge of him. By uncritically following its reflection, reason understood the contrary of the meaning of God's words, that through reflection reason should come to know that it can know God only by God and only when God makes it see things as they are in themselves (*al-amr ʿalā mā huwa ʿalayhi*). Ibn al-ʿArabī emphasizes that not every rational faculty is capable of possessing knowledge of things as they are in themselves, and that this knowledge is preserved for the rational faculties of the saints.[27] God commands reason to reflect, but he warns it against subjugating itself to the categories of reflection and the proofs that are based on them. When reason is liberated from its self-imposed enslavement it is then prepared for seeing things as they are in themselves through a type of reflection that can be called, following Carl J. Kalwaitis, "radical reflection." Kalwaitis explains the meaning of radical reflection as follows:

> If we want to experience that upon which we reflect, then we cannot go anywhere. We cannot use what is before us to accomplish this or that because we do not want to see what is expected to be there, but rather what *is* there. Radical reflection, i.e., philosophical thinking, requires that we, as Heidegger put it, "listen" in order to "let ourselves be told something."[28] Needless to say, "listening" in this context is much more than acoustic perception. It is, rather, an openness that does not obstruct and, therefore, allows us to leave "everything as it is." This fundamental receptivity enables us to belong (*gehören*) and respond to what we hear (*hören*) so that we can experience the matter (thought about), rather than impose ourselves on it.[29]

According to Ibn al-ʿArabī, only the Perfect Man is capable of radical reflection, for he has made the Real his hearing and his sight, since he belongs to the Real in his entirety: "So also are His words, *be not as those who say, 'We hear,' but they hear not* [8:21], even though they hear. Consider this blaming–how similar it is to the furthest limit of praise bestowed on the one whose hearing and eyesight are the Real! When the Real is someone's hearing, he necessarily hears, for he does not hear except through his Lord. *So he hears not through himself.* But it is not correct for him to be a locus for the He-ness of his Lord, so his entity is the being [*wujūd* in Chittick] of the Real, and the property belongs to the possible thing, for that is its trace."[30]

The Perfect Man has made the Real his hearing and his sight. In the same manner, the Perfect Man has become the ears through which the Real hears and the eyes through which the Real sees. The Perfect Man has become the perfect actualization of the notion of permeation between the Real and creation and the possessor of perfect witnessing. Ibn al-ʿArabī describes the Perfect

Man as a person who is destitute of every limited form and is no longer a "possessor of riches." To become a possessor of riches is to adhere to the forms that delimit the Real. Such adherence imprisons the one who witnesses him through the delimited forms:

> When the Real delimits Himself within a form to the recipient of self-disclosure, without doubt the form delimits the viewer. He is with each viewer in a form that is not seen by any other viewer. Hence, no one sees Him nondelimited by existence *except him who is destitute, him from whose witnessing all forms have disappeared.* . . . The Prophet, the possessor of perfect unveiling said: "The possessors of riches are imprisoned," and he who is imprisoned is delimited. But he who is destitute has no riches to delimit or imprison him, so he is not delimited by this delimitation of the possessors of riches. Hence he is nearer to the divine form through nondelimitation than are the possessors of riches, since they are delimited.[31]

The possessors of riches are those who delimit the Real. Those who declare God's comparability to a certain form of creation are possessors of riches. Those who declare God's incomparability to creation are also possessors of riches, since they delimit the Real with the attitude of nondelimitation. As for the Perfect Man, he binds God with both the attributes of comparability and the attributes of incomparability. Thus, says Ibn al-ʿArabī, the Perfect Man shares with the philosophers in what they know, namely, that God should not be compared to creation, but exceeds them in what they fail to acknowledge, namely, that God is not limited even by the limitation of incomparability.[32] William Chittick says that for Ibn al-ʿArabī the attitude of incomparability represents the view of the rational faculty, which affirms God's Unity, while the view of comparability represents the view of imagination, which perceives God's self-disclosures in creation.[33] It is important to keep in mind, however, that for Ibn al-ʿArabī the attitude of imagination is a kind of a third attitude that combines both comparability and incomparability. Chittick is aware of this, of course, and emphasizes that imagination is an intermediary reality standing between the spiritual and the natural and that the possessor of imagination, the Perfect Man, keeps vacillating between the attitude of comparability and the attitude of incomparability. As a result, the Perfect Man succeeds in perceiving the real nature of God's self-disclosures, which is He (creation is the Real) / not He (creation is not the Real).[34]

Ibn al-ʿArabī says that the Perfect Man binds the Real with both the attitude of incomparability and the attitude of comparability. This may seem inconsistent with his insistence that the Perfect Man is he who does not delimit or bind the Real. However, the inconsistency disappears once we understand that the Real is above all limitations, which implies that he is limited by all limitations. Between the Real as limited and the Real as unlimited there is what Izutsu describes as complete reciprocal ontological permeation.[35] By acting as a Supreme Barzakh between the Real and creation, the Perfect Man represents this reciprocal permeation in its most perfect form. The Perfect Man becomes a polished mirror, faithfully reflecting beliefs based on the attitude of declaring the Real comparable to creation and beliefs based on the attitude of declaring the Real incomparable to creation. The Perfect Man becomes a Prime Matter, a Receptacle for all forms of beliefs: "Be careful not to bind yourself to one specific belief and deny all others. This way you miss a great benefit, since you leave out the knowledge of reality as it is in itself. Make yourself a Prime Matter for all forms of belief. God is greater and wider than to be limited to one specific belief."[36]

Prime Matter is a nonexistent thing. Its nonexistence, however, is not the simple negation of existence, but rather includes the negation of existence as a transcended moment. Each form in which Prime Matter manifests itself represents a moment of transcending another form in which it manifests itself. Acting as Prime Matter, the Perfect Man becomes a locus of manifestation in which all forms of belief about the Real are manifested as transcended moments. These forms of belief, which resemble transcended moments in the intellectual growth of the Perfect Man, can be reduced eventually to two fundamental moments: the moment in which the Real is represented as related to the finite forms of manifestation, and the moment in which the Real is represented as totally unrelated to any finite form of manifestation.[37] In the knowledge of the Perfect Man, these two fundamental moments are represented as transcended moments. The outcome of this transcendence is a synthesis between the infinite and the finite representations of the Real, a synthesis in which finitude and infinitude abide in a state of active reciprocal permeation. This active synthetic reciprocity constitutes the essence of each and every moment in the self-manifestation of the Real. It is the essence of Time, since each moment of time designates a passage of the Real from the state of nonmanifestation to a state of manifestation. The Perfect Man, who is a faithful representative or representation of this perpetual synthetic activity, is the Son of Time, as Stephen Hirtenstein explains:

> [The Perfect Man] is the Son of the Instant, *Ibn Waqt*. The Shaykh describes such a one as "he whose instant has become unblemished. He has become no longer ill and so he does not aim. In fact the conjecture (*wahm*) does not indeed come to the fore because it concludes in knowledge." He is no longer ill because he knows and sees that there is only One Being—he does not attribute existence to himself since he has found that his self is but the expression of the One Self.

> He does not aim since that would imply a gap between what he is and what he will be, for he has penetrated beyond the appearance of form. Such a man is in complete accordance with the times, with the needs of the times. The story of Abraham exemplifies the "concluding in knowledge," where the power of love strips the manifestation of light of any inherent existence, so that there is no confusion possible of the form with its reality. *This penetration beyond the appearance of form does not negate the form, but assigns to it its proper place and dignity.*[38]

The Perfect Man is the Son of Time, and Time is identical with the world as Ibn al-ʿArabī says.[39] Hence, the Perfect Man is the Son (epitome) of the world. By knowing himself, the Perfect Man comes to know that he is a dividing line between the temporality (*ḥudūth*) of the world, and the eternity (*qidam*) of the Real, that is, between finitude and infinity. The dividing line between finitude and infinity is the moment of creation. Creation is the human being as Ibn al-ʿArabī says,[40] meaning that the human being is the ultimate purpose or the final cause of creation. The Real created the world because he loved to be known, that is, because he loved to realize himself, and the Perfect Man assists the Real in achieving this realization.[41] The Perfect Man comes to know the Real by differentiating him from creation, that is, by differentiating the infinite from the finite. To differentiate the infinite from the finite is to know the Limit that brings them together while at the same time keeping them separate. The Limit that brings the finite and the infinite together resembles the instant of time (*al-ʿān*), which is the essence of the past time, that is, the time of the manifestation of the Real that has come to be, and future time, that is, the time of the manifestation of the Real that has not come to be. As such, the present state designates the Being of the Real, since the Being of the Real is the Essence of all that has come to be and all that will ever be. In the following, I will elaborate on the logic that leads the Perfect Man to the knowledge of the Being of the Real, which is the knowledge of the Limit between his finite being and his infinite being.

The Logic of the Knowledge of Perfection

In the previous section I mentioned ʿAbdullah Yūsuf ʿAlī's view that Abraham's reasoning in Q 6:76-78 is directed against the superstitious beliefs of his people, and that his statements may be seen as premises of his arguments against polytheism rather than stages in his spiritual enlightenment. I tried to show that, viewed from Ibn al-ʿArabī's standpoint, this view misses the whole thrust of Abraham's reasoning. For according to Ibn al-ʿArabī, Abraham's main argument was directed not only against polytheism, but also against the sort of rational reflection that leads to polytheist and other limited ways of knowing the Real. According to Ibn al-ʿArabī, both the possessors of religious faith and the possessors of rational proofs are deviators from the Way of knowing the Real as much as the polytheist is. There are actually no straight ways to lead to the Real since, for Ibn al-ʿArabī, a straight way is always "circularly straight" (*mustaqīm al-istidāra*): "The follower of the straight (*musṭaṭīl*) way is necessarily bending and drawn away from his aim, seeking that in which he *is* . . . while the follower of the circular (*dawr*) movement, the perplexed who perpetually circulates around the center, does not have a beginning nor an end to limit him."[42]

On the basis of this view, Ibn al-ʿArabī argues that the Perfect Man is he who embraces all ways of knowing the Real, including the way of heresy (*ilḥād*), since heresy is only another deviating way of knowing the Real, a way that is also based on negating other ways of knowing him:[43]

> You worship only what you set up in yourself. This is why doctrines and states differed concerning Allah. Thus one group says that He is like this and another group says that He is not like this, but like that. Another group says concerning knowledge [of Him] that the color of water is determined by the color of the cup. . . . So consider the bewilderment that permeates (*sāriyya*) every belief. Thus the perfect is he whose bewilderment has amplified, and whose regret has become constant. He does not obtain the object of his worship, since what he seeks cannot be obtained, and since he has searched for the Way of Him, Whose Way is unknown. He who is more perfect than the perfect is he who believes in every belief concerning Him. He recognizes Him in [religious] faith (*īmān*), in rational proofs (*dalā'il*) and in heresy (*ilḥād*). After all, *ilḥād* is also deviating from one particular belief in favor of another particular belief.[44]

The Perfect knows that the Way is incapable of being known, but he who recognizes the Way in all the (deviating) ways of knowing the Real is even more perfect than the Perfect. There is a rational procedure that is involved in realizing the Way. The following discussion will be devoted to this procedure. But first I wish to emphasize that it is not, strictly speaking, by rational means that the Perfect Man arrives at realization. Rather, the rational procedure in question provides the Perfect Man with a recognition that extends beyond the rational. Although transcending the rational procedure, this recognition still provides for its theoretical justification. Before I proceed, I must warn the reader of some difficulty that might be experienced in the discussion. The difficulty is partially due to the complexity that is involved in attempting to grasp the epistemological passage from a rational level to one that extends beyond the rational, and the ambiguity of the paradoxical relation that connects the two levels. Luckily we have in the literature about Ibn al-ʿArabī a similar discussion of the subject in question, provided by Izutsu.[45]

The *way* is the term that Izutsu employs as a translation for the Tao. Izutsu considers the notion of the Tao, as it is employed in the works of Lao Tzu and Chuang Tzu, as the equivalent of Ibn al-ʿArabī's notion of the Supreme Barzakh. He brings Chuang Tzu's analysis of the process of the gradual development of the human mind toward Taoist perfection, that is, toward the Absolute. As I am going to show, Chuang Tzu's account of the reasoning that leads to Taoist perfection bears a striking similarity to Ibn al-ʿArabī's account of the reasoning that leads the Perfect Man to the knowledge of the Supreme Barzakh. Izutsu presents Chuang Tzu's theoretical analysis as culminating in an argument that establishes that the Absolute is the negation-of-negation-of-negation, that is, the negation of the Absolute's being Nothing, which is the negation of Being.[46] Chuang Tzu's argument is the following:

> So we posit Beginning. But the moment we posit Beginning, our Reason cannot help going further back and admit the idea of there having been no Beginning. Thus the concept of No-Beginning is necessarily established. But the moment we posit No-Beginning, our logical thinking goes further back by negating the very idea which it has just established, and admits the idea of there having been no "there-having-been-no-Beginning." The concept of "No-No-Beginning" is thus established. . . . In the same manner, we begin by taking notice of the fact that there is Being. But the moment we recognize Being, our Reason goes further back and admits that there is Nonbeing or Nothing. But the moment we posit Nonbeing we cannot but go further back and admit that there has not been from the very beginning Nonbeing. The concept of No-[Nonbeing] once established in this way, the Reason goes further back and admits that there has been no "there-having-been-no-Nonbeing" (i.e., the negation of the negation of Nonbeing, or No-[No Nonbeing]).[47]

Reflection begins from the simple notion of Being. (1) We reflect on Being as the limit beyond which there is nothing. This reflection compels our reason to go further back and think about Nonbeing, or the negation of Being. (2) We reflect on the notion of Nonbeing, and realize that the very fact that we can think about this implies that Nonbeing is No Nonbeing. Hence the negation of the negation of Being is established. (3) We reflect on this negation of the negation of Being as the limit beyond which there is nothing. This reflection results in the negation of the negation of the negation of Being. This third moment of reflection indicates the limit of rational reflection. For no matter how far reflection goes back it always generates three basic results. Its first reflective move yields Nonbeing, its second move yields Being, and its third move yields Nonbeing. Nonbeing will always be the starting point and the end point of the process of reflection. Inasmuch as the third reflection indicates the limit of rational reflection we may, as Izutsu suggests, regard the result of this reflection, that is, the negation of the negation of Nonbeing, as the logical counterpart of the metaphysical Nothing, which is the transcendent Nothing that is beyond both Being and Nonbeing.[48]

It is important to keep in mind that it is not through rational reflection as such that we have arrived at the logical formulation of a Principle that transcends Being and Nonbeing. For rational reflection as such can only go back from negation to the negation of negation to the negation of negation of negation ad infinitum. From this potential infinite reaching further back no concluding formulations could be obtained. If there is a conclusion that we may draw from the potentially infinite process of negations, it is that the moment of recognition that there is a Principle which transcends both affirmation and negation (transcends both Being and Nonbeing) is not the outcome of rational reflection as such, but that it rather transcends the very rational reflection that leads to it.

Ibn al-ʿArabī often cites Q 8:17: "You did not throw, when you threw, but God threw"[49] as his favorite example for illustrating the kind of reasoning that leads to perfection. In the following, I will cite two passages in which Ibn al-ʿArabī provides an analysis of the verse and examine the main points of his analysis:

> God the Almighty said: "You did not throw [when you threw but Allah threw]." He negated "when you threw," then He affirmed what He negated. Then He said, "But God threw" negating what He affirmed. Hence, the affirmation of "throwing" has become a Middle (*wasaṭ*) between two limits [extremities] of negation (*ṭarafyy nafy*). The Middle is limited (*maḥṣūr*) between two identical negations, and therefore, it cannot hold its affirmation. Limitation (*ḥaṣr*) rules over it, especially when the second negation adds to the first negation the affirmation of the throwing to Allah and not to the Middle (i.e. to Muḥammad). The attribution of the throwing as it is witnessed by the senses is affirmed to Muḥammad in virtue of Muḥammad's immutability (*thubūt*) in the Word of the Real (*kalimat al-Ḥaqq*). As he is a thrower/not a thrower, so he is in the Word of the Real Muḥammad/not-Muḥammad, since if he were to be Muḥammad, as his form witnesses, then he would be a thrower, as his throwing witnesses.[50]

The process of reflection begins with the simple notion of throwing. (1) "You did not throw" is the negation of attributing the act to Muḥammad. Not throwing is established. (2) "When you threw" signifies the negation of the negation of attributing the act to Muḥammad. The negation of not throwing is established.

(3) "But Allah threw" is the negation of the negation of the negation of attributing the act of throwing to Muḥammad. The negation of the negation of not throwing is established. The negation of throwing is established twice, whereas its affirmation is established only once. Furthermore, the affirmation (of throwing) is established only in the middle of two negations. This will also be the case no matter how much further we proceed in the process of reflection. We will always have an affirmation (limited) between two negations.

Ibn al-ʿArabī says that attributing the act of throwing is affirmed to Muḥammad by virtue of Muḥammad's immutability in the Word of the Real. Muḥammad is the existential individuation of his immutable entity (*ʿayn thābita*). His immutable entity, like all the immutable entities of all other creatures, is in the Word of the Real.[51] Ibn al-ʿArabī mentions the Word in the opening sentence of the *Futūḥāt*. He says that God brought things into being from nonbeing and the negation of nonbeing (*ʿan ʿadam wa-ʿadamuh*) through the Word, so that we come to know in what sense the temporality and the eternity of things is to be distinguished from the temporality and the eternity of God, and realize the true meaning of God's priority to existence. The being of Muḥammad, as well as the being of all things, belongs to God's Being. But the manifestation of God's Being is dependent on the Word, since God can manifest himself only by granting his Being to the immutable entities that preexist in the Word.

By coming to know the Word, the Perfect Man comes to know himself, since he is the Word.[52] As John Little says, the Word is "the dialectical process of Divine Self-manifestation and Self-realization."[53] The emphasis here is on the dialectical aspect of the process, which indicates infinitude and transcendence. The Self-manifestation of the Real is infinite, and so the self-realization of the Perfect Man must be infinite as well in order to faithfully represent the moments of the self-disclosures of God. Although the dialectical process can be given expression in a rational formula, the process itself, which is the essence of the paradoxical correlation that holds between the Real and creation, transcends all rational formulations. Ibn al-ʿArabī makes it clear that it is an essential characteristic of the follower of the path of perfection to suffer constantly from bewilderment and regret, since the object that he seeks to know is infinite and, as such, can never be conceptually restricted.[54] He makes this point clear in the following passage in which he analyzes Q 8:17:

> He affirmed you, negated you, misguided you and guided you. He made you bewildered in what He made certain to you. Thus, you have ascertained but bewilderment. You knew, therefore, that the affair is all bewilderment, and that deviation (*ḍalāl*) is the same as guidance (*hudā*). He said: "You and not-you" and "You did not throw when you threw but God threw," affirming both that Muḥammad is the only thrower and that Allah is the only thrower. But, then, what has become

> of Muḥammad? He negated him and affirmed him. Then He negated him [for the second time]. Muḥammad is affirmed in His saying: "When you threw" between two negations: an eternal negation in His saying: "You did not throw" and an ever-lasting negation in His saying: "But Allah threw." Thus, the affirmation of Muḥammad in this verse is like the instant of time (*al-ān*), which is the eternal Being (*wujūd*) between the two times, between the past time, which is a realized (*muḥaqqaq*) Nonbeing, and the future time, which is absolute (*maḥḍ*) Nonbeing. . . . He rendered him an affirmed Middle between two negations, so he resembled the instant of time (*al-ān*) that is Being. Being (*wujūd*) belongs to Allah not to Muḥammad, since He is Who possesses permanent Being in the past, in the present state (*ḥāl*), and in the future time. Conjectured (*mutawahham*) delimitation (*taqyīd*) is removed from Him.[55]

The verse: "You did not throw, when you threw, but Allah threw" consists of an affirmation of the attribution of throwing to Muḥammad (limited) between two negations. The affirmation of the attribution of throwing to Muḥammad is an affirmation of his being. That is, his act signifies his existence. The being of Muḥammad is limited between a Nonbeing that has been realized (*muḥaqqaq*) and absolute (*maḥḍ*) Nonbeing. The Nonbeing that has been realized is the negation of Being in his saying, "You did not throw." The Nonbeing that is Absolute is the negation of the negation of Nonbeing in his saying, "But Allah threw." The first Nonbeing, expressed in his saying, "You did not throw," designates a limited or relative Nonbeing. It is limited because "You did not throw" implies that throwing has already taken place. The second Nonbeing expressed in his saying, "But Allah threw," designates unlimited Nonbeing. It is unlimited because it negates not only limited Nonbeing, but also the negation of limited Nonbeing. Absolute Nonbeing is unlimited because it transcends both limited Nonbeing and the logical consequences that follow from positing limited Nonbeing. In the following passage Ibn al-ʿArabī explains the difference between limited and absolute Nonbeing, emphasizing that absolute Nonbeing is more significant at signifying God and making him known than limited Nonbeing:

> Absolute (*maḥḍ*) nonexistence is more eminent than relative nonexistence in a certain respect, since in its magnification of God and in the strength of its signifying Him, it does not receive being. It remains as it is in its root and entity, out of jealousy lest it become an associate of the Divine Side in relation to the attribute of being, and lest the Names that are ascribed to God be ascribed to it. . . . After all, absolute nonexistence is better at making known what is worthy of God than relative nonexistence, because it has the attribute of eternity without beginning

> in His being. This is the description of the Real by the negation of Firstness, which is the description of nonexistence, in that being is negated from it through its own essence. Hence nothing other than God makes God known with greater knowledge than does absolute nonexistence.[56]

Absolute Nonbeing is better at making God known than relative Nonbeing because it has the attribute of eternity without beginning, that is, because it transcends the qualified negation (the negation that implies affirmation) of Firstness. Nevertheless, God is described as the First (*al-Awwal*) and the Last (*al-Akhir*). The question is how Firstness (a*wwaliyya*) is negated from God and yet is a description of him. The answer is that the Firstness and the Lastness of God are identical on account of God's being a barzakh between his two names, the First and the Last. As such, God is the Essence of both. He is like the instant of time (*al-ān*) that can be divided into past time and future time, although it is the present state (*ḥāl*) in both. In the verse "You did not throw, when you threw, but Allah threw," the affirmation of the being of Muḥammad signifies the Being of God. The Being of God is a Limit between his finite being in the past, which is expressed in the conditional negation of Muḥammad's being, and his infinite Being in the future, which is expressed in the absolute negation of Muḥammad's being. The situation of Man's being, which is the conclusion of the situation of creation in general, is a sign or an indication of the situation of the Being of God. In both cases it is the limit situation. The limit situation will be the subject of the discussion of the next chapter.

CHAPTER 8

The Limit Situation

In this chapter I provide an account of the limit situation as it is presented in chapter 451 of the *Futūḥāt*. First I provide a translation of the chapter followed by a brief interpretation of the key concepts in its title.[1] Then, I elaborate on the problem of the relationship between the manifest and the nonmanifest aspects of reality, or, the "paradox of infinity." Finally, I present the limit situation, a situation in which the Real and creation are intertied through the Supreme Barzakh.

On Knowing the Waystation of "In The Articulations is the Knowledge of the Stairs"

You should know that the possible things are *the words of God that do not run out* (Q 31:27).[2] Through the possible things the capacity of the words for manifestation is revealed, a capacity that is never exhausted. They [the possible things] are compound things, since in their compoundness lies their capacity for bestowing benefits. They have emerged from a composition that is expressed in the Arabic language with the word *Be* (Q 16: 40). . . .[3]

They are in the manifest domain in correspondence to what they are in the nonmanifest domain. In the nonmanifest domain they are in the collective form that comprises all the forms in which they fluctuate (*tataqallab*) in the manifest domain. In its turn the fluctuation (*taqlīb*) in the manifest domain is in correspondence to a fluctuation that is infinite in the nonmanifest domain. This [infinite] fluctuation [appears] in the manifest domain instant by instant, since the infinite cannot enter into [manifest] existence [entirely]. For the infinite does not come to an end, so it does not halt at a limit.

The matter within which the words of God, which constitute the world, become manifest is the Breath of the All-Merciful. . . . You should know that when God made manifest His words, He assigned to them levels. Among them are the luminous, the fiery, and the earthy spirits. They have diverse levels, but He made them halt with themselves in order that they witness themselves. He veiled Himself from them within themselves. Then He ordered them to seek Him, and set up *stairs* upon which they ascend in seeking Him.

He entered for them in these stairs with the ruling property of limit, and assigned for them *hearts through which they employ intelligence* (Q 22: 46). To some of them He assigned reflective thought in order that they reflect. He made one of the means of ascending to Him the negation of similarity from Him in all respects. Then He declared Himself similar to them through them, thus affirming exactly what he negated. Then he demonstrated to them the truthfulness of the report that He reported to them [that He is both similar and not similar to creation]. Their understandings differed according to the difference in the realities of their specific configurations. Thus, each group thought about Him in ways that corresponded exactly to its particular reality. Hence, [the possible things] find in the end but themselves.

Among them are those who say that they are He. Among them are those who believe in the incapacity in this and say, "What is required from us is only that we come to know that He is not known," since this is the meaning of incapacity. Among them are those who say that He can be known in one respect but not in another respect. Among them are those who say that all groups are correct in what they believe. . . .

Creation is tied to God as the possible is tied to the necessary. . . . The Real also is tied to creation in respect of His names, since the divine names seek the world through an essential seeking.[4] Hence, there can be no escape in existence from mutual binding. Just as we are in Him and for Him, so He is in us and for us. Otherwise, He would not be [named] our Lord and Creator. . . . He provides us with assistance in existence and we provide Him with assistance in knowledge. . . . [The Real] is the possessor of the exalted stairs with essential descent, and creation is in descending with essential ascending and mounting the stairs.

Thus, everything in existence must leave traces whether in [the state of] existence or nonexistence. But in reality, nothing leaves traces except relations, which are nonexistent things that possess a

> smell of existence. Hence, nonexistence does not leave traces except through the smells of existence, and existence does not leave traces except through nonexistent relations. . . .
>
> *So there is nothing but intertying and intertwining, as He has alerted us: The leg is intertwined with the leg (Q 75:29). In other words: Our affair is intertwined and knotted with His affair, so we will never be untied from His knot.*
>
> When the two are intertied . . . there must be something that brings them together. This is the Tie. It is nothing other than what is required by the two things through their very essence, and no additional affair of existence is needed.[5] Hence, the two are intertied *in themselves*, since there is nothing but creation and the Real. The Tie must be one of them or both. It is impossible for one of them to possess this property [of intertying] in separation from the other. . . . since it is through both that it becomes manifest, not through one of them in separation from the other. . . .
>
> Despite this intertying, the two things are not likenesses, due to the uniqueness of each thing. Hence, they must be distinguished through something else that is not in one of them [alone] but that through which both things are signified.[6]

In the title of this chapter we find two key terms: *makhārij* and *maʿārij*. *Makhārij* is the plural of *makhraj*, the point in the vocal apparatus through which the letters of the alphabet are articulated. As Chittick points out, Ibn al-ʿArabī draws an analogy between the letters that take shape in the human breath, and the manifestation of Being within the Breath of the All-Merciful (*nafas ar-Raḥmān*).[7] The Breath of the All-Merciful is the matter (*māda*) within which the words of God, which are the world, become manifest. Through breathing, God relieves the constriction of the immutable entities (*aʿyān thābita*) that abide as latent forms in his Breath and that seek to manifest their specific properties in the manifest world. Chittick explains that in the human case, the manner of breathing through the throat and mouth determines in what shape letters are produced. In the same manner, each letter/reality of the cosmos manifests Being in a specific mode different from other modes of manifestation.[8] The term *maʿārij* is the plural of *miʿrāj*. It designates means of ascent, like ladder or stairs. Thus, *makhārij* designates places of articulation through which God's words descend to the cosmos, creating the possible things, and *maʿārij* designates means of ascent through which the possible things ascend in their way back to God. Ibn al-ʿArabī states in the title of the chapter that the articulations (the ways of descent) are identical to the stairs (the ways of ascension). Hence, the Real's descent to creation and creation's ascent to the Real point to the same act. Consequently, the Real and creation are intertied through a state of mutual permeation (*takhallul*) characteristic of the limit situation.

The Paradox of Infinity

> You should know that the possible things are *the words of God that do not run out* (Q 31:27). Through the possible things the capacity of the words for manifestation is revealed, a capacity that is never exhausted. They [the possible things] are compound things, since in their compoundness lies their capacity for bestowing benefits. They have emerged from a composition that is expressed in the Arabic language with the word *Be* (Q 16: 40).

The words of God are the possible things of the world, the materialized forms of the immutable entities that are latent in God's Breath and that become manifest by means of the Word *Be*. Words are relations that join letters, investing them with forms or meanings that the letters do not possess apart from the relation that brings them together.[9] In the same way, the compounded things in the cosmos are combinations of uncompounded things. The ways in which letters can be combined to produce new words are infinite. Likewise, the ways in which the possible things can be compounded from uncompounded realities are potentially infinite. This is why the words of God will not run out.[10] The words of God (the forms of the possible things) are infinite because of their rootedness in the storehouse of the fixed entities (*khazānat al-thubūt*), a storehouse that is unlimited.[11] The storehouse of fixity is the domain of the absent (*al-ghā'ib*). From this domain the words of God are manifested into the witnessed domain in a successive manner:

> They are in the manifest domain in correspondence to what they are in the nonmanifest domain. In the nonmanifest domain they are in the collective form that comprises all the forms in which they fluctuate (*tataqallab*) in the manifest domain. In its turn the fluctuation (*taqlīb*) in the manifest domain is in correspondence to a fluctuation that is infinite in the nonmanifest domain. This [infinite] fluctuation [appears] in the manifest domain instant by instant, since the infinite cannot enter into existence [manifest being]. For the infinite does not come to an end, so it does not halt at a limit.

The possible things in the state of manifestation accord with what they are in the absent domain. But the possible things in the absent domain are infinite. How is it possible then that some possible things are prior or posterior to others?

In other words, how can we say that one infinite is greater than another? Ibn al-ʿArabī introduces this problem in chapter 524 of the *Futūḥāt*: "There is no individual object of knowledge or possible thing that does not continue to pass by *ad infinitum*. Nonetheless, some are posterior to those that are prior, so they fall short of those that are prior to them, and the prior ones are greater than they. But neither [the prior nor the posterior] is described by finitude in its continuing passage, so being greater and falling short both may occur in that which is infinite."[12]

Chittick points out that Ibn al-ʿArabī is referring here to "the paradoxes that arise when we come to understand that some infinities are greater than others, even though this is rationally impossible."[13] Ibn al-ʿArabī's meaning can be clarified by referring to the theologians' argument against the philosophers' doctrine of the eternity of the world. The theologians argue that the assumption that the world is infinite leads to the impossible consequence that an infinite time must have elapsed up to any present moment. This is impossible, however, since infinite time cannot actually come to be. Furthermore, the assumption of the infinity of the time of the world leads to the conclusion that one infinite is greater than another. For it must be the case that the infinity of the time that presumably has elapsed up to a given point is either greater or lesser than another infinity that must have elapsed up to another given point, since the two points are separated from each other by a time interval that can be measured in terms of more or less. This is inconceivable, however, since one infinite cannot be greater than another infinite. Therefore, the world must be limited in time.

For Ibn al-ʿArabī, to say that the world is limited in time is to express only half the truth. The world, according to him, consists of the manifested forms of the possible things, which are the existential individuations of their fixed entities that dwell in the Essence of God. These fixed entities are infinite in the sense that being never ceases to pass over them. In virtue of the eternal passage of being over the fixed entities, their existential individuations, which are nothing other than the possible things in the state of manifestation, must be characterized by infinitude. On the other hand, the possible things have their specific realities, which distinguish them from each other. In virtue of possessing these specific realities, the possible things are finite. Thus, the possible things, or, the world that consists of them, must be both finite and infinite. But how can the same world be finite and infinite? Ibn al-ʿArabī treats this problem by resorting to the notion of the *thingness* (*shay'īyya*) that is prior to both essence and existence. The thingness of the world's being comes from the Real, whose Being transcends the finitude of the existence of the possible things and the infinitude of their fixed essences. In virtue of the Being of the Real, which is beyond finitude and infinitude, it is possible to characterize the world as both finite and infinite. I will employ the following passage from chapter 524 to clarify this point:

> The Real does not have being through passage that He might be qualified by finitude or infinitude, for He is the entity of being. It is the existent thing that is qualified by [being's] passage over it. When passage over something continues without end, while it is finite in its own entity in respect of being an existent thing—because in its own entity it has a reality, through which it is distinct from everything that does not have this reality that makes it it, and this is nothing but the entity of its it-ness—this is the existent thing, and it is not described by finitude, but it is also not described as being infinite, because of its being. So in respect of being finite, it is infinite. . . . Being is all letters, words, chapters, and verses. . . . It does not become qualified by nonexistence, because nonexistence is the negation of thingness, but thingness is intelligible both in being and in fixity, and there is no third level.[14]

The Real is not qualified by finitude or infinitude, since he is the *entity of being*, not a thing that acquires being. The entity of being, to be distinguished from the being of the entity, is the thingness that is intelligible in both existence and essence, that is, in the entity's existence in the manifested domain and in the entity's immutability in the domain of the absent. The Being of the Real passes through all entities, that is, through immutable (nonexistent) entities and manifest (existent) entities. The Being of the Real is beyond both the existence, that is the finitude, and the nonexistence, that is, the infinitude, of the entities. It is the Limit that brings together the finite and the infinite. It is with this property of the Limit that the Real enters for the possible things through the stairs (*maʿārij*), which are the ascending levels of reality that the Real designates for them. The possible things ascend these stairs in their way to the Real. This process of the ascent of the possible things through the rising levels of reality corresponds to the process of the descending of the Real to the possible things. In both cases the process is infinite, as it never comes to an end. And yet, the levels of reality, which are designated for the possible things and which are identical to the levels of reality of the descending of the Real, are differentiated in terms of priority and posteriority. This, however, ceases to be impossibility, once we understand that when the Real, who is the Supreme Barzakh between finitude and infinitude, enters the levels of reality with the property of the Limit, he makes them in the likeness of himself, that is, beyond finitude and infinitude.

The Limit Situation

> You should know that when God made manifest His words, He assigned to them levels. Among them are the luminous, the fiery, and the earthy

> spirits. They have diverse levels, but He made them halt with themselves in order that they witness themselves. He veiled Himself from them within themselves. Then He ordered them to seek Him, and set up stairs upon which they ascend in seeking Him. He entered for them in these stairs with the ruling property of limit, and assigned for them *hearts through which they employ intelligence* (Q 22: 46). To some of them He assigned reflective thought in order that they reflect.

The Real manifests his words in the forms of the possible things and determines for them levels of reality. The levels of reality are diverse in relation to each other. They are ranked in an order of priority or posteriority, following the difference in their specific configurations. However, in relation to the Infinite (the Real) they are finite. Furthermore, the Real veils himself from the possible things (the finite entities) within them. Due to this situation, which is nothing but the limit situation, the possible things are engaged in a process of ascension that can be characterized by both finitude and infinitude. The process is finite, due to the fact that the possible things which take part in it must halt with themselves in respect of their specific configurations. The process is also infinite, due to the fact that it is driven by the Infinite, who is veiled from the finite things within them.

To some of the possible things the Real assigns intelligence and reflective thought, which are means of ascent to knowing him. One of these means, by which the possessors of reflection ascend to the knowledge of the Real, is the negation of the similarity between him and creation. Another means of ascent is the affirmation of the similarity between the Real and creation. This is nothing but the negation of the negation of the similarity between them. Once the Real has negated his negation, that is, once the infinite Real has identified himself with the finite, from which he has differentiated himself, he has revealed the true meaning of infinity and the truth about the reports that declare his being beyond both finitude and infinitude, or, beyond both transcendence and immanence. Ibn al-ʿArabī mentions four types of possessors of reflection: (1) Those who say that they are he. (2) Those who say that knowledge is coming to know that he cannot be known. (3) Those who say that he is known in one respect but incapable of being known in another respect. (4) Those who say that all groups are correct in what they believe. The attitude of the first group can be identified with the attitude of declaring God comparable (*tashbīh*). Ibn al-ʿArabī's following words indicate that he agrees partially with this group:

> Creation is tied to God as the possible is tied to the necessary. . . . The Real also is tied to creation in respect of His names, since the divine names seek the world through an essential seeking. Hence, there can be no escape in existence from mutual binding. Just as we are in Him

> and for Him, so He is in us and for us. Otherwise, He would not be [named] our Lord and Creator. . . . He provides us with assistance in existence and we provide Him with assistance in knowledge. . . . [The Real] is the possessor of the exalted stairs with essential descent, and creation is in descending with essential ascending and mounting the stairs.

Since the possible thing is dependent in its very existence on the Necessary, the first group must be correct in claiming that they are he. Ibn al-ʿArabī says that the Real is also tied to creation. But he makes it clear that he is tied to his creation only in respect of his Names. Consequently, it is only in this respect that he is known. Hence, the third group must be correct in claiming that he is known in one respect but unknown in another respect. Although Ibn al-ʿArabī thinks that those who say that creation is identical to the Real and those who say that the Real is known in one respect but unknown in another respect are correct, he identifies his own position with those who say that knowledge is coming to know that the Real is not known, and (even more strongly) with the position of those who say that every group is correct in what they maintain. In agreement with those who say that knowledge is coming to know that the Real cannot be known, Ibn al-ʿArabī often cites a saying attributed to Abū Bakr al-Ṣiddīq: "The most knowledgeable of the knowers is he who knows that he knows what he knows and that he does not know what he does not know. The Prophet said, 'I count not Thy praises before Thee,' since he knew that there is something that cannot be encompassed. Abū Bakr said, "Incapacity to attain comprehension is itself comprehension." In other words, he comprehended that there is something which he is incapable of comprehending. So that is knowledge/not knowledge."[15]

Those who hold the attitude that incapacity to comprehend is comprehension have attained sound understanding of God's prescription to the rational faculty to come to know him through reflection. Through sound reflection, the possessors of knowledge see that reason delimits everything that it knows, while the divine Essence remains beyond delimitation. Thus they come to know that the only knowledge about God that reflection can provide to reason is the knowledge of what God *is not*.[16] Perhaps the best account of this attitude, which prescribes knowing the Real through coming to know that he is incapable of being known, can be found in the writings of the medieval philosopher and theologian Cusanus (d.1464). Consider his following words:

> Therefore, it is not the case that by means of likeness a finite intellect can precisely attain the truth about things. For truth is not something more or something less but is something indivisible. Whatever is not truth cannot measure truth precisely. (By comparison, a noncircle [cannot measure] a circle, whose being is something indivisible.)

> Hence, the intellect, which is not truth, never comprehends truth so precisely that truth cannot be comprehended infinitely more precisely. For the intellect is to truth as [an inscribed] polygon is to [the inscribing] circle. The more angles the inscribed polygon has the more similar it is to the circle. However, even if the number of its angles is increased by infinitum, the polygon never becomes equal [to the circle] unless it is resolved into an identity with the circle. Hence, regarding truth, it is evident that we do not know anything other than the following: viz., *that we know truth not to be precisely comprehensible as it is.* For truth may be likened unto the most absolute necessity (which cannot be either something more or something less than it is), and our intellect may be likened unto possibility. Therefore, the quiddity of things, which is the truth of beings, is unattainable in its purity; though it is sought by all philosophers, it is found by no one as it is. *And the more deeply we are instructed in this ignorance, the closer we approach to truth.*[17]

Like Ibn al-ʿArabī, Cusanus thinks that "philosophers who have endeavored to make known the ever-knowable Essence of God have expended useless efforts, since they have not entered into the field of learned ignorance," in which they come to know that "the better someone knows that knowledge about God's Essence cannot be had, the more learned he is."[18] Cusanus thinks that the quiddity of things, which is their truth, is unattainable. This accords with Ibn al-ʿArabī's view that the realities of the fixed entities are unknown since, like the Essence of the Real, they are characterized by infinitude. The fixed entities are infinite in the sense that the self-disclosures of the Real's Infinite Being through these entities are endless.[19] The essences of things, therefore, are unknown in as much as the Infinite Essence of the Real is unknown, that is, in as much as the self-disclosures of the Real never cease to pass over them. In the same way, Cusanus says that although the quiddity of things "is sought by all philosophers, it is found by no one as it is." The quiddity of the possible things can never be found as it is, because the possible things are never actually what they are potentially. Moreover, Like Ibn al-ʿArabī, Cusanus characterizes the Essence of God as that which is prior to the difference between actuality (existence) and potentiality (nonexistence), and to the difference between being and nonbeing.[20]

According to Cusanus, the Essence of God can never be found, since it is beyond all limits.[21] Ibn al-ʿArabī also thinks that God's Essence transcends all limits, but his understanding of this transcendence seems somewhat different from that of Cusanus although proceeding from the same starting point, as Andrey Smirnov makes clear.[22] Smirnov explains that for Cusanus the indefinableness of God implies that God is beyond all limitations, while for Ibn al-ʿArabī the indefinableness of God implies that God *encompasses* all limits.[23] He emphasizes, however, that Cusanus and Ibn al-ʿArabī share the same understanding concerning the nature of the knowledge of the Real. Both thinkers hold that the Real is unknown or indefinable. According to Cusanus, this is because God is not defined by any definition, whereas according to Ibn al-ʿArabī, it is because God is defined by all definitions.[24] Cusanus's view regarding the "unknowledgeability" of God is identical, in a sense, to the view of the second group of the possessors of rational reflection, which declares God incomparable (*tanzīh*). This view can be contrasted with the view of the first group of the possessors of rational reflection, who say that they are he, and that expresses itself in terms of declaring God comparable (*tashbīh*). Although Ibn al-ʿArabī thinks that both groups are partially correct, his view comes closer to the view of the second group. Consequently, his final position must be identified with the view of the fourth group of the possessors of rational reflection, the view of those who say that all groups are correct in what they maintain.

Ibn al-ʿArabī says that the Real gives us assistance in being, and we give him assistance in knowledge. The meaning of this statement is that except for the Real the possible things will not exist and except for the possible things the Real will not be known. In giving existence to the possible things, the Real situates them in ascending levels of reality. These culminate in the level of reality that is specific to human beings. Human beings possess rational reflection as they employ their rational reflection in making their way to the root of their being. The root of their being is in the Knowledge of the Real, since it is in the storehouse of the Knowledge of the Real that they exist as fixed or immutable entities. Human beings ascend to the knowledge of their fixed entities. But their fixed entities constitute the Essence of the Real. Hence, by ascending to their fixed entities, they actually ascend to the Essence of the Real. In their ascent, they can be divided concerning the knowledge of the Real into three main groups. One of these groups knows him through the attitude of comparability. Another group knows him through the attitude of incomparability. The remaining group knows him through an attitude that can be called the attitude of complementarity. This attitude holds that each of the contradictory views regarding the knowledge of the Real can be correct from a different perspective, despite the fact that the two views are exclusive to each other.

The attitude of complementarity comes very close to the true knowledge about the Real, except that it errs in thinking that the Essence of the Real can be known in a finalized manner. Its assumption is that gathering complementary aspects from the first and the second attitudes of knowledge could obtain a complete or finalized knowledge of the Real. The attitude of complementarity has come very close to the true knowledge of the Real except that it does not seem to be sufficiently rooted in what Cusanus called "learned ignorance." In its turn, the attitude of learned ignorance fails to explicitly emphasize the respect in which the Real must also be limited by every limit. This is actually a common shortcoming of both the attitude of complementarity and the attitude of learned ignorance. For the Real is not only absolutely unlimited, but also absolutely limited, and he is not limited *in one respect* and unlimited *in another respect*, but rather limited and unlimited absolutely: "Upon hearing this from us, our companion Tāj al-Dīn al-Akhlāṭī said: 'Rather He is the (very) opposites,' telling the truth, since the saying of Kharrāz [I knew God by His gathering between the opposites] makes you think that there is an entity which is added to the opposites, and which accepts both. The affair in itself is not like that, since He is the (very) opposites and no entity is added to that. The Manifest is the same entity as the Nonmanifest, the First, and the Last; the First is the same entity as the Last, the Manifest, and the Nonmanifest."[25]

The saying of Kharrāz makes one think that the complementarity between the two opposites, the manifest and the nonmanifest, is contained in an entity that is other than the two opposites. And although this is justified in some sense there is a sense in which the presentation of the Real as merely other than the two opposites lessens the paradoxicality that is intrinsic in Reality. That is why Ibn al-ʿArabī finds it imperative to emphasize that the Real is not different from the Manifest or the Nonmanifest. Given this curious paradoxicality, there is need for the Tie, the Barzakh that brings the two opposites together while keeping them separate:

> When the two are intertied . . . there must be something that brings them together. This is the Tie. It is nothing other than what is required by the two things through their very essence, and no additional affair of existence is needed. Hence, the two are intertied in themselves, since there is nothing but creation and the Real. The Tie must be one of them or both. It is impossible for one of them to possess this property [of intertying] in separation from the other . . . since it is through both that it becomes manifest not through one of them in separation from the other.

Ibn al-ʿArabī's words might be confusing. He is saying that there *is* something that ties the Real to creation, but that this thing *is not* something added to the Real and creation. He is actually stating that there is something and that this something is nothing. Although this statement cannot be comprehended rationally, it is, nevertheless, the closest definition of the limit situation. The definition is stated paradoxically, but only the paradoxical form in which it is expressed can guarantee the proper understanding of the possibility that the Real is comprehended as absolutely limited and also as absolutely unlimited. Ibn al-ʿArabī says that in his own mystical experience he arrived at the limit situation in a nocturnal ascension through the Seven Heavens to the Lotus Tree of the Limit:

> So when I had left (the Temple), I came to the *Lotus-Tree of the limit* (53:14), and I halted amongst its lowest and its loftiest branches. Now "it was enveloped" (53:16) in the lights of (good) actions, and in the shelter of its branches were singing the birds of the spirits of those who perform (those) actions, since it is in the form of Man. As for the four rivers (flowing from its roots, as described in the *ḥadīth*), they are the four kinds of divine knowledge "granted as a gift" (to man), which we mentioned in a part (*juz'*) we called "the levels of the forms of knowledge given freely (by God)."[26] Now when that happened to me I exclaimed: "Enough, enough! My (bodily) elements are filled up, and my place cannot contain me!," and through that (inspiration) God removed from me my contingent dimension. Thus I attained in this nocturnal journey the inner realities (*maʿānī*) of all the Names, and I saw them all returning to One Subject and One Entity: that Subject was what I witnessed, and that Entity was my Being. For my voyage was only in myself and only pointed to myself, and through this I came to know that I was a pure "servant," without a trace of lordship in me at all.[27]

The Lotus Tree of the Limit is in the form of the Perfect Man. The Four Rivers flowing from the roots of the Lotus Tree of the Limit are the four kinds of divine knowledge given to human beings. When Ibn al-ʿArabī reached the Limit his place could not contain him anymore and his limited nature was removed from him. Then he came to realize that he had attained in his journey the inner realities of all the Beautiful Names of the Real. Moreover, he realized that all the Names refer to one entity, and that that entity was nothing but himself. The Perfect Man has come to the knowledge of the self, which is nothing but the knowledge of the Names, the Limits that tie the Real to his creation: "If the door consists of a Real and a creation, that is, you and your Lord, such that the affair has become confused for you, then your entity has not become distinct from your Lord. You will not distinguish Him as long as the door remains unopened. The opening itself will give you knowledge of the door and of the difference between the two leafs. Thus you will know your essence and know your Lord. This is the Prophet's words, "He who knows himself knows his Lord." So there is awareness when the door is closed, and knowledge when the door is opened."[28]

The Real is the Nonmanifest Essence (*al-bāṭin*) that is identical to the Manifest Creation (*al-ẓāhir*) and that is also distinguished from his manifestation. His Reality is, therefore, a Liminal Reality. And in order to comprehend this Reality there is a need for an activity that is also liminal in the sense that it combines both activity and reception of activity. This is the act of the opening mentioned in the cited above passage. This activity is characteristic especially of the limit situation, and its author is the perfect human being. Jandī, one of the interpreters of Ibn al-ʿArabī's *Fuṣūṣ al-Ḥikam* provides an excellent summary of Ibn al-ʿArabī's depiction of this activity:

> You should realize that the Root Reality, which is the origin of the human reality, receives through Her own reality both activity and reception of activity, both manifestation and nonmanifestation. For, indeed, these relationships are the modalities of Her own Essence. Hence they do not change or disappear. This one, all-comprehensive Reality demands the *barzakh*-reality that brings together nondelimitation and delimitation, entification and nonentification, manifestation and nonmanifestation, activity and reception of activity. The human *barzakh*-reality receives the activity of the Entity between the First Entification and the Nonentification of the Essence. She [the *barzakh*-reality] brings together these two while keeping them separate. [29]

Conclusions

I have presented what I think is an essential concept in Ibn al-ʿArabī's mystical philosophy, namely, the concept of the Limit (barzakh). I have conducted this presentation as systematically as possible and within the limitations of the subject matter of the study. The task was not an easy one, as readers of Ibn al-ʿArabī can imagine. This is not, however, to rid myself of the full responsibility for mistakes that have been committed in the work or for the criticism that it might invoke. This must be the case not only regarding Ibn al-ʿArabī, but also in relation to other thinkers that I have dealt with in this work such as Ghazālī, Ibn Sīnā and Ibn Rushd. The discussion of these thinkers, conducted in chapters 2 and 3, covered a somewhat familiar material that has received extensive treatment, not to mention that the very attempt to link Ibn al-ʿArabī's concept of the Limit to philosophical disputations might raise some reservations partly because of his critical stand from philosophical thought.

Such reservations are based, in my view, on methodological worries rather than on matters of essence. Concerning the first point, it should be emphasized that although the material presented in chapters 2 and 3 is somewhat familiar, the special manner of presenting this material, which aims to relate central themes in Islamic philosophy and theology to Ibn al-ʿArabī's thought and, in particular, to his concept of the Limit, adds to the study of Ibn al-ʿArabī something that is, in my opinion, terribly missing and that is also at the heart of his mystical philosophy, namely, relationality. Of course Ibn al-ʿArabī's critical stand and even proclaimed distance from the rational philosophers is something that the researcher must be aware of. However, it is totally unclear, at least to the author of this work, why a certain scholar should establish his view concerning Ibn al-ʿArabī's stand from philosophical thought on the basis of some anecdote that depicts him tossing away a philosophy book,[1] for instance, and not on the basis of his words in defense of philosophical activity.[2] In a sense, this selective reading of Ibn al-ʿArabī seems as rather taking him out of context?[3]

Still there seems to be another sense in which scholars' reluctance to linking Ibn al-ʿArabī to the philosophical tradition, which seems like taking him out of the general context of the Islamic medieval intellectual tradition, might enjoy some sort of methodological justification. For scholars of Ibn al-ʿArabī know well how difficult and, in some places, impossible his writing style renders the mission of reconstructing his arguments in the context of a philosophical discussion.[4] The reader must be aware how in several places of this work, where I endeavored to make the comparisons more direct, I had to bring one statement from a certain chapter of Ibn al-ʿArabī's voluminous *Futūḥāt*, and then another statement from another chapter of the same work or even from a different work. Hence, I must express my full understanding of views critical of relating Ibn al-ʿArabī to the Islamic or Greek philosophical thought. At the same time, I must express also my full confidence that this is something that should be attempted even if some sacrifice in terms of clarity of exposition is called for.

One possible criticism is that the work seems to be highly sympathetic with and not nearly sufficiently critical of Ibn al-ʿArabī's thought. One reason for this highly sympathetic stand is my conviction that involving a heavy criticism of Ibn al-ʿArabī at a stage when his mystical thought has not been properly or systematically exposed and analyzed might only add to the confusion of readers who must be having difficulties understanding his complex thought in the first place. Every reader of Ibn al-ʿArabī knows how unsystematic and convoluted his writing style is.[5] Hence, I think that at the present stage it is important to bring some order into his work rather than bombard it with heavy and immature criticism, thus causing it to appear even more obscure.

My general aim in the work has been to explore a unique concept (the concept of the Limit) in Ibn al-ʿArabī's thought rather than merely provide a summary of the main themes of his mystical philosophy. Although I have presented Ibn al-ʿArabī in the context of Islamic philosophical and theological traditions, my broader aim was to employ the Limit concept in order to relate the mystical thought of Ibn al-ʿArabī to different ancient, medieval, and modern intellectual inquiries. In the attempt, I experienced more than once the frustration of a scholar who seeks to trace a philosophical notion back to its roots and finds that this task is incomparably more difficult than performing the opposite one, which has been worked out to death in our modern and postmodern thought, namely, purifying philosophical thought of its mystical and metaphysical roots. Add to this that the radical paradoxicality of the notion of the barzakh has rendered the attempt of defining it very strenuous and more problematic than what meets the reader's eye.

Two reasons made me persevere in performing this task despite the many difficulties surrounding it. The first reason has to do with the present situation of philosophical thought. It is hardly a discovery that present philosophical thought is undergoing a serious crisis. The question is, of course, what is the cause of the crisis and how can we make our way out of it? My main assumption, which I tried to establish in this work on the basis of views of professional philosophers as well as scholars who are not necessarily members of philosophy departments, is that philosophical thought is not progressing because it has disconnected itself from its roots in medieval and ancient thought. On the basis of this assumption and with the help of Ibn al-ʿArabī's unique concept of the Limit I have tried to show not only that modern philosophy was incorrect in assuming that ancient and medieval thought belonged to the history of ideas, but that certain ancient and medieval notions can still be our guide in ridding us of our present intellectual predicament. This is despite the unsystematic, ambiguous, and, as some like to say, primitive ways in which these notions had been expressed.

The second reason has to do with the striking indications that I have detected for the existence of the notion of the Limit in literature from almost all periods and in various fields of human intellectual history. Consider, for instance, the following citation from a text of ancient religion in which the paradoxical notion of the Limit is stated most explicitly:

> It is thus revealed in the Good Religion that Ohrmazd was on high in omniscience and goodness. For boundless time He was ever in the light. That light is the space and place of Ohrmazd. Some call it Endless Light. . . . Ahriman was abased in slowness of knowledge and the lust to smite. The lust to smite was his sheath and darkness his place. Some call it Endless Darkness. And between them was emptiness. They both were limited and limitless: for that which is on high, which is called Endless Light . . , and that which is abased, which is Endless Darkness—those were limitless. (But) at the border both were limited, in that between them was emptiness. There was no connexion between the two. Then both two Spirits were in themselves limited. On account of the omniscience of Ohrmazd, all things were within the knowledge of Ohrmazd, the limited and the limitless; for He knew the measure of what is within the two Spirits.[6]

Endless Light and Endless darkness are limitless entities. At the border, however, both are limited in that between them there is emptiness. Between the two entities there is a third thing, which is nonexistent. This is the border that separates between the two entities. That is why it is said in the text that "there was no connexion between the two" entities. However, through that very nonexistent border the two entities are rendered limited.[7] Another example from a text of religion that bears a striking similarity to Ibn al-ʿArabī's paradoxical concept of the Limit is the following: "[He] first brought forth [Monogenes and Limit]. And Limit [is the separator] of the All [and the confirmation of the All]. . . . [And they say concerning] him: [. . . He is the manifest, but invisible] to [them while he remains within Limit]. And he possesses [four] powers: a separator [and a] confirmer, a form-provider [and a substance-provider]."[8]

The following is another example from Plato. It deals with the notion of the Instant, a notion that Ibn al-ʿArabī employed as one of his favored illustrations of the Limit. Notice the striking similarity between the paradoxical expression of the notion of the Instant in Plato's *Parmenides* and the paradoxical expression of the notion of the Limit in Ibn al-ʿArabī. A comparison between Plato's and Ibn al-ʿArabī's notions of the Instant deserves a special treatment. Here, however, I will simply cite the example and leave the reflection on it to the reader's imagination:

> The word "instant" appears to mean something such that *from* it a thing passes to one or other of the two conditions. There is no transition *from* a state of rest so long as the thing is still at rest, nor *from* motion so long as it is still in motion, but this queer thing, the instant, is situated between the motion and the rest; it occupies no time at all, and the transition of the moving thing to the state of rest, or of the stationary thing to being in motion, takes place *to* and *from* the instant. Accordingly, the one, since it both is at rest and is in motion, must pass from the one condition to the other—only so can it do both things—and when it passes, it makes the transition instantaneously; it occupies no time in making it and at that moment it cannot be either in motion or at rest.[9]

Finally, consider the criticism that the author of the following passage directs against Descartes, the father of modern philosophy, especially his attempt to rid modern thought of the symbolic (liminal) meaning of the phenomenon of the rainbow. The attempt has failed, it seems, and scientists, like the writer of the following words, are returning to the unified roots of the human thought, even as these roots extend to mystical forms of expression: "Until the 17th century in France, the rainbow was still primarily known as 'iris' in honor of the Greek messenger goddess. It was Rene Descartes who finally replaced that ancient name with the more prosaic, mundane phrase 'arc-in-the-sky.' However, although Descartes extensively evicted Iris from her heavenly abode, she still lives on in one private part of the universe. For, each person has a modest ring of color in his/her eye, a ring that divides a white exterior and a black interior, and serves as a threshold, open door, and bridge between outer and inner worlds of reality."[10]

The research on medieval Arabic thought has not received the serious attention that it deserves. This is despite the fact that some scholars nowadays are showing some promising interest in the research. Yet the effort that has been invested is not nearly sufficient. There are some signs that special attention is being given recently to Ibn al-ʿArabī's mystical thought and special effort is being invested in studying his work. The scholars who are involved in the effort are working with complex material and under unfavorable conditions. Both the source that they are working with and the scarcity of the tools of analysis at their disposal make their work precarious. This is perhaps the reason why the most distinguished individual among them and the one who made the greatest contribution to date to the research on Ibn al-ʿArabī, William C. Chittick, exercises caution and works with extra care, as he tries to speak for Ibn al-ʿArabī as Ibn al-ʿArabī would speak for himself, and to avoid taking his words out of their proper context. Perhaps the writer of these words has not been sufficiently careful in following the standards of extra carefulness in dealing with Ibn al-ʿArabī. However, I hope that the work has managed, nonetheless, to contribute to such a difficult and complex field of study.

Notes

Introduction

1. This story is brought from *Risāle-i Mi ʿmāriyye: An Early 17th Century Ottoman Treatise on Architecture,* trans. Howard Crane (Leiden: E. J. Brill, 1987), 24–26.
2. Ibid., 26.
3. Quoted from Ibn al-ʿArabī's *Fuṣūṣ al-Ḥikam* in Claude Addas, *The Quest for the Red Sulphur: The Life of Ibn ʿArabī*, trans. Peter Kingsley (Cambridge: The Islamic Texts Society, 1993), 74–75.
4. The other version in *Rūḥ al-Quds* reads, "Next I noticed a man who was tall, with a broad face, white hair and a large beard, and who had his hand on his cheek. I chose to address myself to him and ask him the reason for this gathering. He said to me: 'They are all the prophets from Adam down to Muḥammad; not a single one of them is missing.' I asked him: 'And you? Which of them are you?' He replied: 'I am Hūd, of the people of ʿĀd.' I said: 'Why have you all come?' He answered: 'We have come to visit Abū Muḥammad.' On waking, I inquired about Abū Muḥammad Makhlūf [al-Qabā'ilī] and learned that on that very night he had fallen ill. He died a few days later." Addas, *The Quest for the Red Sulphur*, 75.
5. Ibid., 76.
6. Michel Chodkiewickz, *Seal of the Saints: Prophethood and Sainthood in the Doctrine of Ibn ʿArabī*, trans. Liadain Sherrad (Cambridge, England: Islamic Texts Society, 1993).
7. Ibid., 77.
8. I provide a discussion of the encounter between Khaḍir and Moses from Ibn al-ʿArabī's perspective in chapter 4.
9. William C. Chittick, *The Self-Disclosure of God: Principles of Ibn al-ʿArabī's Cosmology* (Albany: State University of New York Press, 1998), 378 (Hereafter cited as SD); Muḥyiddīn Ibn al-ʿArabī, *al-Futūḥāt al-Makkiyya*, 4 vols. (Beirūt: Dār Ṣādir, 1968) 2, 90: 30–35 (Hereafter cited as F).

10. SD, 196–197; F, 3, 283: 15–28.
11. According to Lane's Arabic-English Lexicon, *dahr* signifies a long unlimited time, or an extended indivisible space of time, or duration without end. Edward William Lane, *An Arabic-English Lexicon,* 8 vols. (Beirūt, 1968), 3:923.
12. SD, 128–129; F, 3, 546: 34–38. The line has two limits, the limit as its beginning and the limit as its end. In the case of the circle, any limit that we may assume on its circumference signifies both the point of its beginning and its end, that is, the limit as beginning and the limit as end are one.
13. SD, 407, n. 29.
14. William C. Chittick, "Spectrums of Islamic Thought: Saʿīd al-Dīn Farghānī on The Implication of Oneness and Manyness," in *The Heritage of Ṣūfism,* ed. Leonard Lewisohn, 3 vols. (Oxford: One World, 1999), 2:203.
15. Sachiko Murata, *The Tao of Islam: A Source Book on Gender Relationships in Islamic Thought* (Albany: State University of New York Press, 1992), 63–64.
16. Dialectic originates from the Greek expression for the art of conversation and as the internal dialogue of the soul with itself. Zeno of Elea (fifth century B.C.) made use of the dialectical arguments (his famous paradoxes) for refuting the hypotheses of opponents by means of indirect logical arguments and through drawing unacceptable consequences from them. The sophists employed this method of argumentation as a mere instrument for winning a dispute. In contrast to the sophists, the use that Socrates made of dialectical argument, a major element in which was the *elenchus* (cross-examination which refutes the opponent's argument by drawing a contradiction from it), was professed for seeking the truth. In Plato dialectic became the supreme philosophical method and the highest of human arts, as it consisted of two complementary components: division and synthesis. See Roland Hall, "Dialectic," in the *Encyclopedia of Philosophy*, ed. Paul Edwards, 8 vols. (New York: Macmillan and Free Press, 1967), 2: 385–386. As I am going to show in this work there is much that is common between the dialectical methods of Zeno, the sophists, Socrates, and Plato and the methods of certain Islamic thinkers, especially Ghazālī and Ibn al-ʿArabī .
17. Similar to Hegel's "thesis-antithesis-synthesis" principle. The reservation stated here against identifying Ibn al-ʿArabī's way of thinking with certain Hegelian principles does not imply dismissal of the remarkable similarity between the two thinkers. For example, I find the resemblance between Hegel's dialectic of Lordship and Bondage (see G. W. F. Hegel, *Phenomenology of Spirit*, trans. Arnold. V. Miller [Oxford: Clarendon Press, 1977], 111–119.) and Ibn al-ʿArabī's conception of the relationship between the Lord (*rabb*) and His vassal (*marbūb*) very striking and it deserves to be treated in an independent study.
18. Abū al-ʿIlā ʿAffīfī, *The Mystical Philosophy of Muḥyiddīn-Ibnul ʿArabī* (Lahore: Sh. Muḥammad Ashraf, 1964), 18.
19. Several interpretations may be provided for what constitutes rationalism. Here I bring the following two:

a. The position that reason has precedence over other ways of acquiring knowledge, or that it is the unique path to knowledge. Daniel Garber, "Rationalism," in *The Cambridge Dictionary of Philosophy*, ed. Robert Audi (Cambridge: Cambridge University Press, 1995), 673.

b. The position that stresses the abilities of human rationality to attain a coherent, logically consistent, conceptually precise, and systematically comprehensive grasp of the whole of reality. See Mario Bunge, "Seven Desiderata for Rationality," in *Rationality: The Critical View*, ed. Joseph Agassi and Ian Charles Jarvie (Boston: Martinus Nijhoff Publishers, 1987), 5–10.

20. Scholasticism is the tradition that arose in the medieval universities and is associated with the methods and thoughts of the major philosophers of the thirteenth and fourteenth centuries. It remained dominant in European philosophy until the fifteenth century, when it gave way to Renaissance humanism, rationalism, and empiricism. See John Haldane, "Scholasticism," in *The Oxford Companion to Philosophy*," ed. Ted Honderich (Oxford: Oxford University Press, 1995), 802. As Phillip Rosemann points out, a significant movement of scholarly interest in medieval philosophy began in the last century in Catholic circles that hoped to find in the thought of the Scholastics the means to stand against the "dangers of modernity." The significance of this movement was lifted in 1879 when Pope Leo XIII defined Scholasticism as the official Catholic philosophy. Phillip Rosemann, "A Change of Paradigm in the Study of Medieval Philosophy: From Rationalism to Postmodernism," *American Catholic Philosophical Quarterly* 72 (1998): 61. There have been serious efforts at reviving the teaching of the philosophers of scholasticism, and newscholasticism (or neoscholasticism) is the most significant among them.

21. Especially *Understanding Scholastic Thought with Foucault* (New York: St. Martin's Press, 1999) and "Change of Paradigm," 58–73.

22. Rosemann, "Change of Paradigm," 64.

23. Ibid., 69–70. Peter Von Sivers applies the same criticism to analytical thinking. In an unpublished paper entitled "Belief in Anything: Construction of Meaning at the End of the Twentieth Century," 8–9, he writes, "Instead of atomizing units into their component parts, as analytical thinking attempts to do, one views the units as wholes within larger contexts, without dissolving them. This view of wholes in contexts is articulated through the medium of narration, that is, one tells a story with a beginning, middle and an end thereby suggesting a congruity between the perceived wholes, their contexts, and the unity of the story."

24. Peter Young, "Ibn ʿArabī: Towards a Universal Point of View," *Journal of the Muḥyiddīn Ibn ʿArabī Society* 25 (1986): 89–90.

25. William C. Chittick, *The Ṣūfī Path of Knowledge* (Albany: State University of New York Press, 1989), ix. Hereafter cited as SPK.

26. Aristotle, *Aristotle's Metaphysics*, trans. Hippocrates G. Apostle (Bloomington: Indiana University Press, 1973), 5. 17, 1022a.

27. In the part that deals with the "Antinomy of Pure Reason" of the *Critique of Pure Reason* Kant first sets out a series of pairs of contradictory metaphysical doctrines. He then produces proofs for each pair, maintaining that if we adopt the dogmatic standpoint of the parties to the dispute, we can show, for example, that the world has a beginning in time (thesis) and also that it has no beginning in time (antithesis). See William Henry Walsh, "Kant," in *The Encyclopedia of Philosophy*, ed. Paul Edwards, 8 vols. (New York: Macmillan and Free Press, 1967), 4: 316.

28. Complementarity is the view of the quantum physicist Neils Bohr. See Max Jammer, *The Philosophy of Quantum Mechanics: The Implications in Historical Perspective* (New York: Wiley, 1974), 106.

Chapter 1. Ibn al-ʿArabī's Liminal (*Barzakhī*) Theory of Representation: An Outlook from the Present Situation

1. Notice the similarity between the barzakh and the Tibetan *bardo*, which signifies a transition or a gap between the completion of one situation and the onset of another. *Bar* means "in between" and *do* means "suspended" or "thrown." See Sogyal Rinpoche, *The Tibetan Book of Living and Dying*, ed. Patrick Gaffney and Andrew Harvey (New York: HarperCollins, 1994), 102.
2. ʿAbdullah Yūsuf ʿAlī, *The Meaning of the Holy Qur'ān*, 6th ed. (Beltsville, Md.: Amana, 1989), 901–902. The barzakh is presented in this verse as a limit that separates between two bodies of water. This act of separating is depicted in ancient myths as signifying the beginning of the process of creation. For example in the Babylonian epic of creation we read:

> When above the heaven had not (yet) been named,
> (And) below the earth had not (yet) been called by a name;
> (When) Apsū primeval, their begetter,
> Mammu, (and) Ti-āmat, she who gave birth to them all,
> (Still) mingled their waters together,
> And no pasture land had been formed (and) not (even) a reed march was to be seen;
> When none of the (other) gods had been brought into being;
> (When) they had not (yet) been called by (their) name (s, and their) destinies had not (yet) been fixed,
> (At that time) were the gods created within them.

Cited in Ewa Wasilewska, *Creation Stories of the Middle East* (London: Jessica Kingsley, 2000), 50. Apsū personifies sweet waters; Tiāmat personifies salt waters. Ibid.
3. Henry Corbin, *Spiritual Body and Celestial Earth: From Mazdean Iran to Shiʿite Iran* (Princeton, N.J., Princeton University Press, 1977), 172.
4. F, 1, 119: 4. SPK, 136.
5. Max Jammer considers this thesis a precursor to Neil Bohr's quantum *complementarity thesis*. Jammer, *Philosophy of Quantum Mechanics*, 106.
6. Alfred North Whitehead, *Modes of Thought* (New York: Free Press, 1968), 174. This is so, provided that we regard reason as part of the activity of rationalizing the mystical and not the other way around. No attempt will be made here to present the activity of rationalizing the mystical in finalized terms but rather as a constant activity of finalization.
7. Plato, *The Collected Dialogues*, ed. Edith Hamilton and Huntington Cairns (Princeton, N.J.: Princeton University Press, 1994), Letter vii, b: 4–10. Hereafter cited as TCD.
8. TCD, xv.
9. I think that Plato's *Parmenides* was an attempt to offer a resemblance of such a process of representation. We find Parmenides expressing his reluctance to engaging himself in what he characterizes as a heavy and tiring process of representation. TCD, *Parmenides*, 136d.
10. Quoted from Timothy Beardsworth's *A Sense of Presence* (1977) in William P. Alston, *Perceiving God: The Epistemology of Religious Experience* (Ithaca, N.Y. and London: Cornell University Press, 1991), 18.

11. Alston, *Perceiving God*, 14.
12. Sara Sviri, *The Taste of Hidden Things: Images on the Ṣūfī Path* (Inverness, Calif. Golden Ṣūfī Center, 1997), 150.
13. I find this similar, in a way, to what is described in the following words by physicist Neils Bohr: "I get to think about my own thoughts of the situation in which I find myself. I even think that I think of it, and divide myself into an infinite regressive sequence of 'I's who consider each other. I do not know at which 'I' to stop as the actual, and in the moment I stop at one, there is indeed another an 'I' which stops at it. I become confused and feel a dizziness as if I were looking down into a bottomless abyss, and my ponderings result finally in a terrible headache." Quoted in John Honner, *The Description of Nature: Neils Bohr and the Philosophy of Quantum Physics* (Oxford: Clarendon Press, 1987), 4.
14. SD, xi.
15. Michael G. Carter, "Infinity and Lies in Medieval Islam," in *Philosophy and Art in the Islamic World*, Orientalia Lovaniensia Analecta, ed. U. Vermeulen and D. De Smet, vol. 87 (Leuven: Uitgeverij Peeters, 1998), 235.
16. Ibid., 237. *Mutakallimūn* = Islamic scholastic theologians.
17. Carter mentions another "heresy" of another philosopher, Ibn Sīnā, which is established on a conceptual interpretation of the term *possible-of-existence* as that which may or may not exist. Carter says that Ibn Sīnā's interpretation, in combination with his "innocent" deduction that everything which is possible *must* eventually happen (or else be impossible!) . . . puts God in a double bind which no orthodox Muslim could be at ease with." Ibid., 337.
18. Ibid., 240.
19. Ibid., 241.
20. Ibid., 242.
21. Ibid.
22. Ibid., 241.
23. For a concise account of the Liar and other related paradoxes, see Richard M. Sainsbury, *Paradoxes* (Cambridge: Cambridge University Press, 1995), 111–119.
24. See Simon Van Den Bergh's introduction to Ibn Rushd's *Tahāfut al-Tahāfut* (*The Incoherence of the Incoherence*), 2 vols. (Oxford: Oxford University Press, 1954), 1: 215. Hereafter cited as TT. Unless otherwise stated, reference will be to vol.1.
25. F, I, 304: 22–32.
26. On the basis of similar analysis I have argued that the barzakh constitutes Ibn al-ʿArabī's proof for the Unity of Being. See Salmān Bashier, "Proofs of the Existence and the Unity of God in Greek and Islamic Thought, with an Emphasis on Ibn al-ʿArabī's Barzakh Concept and Its Role in Proving God's Existence and Unity," *Transcendent Philosophy* 2 (2001): 29–51
27. John Renard points out that the term *liminality* is derived from the Latin *limen*, "threshold." John Renard, *Seven Doors to Islam: Spirituality and the Religious Life of Muslims* (Berkeley: University of California Press, 1996), 36. According to Annemarie Schimmel, the threshold signifies for many Muslims a sacred symbol and a liminal phenomenon. Muslims avoid touching the threshold. The bride in Muslim India is carried over the threshold into her new home, and the devotee is warned not to step on the threshold of the master's abode. Annemarie Schimmel, *Deciphering the Signs of God:*

A Phenomenological Approach to Islam (Albany: State University of New York Press, 1994), 50. In a sense, the threshold in the mentioned examples enjoys the status of a nonexistent entity (it is not touched, it is crossed over). However, through that very seeming nonexistence the threshold holds the otherwise unidentified distinction between the sacred and the profane intact.

28. Rorty seems to have prophesized the death of philosophy already at the end of *Philosophy and the Mirror of Nature:* "Whatever happens, however, there is no danger of philosophy's 'coming to an end.' Religion did not come to an end in Enlightenment, nor painting in Impressionism." Richard Rorty, *Philosophy and the Mirror of Nature* (Princeton, N.J.: Princeton University Press, 1979), 394. For further discussion, see Bob Brandom, introduction to *Rorty and his Critics*, ed. Robert B. Brandom (Malden, Mass.: Blackwell., 2000), x. Hereafter *Rorty and his Critics* will be cited as RC.

29. Graham Priest, *Beyond the Limits of Thought* (Cambridge: Cambridge University Press, 1995), 255.

30. Hilary Putnam, *Reason, Truth and History* (Cambridge, Cambridge University Press, 1981), ix.

31. Ibid., x.

32. Ibid., 106. The logical positivists used the term *analytic* to account for logical and mathematical truths.

33. Hilary Putnam, "Richard Rorty on Reality and Justification," in RC, 86.

34. Michael P. Lynch, *Truth in Context: An Essay on Pluralism and Objectivity* (Massachusetts: MIT, 1998), 146.

35. Putnam, "Richard Rorty on Reality and Justification," 83–84.

36. Rorty, "Universality and Truth," in RC, 1.

37. Jürgen Habermas, "Richard Rorty's Pragmatic Turn," in RC, 31.

38. Ibid., 32.

39. For Rorty, "analytic philosophy" and "linguistic philosophy" can be used interchangeably. He defines linguistic philosophy as follows: "The view that philosophical problems are problems which may be solved (or dissolved) either by reforming language, or by understanding more about the language we presently use." See Richard Rorty's introduction to *The Linguistic Turn: Recent Essays in Philosophical Method*, ed. Richard Rorty (Chicago: University of Chicago Press, 1967), 27.

40. Habermas, "Richard Rorty's Pragmatic Turn," 33.

41. Rorty, "Universality and Truth," 15.

42. Habermas, "Pragmatic Turn," 35.

43. Rorty, *Philosophy and the Mirror of Nature*, 132.

44. Rorty, "Response to Michael Williams," in RC, 214.

45. Ibid., 216.

46. F, 2, 523: 10.

47. Paul E. Walker, "Platonisms in Islamic Philosophy," *Studia Islamica* 79 (1996): 5–6.

48. Rorty, "Universality and Truth," 9.

49. See SD, 347. Ibn al-ʿArabī says, "The . . . interpreter 'crosses over' . . . by means of what he says. In other words . . . he transfers his words from imagination to imagination, since the listener imagines to the extent of his understanding. Imagination may or may not coincide . . . with imagination. . . . If it coincides, this is called his 'understanding' (*fahm*); if it does not coincide, he has not understood. . . . We only make this allusion

to call attention to the tremendousness of imagination's level, for it is the Absolute Ruler (*al-ḥākim al-muṭlaq*) over known things." SPK, 119. F, 3, 454.
50. F, 4, 65: 32.
51. F, 2, 518: 12.
52. See F, 2, 525: 29.
53. F, 1, 159: 11–15.
54. Habermas, "Pragmatic Turn," 33.
55. Gerald T. Elmore, *Islamic Sainthood in the Fullness of Time: Ibn al-ʿArabī's Book of the Fabulous Gryphon* (Boston: E. J. Brill, 1999), 344–345. Arabic words dropped from Elmore's translation.
56. Steven M. Wasserstrom, *Religion after Religion: Gershom Scholem, Mircea Eliade and Henry Corbin at Eranos* (Princeton, N.J.: Princeton University Press, 1999), 243. Hereafter cited as RR.
57. Ibid., 239–240.
58. Ibid., 238.
59. I think that a proper response to both Wasserstrom and Rorty in this regard, a response that fits neatly into Ibn al-ʿArabī's notion of the Unity of Being, can be found in the following statement by Jürgen Habermas: "The metaphysical priority of unity over plurality and the contextualistic priority of plurality above unity are secret accomplices." Quoted in Rorty, "Universality and Truth," 18.
60. RR, 155.
61. Addas, *The Quest*, 10.
62. RR, 163, 172.
63. Ibid., 81, 182, 241. Here, I must agree with William Chittick that when reading Corbin's study of the esoteric thought of Ibn al-ʿArabī, one may not know where Ibn al-ʿArabī ends and Corbin begins. Chittick says that Corbin fails to bring out the practical sides of Ibn al-ʿArabī's works, neglecting the fact that Ibn al-ʿArabī established all knowledge on the norms revealed through the Qur'ān and the Law of the Prophet. Chittick has attempted to avoid this shortcoming and his effort has yielded two important works: *The Ṣūfī Path of Knowledge* (1989) and *The Self-Disclosure of God* (1998). In his part, Chittick tries to let Ibn al-ʿArabī's words speak for their own author, limiting himself to literal interpretation as well as concise and very careful commentaries and analysis of Ibn al-ʿArabī's words. Chittick's careful research has opened the teachings of Ibn al-ʿArabī before general readers and scholars and added a crucial contribution to his study. In my view, both the important work that Chittick has accomplished and that done by Corbin are crucial for understanding Ibn al-ʿArabī's thought and for advancing his teachings.
64. Kant defines the goal of rational philosophy as follows: "The greatest and perhaps the sole use of all philosophy of pure reason is therefore only negative; since it serves not as an organon for the extension but as a discipline for the limitation of pure reason, and, instead of discovering truth, has only the modest merit of guarding against error." Immanuel Kant, *Critique of Pure Reason*, trans. Norman Kemp Smith (London: Redwood Press, 1970), 629.
65. RR, 238, 81.
66. RR, 180.
67. Richard Rorty, "Response to Michael Williams," 216.

Chapter 2. Creation ex nihilo, Creation in Time, and Eternal Creation: Ibn Sīnā versus the Theologians

1. Ian Richard Netton, *Allah Transcendent: Studies in the Structure and Semiotics of Islamic Philosophy, Theology and Cosmology* (London: Routledge, 1989), 23. The Qur'ān mentions the word *created* (*khalaqa*) or words derived from it more than thirty times. It also names God "the Creator" (*Fāṭir*) as one of its chapters is called *al-Fāṭir*. See, Ishaq Akintola, "Creation Theories and the Qur'ān," *Islamic Quarterly* 36 (1992): 196.
2. Ibid. Netton mentions Ṭabarī (d. 923), Zamakhsharī (d. 1144) and Bayḍāwī (d. 1286).
3. See discussion in Thomas J. O'Shaughnessy, *Creation and the Teaching of the Qur'ān* (Rome: Biblical Institute Press, 1985), 1.
4. Harry Austryn Wolfson, *The Philosophy of the Kalām* (Cambridge, Mass.: Harvard University Press, 1976), 357. Hereafter cited as PK.
5. Ibid., 358.
6. Oliver Leaman, *An Introduction to Medieval Islamic Philosophy* (Cambridge: Cambridge University Press, 1985), 26.
7. Dominique Urvoy, *Ibn Rushd* (Averroes), trans. Olivia Stewart (London: Routledge, 1991), 82.
8. David B. Burrell, *Freedom and Creation in Three Traditions* (Notre Dame, Ind.: University of Notre Dame Press, 1993), 24.
9. Ibn Rushd, *On the Harmony of Religion and Philosophy*: *A Translation of Ibn Rushd's Kitāb Faṣl al-Maqāl with an Extract from Kitāb al-Kashf 'an Manāhij al-Adilla*, trans. George F. Hourani (London: Messrs. Luzac, 1961), 56–57.
10. See Ibn Rushd's *On the Harmony of Religion and Philosophy*, 45–49. See also discussion in Binyamin Abrahamov, *Islamic Theology: Traditionalism and Rationalism* (Edinburgh: Edinburgh University Press, 1998), vii.
11. The Qur'ān mentions the term *'aql* or terms derived from it more than fifty times.
12. See Ghazālī's third and fourth introductions to *The Incoherence of the Philosophers*, trans. Michael E. Marmura (Provo, Utah: Brigham Young University Press, 1997), 7–9. Hereafter cited as TF.
13. Etienne Gilson, *Being and Some Philosophers* (Toronto: Pontifical Institute of Mediaeval Studies, 1949), 6–7.
14. Ibid., 7.
15. Francis Macdonald Cornford, *Plato and Parmenides: Parmenides' Way of Truth and Plato's Parmenides* (London: Routledge and Kegan Paul, 1951), 33–35.
16. Ruhi Muhsen Afnan, *Zoroaster's Influence on Greek Thought* (New York: Philosophical Library, 1965), 59.
17. Lenn Evan Goodman, "Time in Islam," *Asian Philosophy* 2 (1992): 15.
18. Ibid.
19. Aristotle says, "For if there is to be coming-to-be without qualification, 'something' must—without qualification—'come-to-be out of not-being,' so that it would be true to say that 'not-being is an attribute of some things.' For *qualified* coming-to-be is a process out of *qualified* not-being (e.g. out of not-white or not-beautiful), but *unqualified* coming—to-be is a process of *unqualified* not-being. . . . In one sense things come-to-be out of that which has no 'being' without qualification: yet in another sense they come-to-be always out of 'what is.' For coming-to-be necessarily implies the pre-existence of something

which *potentially* 'is,' but actually 'is not'; and this something is spoken of both as 'being' and as 'not-being.'" Richard McKeon, ed., *The Basic Works of Aristotle* (New York: Random House, 1970), *On Generation and Corruption*, 1. 3, 317b: 1–7, 17–21. Hereafter *The Basic Works of Aristotle* will be cited as BWA.

20. Al-Kindī (d. 866) is considered the exception among Islamic philosophers, since he objected to the doctrine of the eternity of the world. As Jules Janssens points out, al-Kindī's major source in the elaboration of this doctrine seems to be John Philoponus, as his main argument against the eternity of the world is reducible to the demonstration of the impossibility of an actual infinity. Jules Janssens, "Al-Kindī's Concept of God," *Ultimate Reality and Meaning* 17 (1994): 6.

21. Miracle and challenge (*muʿjiza* and *taḥaddī*) were considered correlatives in Muslim usage. See Bernard Weiss, *The Spirit of Islamic Law* (Athens: University of Georgia Press, 1998), 42. Thus it is said that the Prophet vied or contended (*taḥaddā*) with the Arabs by means of the Qur'ān (Lane, *An Arabic-English Lexicon,* 2, 533) in accordance with the challenge in Q 17: 88 posed to humans and Jinns to gather together and produce the like of the Qur'ān, which they will not be able to do. As we will see later in this chapter, the Ashʿarite theologians held that even the occurrence of regular events in the phenomenal world is subject to the divine transcendent decree, which is responsible for their creation each moment anew. It is because we have become used to the occurrence of these events that we ceased to discern their miraculous nature. See Bernard Weiss, *The Search for God's Law: Islamic Jurisprudence in the Writings of Ṣafy al-Dīn al-Amidī* (Salt Lake City: University of Utah Press, 1992), 75.

22. PK, 359–360.

23. Ibid., 362–364.

24. For a brief account of the ideological reasons for Abū al-Ḥasan al-Ashʿarī's dissent from the Muʿtazilite doctrine, see Seyyed Hossein Nasr, "Theology, Philosophy, and Spirituality," in *Islamic Spirituality: Manifestations*, 2 vols., World Spirituality. ed. Seyyed Hossein Nasr (New York: Crossroad, 1991), 2: 399–400. Nasr discusses the reaction that occurred during the ninth century against the rationalism of the Muʿtazilites, following the inquisition (*miḥna*) of the Ma'mūn. A theology was needed that would utilize rational argumentation but remain faithful to orthodoxy. To this task Abū al-Ḥasan al-Ashʿarī addressed himself, founding a new theological school which became the most widespread in the Sunnī world.

25. PK, 374.

26. John Philoponus (or John the Grammarian) was a Greek Philosopher and a Christian theologian, who lived in the sixth century. He made use of Aristotle's *Physics* in order to demonstrate the beginning of the world in time. Most of his arguments appeared in the lost *Contra Aristotelem*, while some are found in his *De aeternitate mundi contra Proclus*, which is a refutation of Proclus's defense of the eternity of the world. The *De aeternitate mundi contra Proclum* contains eighteen books corresponding to Proclus's nonextant work in which he tried to prove the eternity of the world by eighteen arguments. See Seymour Feldman, "Philoponus on the Metaphysics of Creation," in *A Straight Path: Studies in Medieval Philosophy and Culture*, ed. Ruth Link-Salinger (Washington: The Catholic University of America Press, 1988), 74.

27. BWA, *Phys.*, 3. 4, 204a :5–7.

28. Ibid., *Phys.*, 3. 5, 206a: 8–9.

29. Ibid., *Phys.*, 3. 5, 204a: 20–26.
30. Ibid., *Phys.*, 3. 6, 206a: 10–11.
31. See PK, 412. Concerning the view that only a potential infinite can exist, Wolfson refers the reader to Aristotle's *Phys.*, 3. 6, 206a. For another argument by Aristotle to the effect that the infinite can exist only as a potential infinite, see *Aristotle's Metaphys.*, 9. 6, 1048b: 8–18.
32. PK, 414–415. Concerning the principle that it is impossible to traverse the infinite, Wolfson refers the reader to a combination of *Phys.*, 8. 8, 263a: 6, and 8. 9, 265a: 19–20. The principle can be found also in *Metaphys.*, 11. 10, 1066b: 1. Concerning the principle that two infinites cannot be greater than one another, Wolfson says that it is a derivation from Aristotle's principle that the same infinite cannot be many infinities in *Phys.*, 3. 5, 204a: 25–26.
33. PK, 413–414.
34. Ibid., 414.
35. Ibid., 415.
36. Ibid., 417.
37. Ibid., 421.
38. Aristotle says, "But we apprehend time only when we have marked motion, marking it by 'before' and 'after,' and it is only when we have perceived 'before' and 'after' in motion that we say that time has elapsed. . . . When we think of the extremes as different from the middle and the mind pronounces that the 'nows' are two, one before and one after, it is then that we say that there is time." BWA, *Phys.*, 4. 10, 219a: 22–30.
39. Lenn Evan Goodman, "Time in Islam," 14. Ibn Sīnā's argument is based on Aristotle's argument for the eternity of time. See Aristotle's *Metaphys.*, 12. 6, 1071b: 10–12.
40. See discussion of Islamic occasionalism in Mājid Fakhry, *Islamic Occasionalism and its Critique by Averroes and Aquinas* (London: George Allen and Unwin, 1958), 27.
41. Fakhry, *Islamic Occasionalism*, 26–27. Shlomo Pines provides the following summary of the Ashʿarite's atomistic theory: "One of the nuclei of the Ashʿarite system is its atomic theory. Creator and creation are diametrically opposed. God cannot be conceived intellectually, even in a negative fashion; the formula *bilā kayfa* constitutes an effective barrier in the face of any speculation about His nature or attributes. Creation divides up into atoms of matter, qualities, space and time. Every event may be analyzed into discrete moments, completely independent of each other, which have been brought together solely by means of God's will. Qualities exist only for a single instant. Substances persevere only by being continually recreated at every instant: *khalq fī kull waqt*. Implicit in this is the rejection of any natural order." *Studies in Islamic Atomism*, ed. Tzvi Langerman, trans. Michael Schwarz, (The Hebrew University, Jerusalem: Magnes Press, 1997), 2. On the theologians' attempt to validate their doctrine of continuous creation by reference to Q 2: 255, see Lenn E. Goodman, *Avicenna* (London: Routledge, 1992), 110 n.12. Hereafter cited as AV.
42. Michael Marmura, "The Metaphysics of Efficient Causality in Avicenna," in *Islamic Theology and Philosophy*, ed. Michael Marmura (Albany: State University of New York Press, 1984), 187. The philosophers regarded the theologians' atomistic conception of the world as inconsistent with the intelligibility of nature and as infringing upon the validity of natural laws. For if the world is created each moment anew, there can be no connection between one natural state and the one that follows it. When necessary connections

are absent, knowledge about the world becomes impossible. One may argue that even if it is the case that knowledge cannot be obtained about a world that is created continuously, this does not mean that the world does not exist as such. On the other hand, one may argue that in the absence of a unified conception of the world, it would be impossible even to have the very activity of thinking or reflecting on the world started.

43. The theologians claim that there must be a beginning in time for the existence of things in the world; otherwise there will be an infinite number of individuals of different species that actually have come to be. For if each individual has come to be, the whole number of individuals, which succeed each other, must have come to be as well. But it is impossible for an infinite by succession to actually have come to be, since then the infinite number will be limited. The possibility of halting with any of the individual things implies that an infinite time will have expired up to the present time of any given individual. Moreover, with the renewal of time, the number of individuals will increase, but it is impossible for an infinite number to increase. See, Ibn Sīnā, *al-Ishārāt wa al-Tanbīhāt, ma' Sharḥ Naṣīr al-Ḍīn al-Ṭūṣī* [*Book of Remarks and Admonitions, with the commentary of Naṣīr al-Ḍīn al-Ṭūṣī*], ed. Sulaymān Dunyā, 4 vols. (Cairo: Dār al-Ma'ārif, 1957), 3: 106–107. See also Ḥusām Muḥyiddīn al-Alwasī, *Ḥiwār bayna al-Falāsifa wa al-Mutakallimīn* (Baghdād: Maṭba'at al-Zahrā', 1967), 81–85.

44. Alwasī, *Ḥiwār*, 81–82.

45. Ibid., 84. By a "nonexistent" infinite Ibn Sīnā means a potential infinite.

46. Alwasī, *Ḥiwār*, 85.

47. Ibn Sīnā, *Ishārāt*, 3: 114–115.

48. Ibn Sīnā's full argument for the preexistence of time can be found in *al-Najāt*, ed. M. Kurdī (Cairo: Sa'adat Press, 1938), 218.

49. See Ibn Sīnā, *al-Najāt*, 213–214 and *Ishārāt*, 3: 88.

50. AV, 78.

51. See Ghazālī's first introduction to TF, 2.

52. AV, 61.

53. Lenn E. Goodman, "Three Meanings of the Idea of Creation," in *God and Creation: An Ecumenical Symposium*, ed., David B. Burrell and Bernard McGinnis (Notre Dame, Ind.: Notre Dame Press, 1990), 94. Also interesting is Goodman's statement that defenders of creation against eternalism, like Ghazālī and Maimonides, did not reject emanation either. Ibid.

54. Richard M. Frank, "Kalām and Philosophy: A Perspective from One Problem," in *Islamic Philosophical Theology*, ed. Parviz Morewedge (Albany: State University of New York Press, 1979), 74.

55. Ibid.

56. Ibid. Frank mentions Nasafī, who criticized Aristotle's logic and was charged with not understanding its foundations.

57. See TF, 9.

58. AV, 65.

59. Leaman, *Medieval Islamic Philosophy*, 30. Leaman's citation is from Ibn Sīnā's *al-Najāt*, ed. Kurdī, 226.

60. Ibid., 29.

61. Ibid. Leaman's citation is from Ibn Sīnā's *al-Najāt*, ed. Kurdī, 226. Leaman says that the philosophical motives of Ibn Sīnā's conflation of necessity and possibility go

back to Aristotle and to what Jaakko Hintikka called "Aristotle's Principle of Plenitude." Hintikka defines Aristotle's Principle of Plenitude as follows: "No unqualified possibility remains unactualized through an infinity of time. Any such possibility thus has been, is, or will be realized." See Jaakko Hintikka, *Time and Necessity: Studies in Aristotle's Theory of Modality* (Oxford: Clarendon Press, 1973), 94.

62. Ibn Sīnā, *The Metaphysica of Avicenna* (*Danish Nameh*), trans. Parviz Morewedge (London: Routledge and Kegan Paul, 1973), 21.

63. See Parviz Morewedge, "Philosophical Analysis and Ibn Sīnā's 'Essence-Existence' Distinction," *Journal of the American Oriental Society* 42 (1972): 425.

64. David B. Burrell, "Creation and Emanation: Two Paradigms of Reason," in *God and Creation: An Ecumenical Symposium*, 35. See also Parviz Morewedge "Philosophical Analysis 426.

65. David B. Burrell, *Knowing the Unknowable God: Ibn Sīnā, Maimonides, Aquinas* (Notre Dame, Ind.: Notre Dame Press, 1986), 20. This seems to contradict what Aristotle says in *Metaphysics*: " We should inquire whether each thing and its essence are the same or distinct. This is useful for our inquiry into *substance*; for each thing is thought to be nothing else but its own *substance*, and the essence is said to be the *substance* of each thing." *Aristotle's Metaphysics*, trans. Apostle, 7. 6, 1031a.

66. Soheil M. Afnan, *Avicenna: His Life and Works* (London: George Allen and Unwin, 1958), 61.

67. See, for example, Francis A. Cunningham, "Averroes vs. Avicenna on Being," *New Scholasticism Quarterly Review of Philosophy* 48 (1974): 196.

68 Etienne Gilson. *Being and Some Philosophers*, (Toronto, Canada: Pontifical Institute of Mediaeval Studies, 1949), 51-52.

69. AV, 49–122.

70. Ibid., 69.

71. Ibid., 70.

72. Ibid., 66.

73. Ibid., 79.

74. Hence, Rahman's statement, which provides a sort of qualification for the view that Ibn Sīnā endorsed the distinction between essence and existence, expresses only half the truth. See his article "Essence and Existence in Ibn Sīnā: The Myth and the Reality," *Hamdard Islamicus* 4 (1981): 3–14.

75. AV, 74.

76. Ibid., 78.

77. Ibid., 77.

78. Ibid., 79.

79. Ibid., 65.

80. Ibid., 73. See Ibn Sīnā, *The Metaphysica of Avicenna,* 21.

81. J. L. Teicher, "Avicenna's Place in Arabic Philosophy," in *Avicenna: Scientist and Philosopher*, ed. G. M. Wickens (London: Luzac and Company, 1952), 39. The curious juxtaposition of the rationalistic and intuitive elements in Ibn Sīnā is also observed in his theory of eternal creation. Teicher explains this point in the context of discussing Ibn Sīnā's doctrine of creation through the process of emanation: "Avicenna's account of the process of emanation forms a cross between intuitive and rationalistic notions. By intuition reality is interpreted as a flux, as a continual movement; hence Ibn Sīnā

describes the first stage of emanation as the 'flowing out' of the first intelligence from God. But he describes quite differently the further stages of emanation. . . . The process of emanation from the first intelligence onwards is due to the acts of self-reflection. . . . Thus intuitive knowledge is replaced by rationalistic modes and reality as a flux by the psychological processes of the rationalistic attitude." Ibid., 42.

Chapter 3. Ibn Rushd versus al-Ghazālī on the Eternity of the World

1. Ghazālī, *al-Munqidh min al-Ḍalāl* [*Deliverer from Error*], ed. Jamīl Ṣalība and Kāmil ʿAyād (Damascus, Syria: Maṭbaʿat Jamiʿat Dimashq, 1960).
2. See Simon Van Den Bergh's introduction to TT, xii. The view that Ghazālī wrote his *Munqidh* in this period of doubt can be supported by reference to Ghazālī's *Munqidh*, ed. Ṣalība and ʿAyād, 80.
3. Ghazālī expressed a critical attitude toward scholastic theology. See, for example, Ghazālī, *Munqidh*, ed. Ṣalība and ʿAyād, 68–70. For a thorough discussion of this subject see Josep Puig Montada, "Ibn Rushd Versus al-Ghazālī: Reconsidering of a Polemic," *The Muslim World* 82 (1992): 14–18.
4. Oliver Leaman, *Medieval Islamic Philosophy* (Cambridge: Cambridge University Press, 1985), 40.
5. William C. Chittick, *The Heart of Islamic Philosophy: The Quest for Self-Knowledge in the Teachings of Afḍal al-Dīn Kāshānī* (Oxford: Oxford University Press, 2001), 30. This view can be supported by reference to Ghazālī's following statement: "The things one seeks to know are not given innately and cannot be caught save in the net of truths that are already achieved. Indeed, no truth is achieved save through two prior truths that are combined and coupled in a particular way and from whose coupling a third truth is achieved, just as birth comes about through the coupling of a stallion and a mare. . . . Thus every true cognition has two particular foundations and there is a way of coupling them, from which coupling of them the acquired knowledge which was sought comes about. It is ignorance of these foundations and the manner of their coupling that precludes the knowledge." Cited from Ghazālī's *Kitāb Sharḥ ʿAjā'ib al-Qalp* [*Book of Commentary on the Wonders of the Heart*] in R. M. Frank, *Al-Ghazālī and the Ashʿarite School* (Durham: Duke University Press, 1994), 25-26. More on Ghazālī's view on logic and the sciences see Michael Marmura, "Al-Ghazālī's Attitude to the Secular Sciences and Logic," in *Essays on Islamic Philosophy and Science*, ed. George F. Hourani (Albany: State University of New York Press, 1975), 100–111.
6. Ibn Rushd, *On the Harmony*, 61.
7. Ibn Ṭufayl, *Ḥayy Ibn Yaqẓān*, trans. Lenn Evan Goodman (New York: Twayne, 1972), 101.
8. Ibid.
9. TF, 7.
10. TT, xii.
11. TF, xxiii.
12. Barry S. Kogan, *Averroes and the Metaphysics of Causation* (Albany: State University of New York Press, 1985), 19.

13. Oliver Leaman, *Medieval Islamic Philosophy*, 39. Leaman expresses the opposite view in *Averroes and his Philosophy:* "Averroes is in the fortunate position of not having to agree with everything his philosophical predecessors propounded." Oliver Leaman, *Averroes and his Philosophy* (Oxford: Clarendon Press, 1988), 15.
14. He says that the dispute between the philosophers and other sects of Islam consists of three parts. There is the part in which the dispute is verbal. It is not necessary, says Ghazālī, to dispute with the philosophers about verbal controversies. The second part is one where the philosophers' doctrine does not contend with any religious principle. The philosophers' statements about the lunar and the solar eclipses are examples of this. Here, again, Ghazālī does not think it necessary to dispute with the philosophers about such matters. The third part is one where the dispute pertains to one of the principles of religion, such as upholding the doctrine of the world's origination, a doctrine that the philosophers, according to Ghazālī, have denied. Ghazālī thinks that it is concerning such topics that one must expose the falsity of the philosophers' doctrine. TF, 5–7.
15. TT, xvi.
16. Ibid. As Mājid Fakhry points out, Ibn Ḥazm, the *Zāhirī* theologian (d. 1064) appears to be the first Muslim theologian to attempt a complete refutation of the doctrine of the eternity of the world, and a proof of its temporality. Majid Fakhry, "The Classical Islamic Arguments for the Existence of God," *The Muslim World* 47 (1957): 137.
17. Except for the fourth proof.
18. TT, 1.
19. Van Den Bergh warns us against the arbitrariness of Ghazālī's presentation of the proofs of the philosophers and the fact that he mixes them up with the arguments of the theologians in such an involved way that the trend is hard to follow. For instance, Ghazālī says that there are two objections to the philosophers' first proof, but he mentions the first objection on p. 3 and the second only on p. 32. TT, xv.
20. Ibid., 21.
21. Ibid., 23–24.
22. Cited from *Iḥyā' ʿUlūm al-Dīn* [*The Revival of the Sciences of Religion*] in Rosalind W. Gwynne, "Al-Jubbā'ī, al-Ashʿarī and the Three Brothers: The Uses of Fiction," *Muslim World* 75 (1985): 134.
23. Kevin Reinhart, *Before Revelation*: *The Boundaries of Muslim Moral Thought* (Albany: State University of New York Press, 1995), 169. Ghazālī uses this and other examples to contest the Muʿtazilite's rational conception of God, the world and the relationship between them. Binyamin Abrahamov's following words explain the meaning of rationalism in the context of the debate between Ashʿrites and Muʿtazilites: "The basis of rationalism is the notion that God and the world can be perceived through the intellect which God creates in man. Concerning God, this perception means that God's existence, His unity and His attributes can be known through reason. Concerning the world, it means that the creation of the world and its structure, man and his actions can be logically understood. From this foundation, it follows that the world is directed according to rational rules and that, hence, even God is subject to these rules. We shall immediately see that according to some Muʿtazilites, God is logically obliged to act in a certain manner." Binyamin Abrahamov, *Islamic Theology: Traditionalism and Rationalism* (Edinburgh: Edinburgh University Press, 1998), 32.

24. *On the Harmony*, 45. Aristotle says in *Physics*, "For we do not think that we know a thing until we are acquainted with its primary conditions or first principles, and have carried our analysis as far as its simplest elements." BWA, 1. 2, 184a: 3–6.
25. See Soheil Afnan, *Avicenna: His Life and Works* (London: George Allen and Unwin, 1958), 106.
26. See TT, 21.
27. Ibid., 9. For example, the sphere of the sun revolves in one year and that of Saturn in thirty years. And so Saturn's revolution is one-thirtieth of the sun's revolution, although the number of Saturn's past revolutions is, like the number of the past revolutions of the sun, infinite
28. Ibid.
29. See previous chapter.
30. TT, 10.
31. Ibid.
32. The syllogism is reconstructed by Barry Kogan in "Eternity and Origination: Averroes' Discourse on the Manner of the World's Existence," in *Islamic Theology and Philosophy*, ed. Michael E. Marmura (Albany: State University of New York Press, 1984), 225.
33. TT, 11.
34. Kogan, "Eternity and Origination," 218.
35. Ibid., 224.
36. TT, 12.
37. Ibid.
38. Ibid., 13.
39. Kogan, "Eternity and Origination," 226.
40. Ibid.
41. TT, 32.
42. Ibid., 35.
43. Ibid., 36.
44. Ibid.
45. Ibid., 37.
46. Ibid., 38. Ghazālī's main concern is to establish that there are no necessary connections between the rational, which is expressed through language, and the real. It may seem that Ghazālī is making a distinction here between essence and existence, but this is exactly the opposite of his meaning. To say that the essence of the world did not exist does not imply that the world existed as a nonexistent essence.
47. Ibid.
48. Ibid.
49. Ibid.
50. Ibid., 39.
51. "Eternity and Origination," 209. The detailed proof for the implausibility of the thesis that time is the measure of the world is reconstructed by Kogan in the same article, 222.
52. Ibid. I must agree here with David Burrell that the manner of Ibn Rushd's refutation of the theologians' argument tends to confirm Ghazālī's critique by establishing an unbridgeable gulf between the deliverances of faith and of reason. David B. Burrell, *Freedom and Creation in Three Traditions* (Notre Dame, Ind.: Notre Dame Press, 1993),

55. Ibn Rushd says that God is not prior to or simultaneous with the world in time, knowing that these two possibilities exhaust the philosophers' rational options for fixing a relation of createdness, or any sort of relation for that matter, between God and the world. However, I would like to indicate a different understanding of the implication of abolishing the sort of rational relation between God and the world. In my view, by doing so Ibn Rushd was opening the way for establishing the (paradoxical) concept of *relationality*, which will be called "barzakh" by Ibn al-ʿArabī.

53. Burrell, *Freedom and Creation*, 55.

54. See Leaman, *Medieval Islamic Philosophy*, 49.

55. TT, 48.

56. Ibid., 44.

57. Ibid., 48.

58. Ibid., 51.

59. Ibid., 54.

60. Ibid., 237.

61. Ibid., 57.

62. Otherwise what sense is there in saying that something is possible of existence if, given an infinite amount of time, it does not enter into existence? See discussion of Ibn Sīnā's distinction between the possible- and the necessary-of-existence in the previous chapter.

63. Leaman, *Averroes and his Philosophy*, 30.

64. TT, 57–58.

65. Leaman, *Medieval Islamic Philosophy*, 51.

66. Ibid.

67. TT, 239.

68. See, Mājid Fakhry, "The Ontological Argument in the Arabic Tradition: The Case of al-Fārabī," *Studia Islamica* 64 (1986): 10.

69. Mājid Fakhry, "The 'Antinomy' of the Eternity of the World in Averroes, Maimonides and Aquinas," *Le Muséon* (1953): 143.

70. Followers of Plotinus and Proclus, mainly Ibn Sīnā and al-Fārābī.

71. Mājid Fakhry, "Rationality in Islamic Philosophy," in *Rationality in Question: On Eastern and Western Views of Rationality*, eds., Shlomo Biderman and Ben-Ami Scharfstein (Leiden: E. J. Brill, 1989), 506.

72. Charles Genequand, "Metaphysics," in *History of Islamic Philosophy, part 2*, Routledge History of World Philosophies, vol. 1, ed., Seyyed Hossein Nasr and Oliver Leaman (London: Routledge, 1996), 793.

73. Ibid., 792.

74. See discussion by Leaman, *Averroes and his Philosophy*, 68–69.

75. Genequand, "Metaphysics," 794. See also Ibn Rushd, *Tafsīr mā baʿd at-Ṭabīʿa* [Commentary on Aristotle's Metaphysics], 3 vols. (Beirūt: Dār al-Mashriq, 1973), 3: 1652.

76. Genequand, "Metaphysics," 794. See also Ibn Rushd, *Tafsīr*, 3: 1648.

77. Genequand, "Metaphysics," 794. Genequand is one of those scholars who affirm that "Ibn Rushd becomes fully intelligible only insofar as we regard him as primarily a successor of Aristotle," and that he "was not the builder of a new system, nor even the systematizer of a scattered body of doctrine and interpretation as Ibn Sīnā was." Charles Genequand, *Ibn Rushd's Metaphysics: A Translation with Introduction of Ibn*

Rushd's Commentary on Aristotle's Metaphysics, Book Lām (Leiden: E. J. Brill, 1984), 58. Most scholars who express similar views tend to present Ibn Rushd as saying that he found the truth with Aristotle, not that he found Aristotle with the truth. The difference between the two assertions becomes significant if we consider that Ibn Rushd was not only an interpreter of Aristotle, but also his defender. Take the problem of the creation of the world for example. Aristotle never used the language of creation ex nihilo in describing the relationship between God and the world. Ibn Rushd, however, claimed that the notion of creation ex nihilo, properly interpreted, is fully consistent with Aristotle's teaching. For a discussion of this subject, see Maḥmūd Qāsim, *Naẓariyyat al-Maʿrifa ʿinda Ibn Rushd wa-Ta'wīlihā ʿinda Tūmas al-Akwīnī* [Ibn Rushd's Theory of Knowledge and Its Interpretation in Thomas Aquinas] (Cairo: Maktabat al-Anglo al-Miṣriyya, n.d.), 92.
78. Charles Genequand, *Ibn Rushd's Metaphysics*, 33, and Ibn Rushd, *Tafsīr*, 3: 1567–1568.
79. Cited in Kogan, *Metaphysics of Causation*, 207.
80. Ibid., 211.
81. Ibid., 206. Mājid Fakhry expresses his view that by adhering to a doctrine of continuous creation, Ibn Rushd makes a concession to the revealed religion. Fakhry, "The 'Antinomy'," 151.
82. Ibid., 212.
83. Cited in Kogan, *Metaphysics of Causation*, 207.
84. Ibid., 212.
85. J. L. Teicher, "Avicenna's Place in Arabic Philosophy," in *Avicenna: Scientist and Philosopher*, ed. G. M. Wickens (London: Luzac and Company, 1952), 46.
86. Ibn Rushd, *Kitāb al-Samā ʿ at-Tabī ʿī*, in *Rasā'il Ibn Rushd* (Maṭbaʿat Da'irat al-Maʿrifa al-ʿUthmāniyya, 1947), 49.
87. Ibid., 46.
88. Teicher, "Avicenna's Place," 47.
89. Aristotle says, "But we apprehend time only when we have marked motion, marking it by 'before' and 'after'; and it is only when we have perceived 'before' and 'after' in motion that we say that time has elapsed. . . . When we think of the extremes as different from the middle and the mind pronounces that the 'nows' are two, one before and one after, it is then that we say that there is time." BWA, *Phys.*, 4. 11, 219a: 22–28.
90. Ibid.
91. *Aristotle's Metaphysics*, trans. Apostle, 5. 17, 1022a.
92. Ibn Rushd, *Kitāb al-Ṣamā*, 48.

Chapter 4. Mysticism versus Philosophy: The Encounter between Ibn al-ʿArabī and Ibn Rushd

1. William C. Chittick, "Mysticism vs. Philosophy in Earlier Islamic History: The al-Ṭūsī, al-Qūnawī Correspondence," *Religious Studies* 17 (1981): 88. For a summary discussion of the difference in methodology between rational philosophers, dogmatic theologians and theoretical Ṣūfism see, Chittick, *The Heart of Islamic Philosophy*, 32.
2. Ibid., 94.

3. Oliver Leaman, "Philosophy vs. Mysticism: an Islamic Controversy," in *Philosophy, Religion and the Spiritual Life*, ed. Michael McGhee (Cambridge: Cambridge University Press, 1992), 178.
4. Ibn Rushd was accused of holding a theory of "double truth," since he seems to have claimed that sacred texts could be subject to different interpretations, and that each interpretation might reveal contradictory aspects (apparent, hidden) of the meaning of the text. However, as Jorge E. Gracia points out, this does not mean that truth is double. Ibn Rushd insisted upon the unity of truth since, according to him, "Truth does not oppose truth but accords with it and bears witness to it." Jorge E. Gracia, "Interpretation and the Law: Averroes' Contribution to the Hermeneutics of Sacred Texts," *History of Philosophy Quarterly* 14 (1997): 143.
5. See previous chapter.
6. Fadlou Shehādī, *Ghazālī's Unique Unknowable God* (Leiden: E. J. Brill, 1964), 57.
7. Chittick, "Mysticism vs. Philosophy," 90.
8. Ibid., 89.
9. Khaḍir (or Khiḍr) is the name of a popular figure who plays a prominent role in many ancient oriental legends and stories, such as the Gilgamish epic and the Jewish legend of Elijah and Rabbi Joshua Ben Levi. The commentators on the Qur'ān, Ḥadīth scholars, and historians collected a mass of statements around Khaḍir and the Qur'ānic story, especially in connection to the Alexander's search for the Spring of Life. The usual account of the story makes Alexander and Khaḍir go their ways separately. In some versions, the latter has a fish with him, as he discovers the miraculous well of the waters of life through the fish becoming alive when it touches the water. In the Arabic explanations of Khaḍir's name, Khaḍir is conceived as belonging to the vegetable kingdom. Khaḍir was told at the Spring of Life that whenever he touches earth it becomes green. There are different views concerning Khaḍir's nature and whether he was considered an apostle in addition to being a prophet, or whether he should be regarded as human or rather an angelic person. Ṣūfī circles regarded him a saint, and held that every age has its Khaḍir. *The Shorter Encyclopaedia of Islam*, eds., H. A. R. Gibb and J. H. Kramers (Leiden: E. J. Brill, 1974), 232–235.
10. F, 1, 152–155. For a useful discussion of the psychomystical implications of the Qur'ānic story of the encounter between Moses and Khaḍir see Sara Sviri, "Where the Two Seas Meet: The Story of Khiḍr," in *The Taste of Hidden Things: Images on the Ṣūfī Path* (Invernes, Calif.: Golden Ṣūfī Center, 1997), 77–101.
11. Henry Corbin provides the most elaborated study of the notion of creative imagination in *Creative Imagination in the Ṣūfism of Ibn ʿArabī*. He devotes a significant part of his work to the discussion of the knowledge obtained by Khaḍir and Ṣūfīs (like Ibn al-ʿArabī), who considered themselves his direct disciples in that they obtained an immediate bond with the Godhead. Henry Corbin, *Creative Imagination in the Ṣūfism of Ibn ʿArabī*, trans. R. Mannheim (Princeton, N.J.: Princeton University Press, 1969), 53–76.
12. F, 1, 153: 17.
13. F, 1, 153: 21–22.
14. William Chittick, *Imaginal Worlds: Ibn al-ʿArabī and the Problem of Religious Diversity* (Albany: State University of New York Press, 1994), 70–71.
15. Renate Jacobi mentions the following meanings of the term *khayāl* (imagination): "As for the *khayāl*, it is to be derived from *khala*, 'to think, surmise or fancy a thing'

(*tawahhama ash-shay*') and signifies, according to Lane (2, 835c), 'an incorporeal form or image.' In his further explanations, mostly quotations from Arabic lexicographers, the following basic meanings can be distinguished. The *khayāl* is anything seen like a shadow, an image in the mirror, for instance, or on water. It is also 'a form imaged to one in the mind,' and it is further 'a fancied image, apparition or specter coming in sleep.'" "The Khayāl Motif in Early Arabic Poetry," *Oriens* 32 (1990): 53. Jacobi discusses the phenomenon of the appearance of the *khayāl* in relation to early Arab poets. she registers the following interesting observation: *khayāl* appeared to the poet in the form of the beloved in the time of the night "when darkness is beginning to fade and dusk is slowly setting in." Ibid., 54. As I am going to make clear in this work, imagination for Ibn al-ʿArabī signified the power of manifesting a spiritual entity in a material form. Imagination is situated at the boundary between the realm of the spiritual and the realm of the material like the *khayāl* of the beloved that appears at the boundary between darkness and light.

16. F, I, 153: 26. This is an important statement which may be related to the discussion in the previous chapter. God's work is an infinite actuality and the world is its finite actualization. Actuality is identical to its actualization from the point of view of God, who is its root. From the point of view of the limited creatures (the limited actualizations of God's action) this might not be realized easily. What is needed is a knowledge that takes them back to the root of creation, or the root of breathing, where God's act and the product of this act are still at the edge of bifurcation. At the root of creation knowledge of God's work (knowledge of actuality) is the same as the knowledge of the world (actualization). It might be said that this was the knowledge that Khaḍir possessed and Moses was after.

17. F, 1, 153: 25–26.

18. The commentators on the Qur'ān explain the "Meeting of the Two Seas" (*majmaʿ al baḥrayn*) in different ways. Some (Bayḍāwī) regard it as the meeting place of the Persian Ocean and the Roman Sea, which points to the Isthmus of Suez. Others (Ṭabarī, Zamakhsharī) say that it is the junction of the Roman Sea with the Ocean, which points to the Straits of Gibraltar. *The Shorter Encyclopaedia of Islam*, 233. ʿAbdullah Yūsuf ʿAlī interprets *majmaʿ al-baḥrayn* as the meeting place of the two seas of the great streams of secular and divine knowledge, which were to meet in the persons of Moses and Khaḍir. ʿAlī, *The Meaning*, 725.

19. The Servant of God is called Khaḍir by the majority of the commentators on the Qur'ān.

20. This is a very special knowledge, by means of which the servant realizes the secret of God's all-comprehensive mercy, which encompasses even those of whom it is said that mercy would not include them. Q7: 156 states unqualifiedly that God's mercy extends to all things, which seems to contradict the Qur'ānic statement that God's mercy includes all humans except those who associate others with Him. More on the notion of God's mercy in Ibn al-ʿArabī see Ronald Nettler, "Ibn ʿArabī's Notion of Allah's Mercy," *Israel Oriental Society* 8 (1978): 219–229.

21. Which will become an obligation imposed on every seeker (*murīd*) who seeks the favor of his Ṣūfī Master, namely, to become a silent follower. The following is ʿAbdullah Yūsuf ʿAlī's interpretation of Q 66: 71–77.

22. ʿAlī, *The Meaning*, 731.

23. Ian Richard Netton, "Theophany as Paradox: Ibn ʿArabī's Account of *al-Khaḍir* in his *Fuṣūṣ al-Ḥikam*," *Journal of the Muḥyiddīn Ibn ʿArabī Society* 11 (1992), 14.
24. Consider the relevance of Carl J. Kalwaitis's following words to the present discussion: "We can see the relation between familiarity and acceptability in the word 'paradox' itself, which is derived from the Greek *paradoxos*. *Paradoxos* means 'contrary to received opinion, beyond expectations, strange, wonderful, enigmatic.' It is a combination of the prefix *para*, meaning 'beyond' or 'contrary,' and the substantive *doxa*. *Doxa* is most often translated as 'opinion,' but we must be careful not to interpret this too narrowly. *Doxa* is essentially what we are referring to as the domain of acceptability, or the accepted way (understanding). For it is derived from *dokein*, which means 'to appear, seem, think (as in suppose),' and is related to *dekesthai*, 'to accept.' From this is derived the English 'document' and 'doctrine.' Thus characteristic of *doxa* is accepting ('This is what we do') and supposing ('It's supposed to be done that way'). Our behavior is in agreement with *doxa* if we meet its expectations. We do not have to wonder about or question it. It is familiar and obvious. It is 'what one does.'" "The Origin of Paradox and its Relation to Philosophical Reflection," *Philosophy Today* 42 (1998): 361.
25. Carl Jung, "The Transcendent Function," in *Jung on Active Imagination*, ed. Joan Chodorow (Princeton, N.J.: Princeton University Press, 1997), 44. It is worth mentioning that Jung provided an interpretation of the Qur'ānic story of the encounter between Moses and Khaḍir in *Concerning Rebirth* (1939). According to him, "Khiḍr symbolizes not only the higher wisdom but also a way of acting which is in accord with this wisdom and transcends reason." See Nicholas Battye, "Khiḍr in the Opus of Jung: The Teaching of Surrender," in *Jung and the Monotheisms*, ed. Joel Ryce Menuhin (London: Routledge, 1994), 167.
26. Brian John Martine, *Indeterminacy and Intelligibility* (Albany: State University of New York Press, 1992), 61.
27. Ibid.
28. Ibid.
29. See Chittick's discussion of the subject of the perpetual renewal of creation in SPK, 96–112.
30. Sara Sviri's following words illustrate the barzakhī nature of Khaḍir's conduct: "Standing at the twilight zone, Khiḍr is a *barzakh*, and isthmus. This 'nowhere-place,' this 'nonexisting line' between here and here, between now and now, does not exist, yet it makes up our reality. It is like imagination, like a dream, like a mirror, reflecting images yet at the same time showing that reality is neither there nor not-there; that everything, including our ideas and notions of God, is both it and not-it." Sara Sviri, "The Obsession with Life: Jung, Khiḍr and the Sūfī Tradition," in *The Guild of Pastoral Psychology*, 273, (2000), 8.
31. *Naʿam lā*. Gerald T. Elmore draws our attention to the absence of conjunction between the two words (yes no), saying that this must imply "folly to the materialist, chaos and evil to the rationalist." Elmore, *Islamic Sainthood*, 51. The second passage is Elmore's translation.
32. See the following note.
33. Elmore remarks that Asin Palacios and Henry Corbin misread this passage, thinking that Ibn Rushd and Ibn al-ʿArabī did not meet on a second occasion. If we accept Elmore's interpretation, then we must consider four encounters between the philosopher

and the mystic rather than three. It is not clear, however, whether Elmore's interpretation can be sustained, especially if we consider the fact that right after this passage Ibn al-ʿArabī says, "Then I wished to meet with him a second time (*marra thāniyya*)." Elmore translates *marra thāniyya* as "on another occasion." But it seems more probable to me that the 'literal meaning' (a second time) is what is meant here.

34. Elmore confirms the view of Roger Arnaldez and Ernest Renan that this statement cannot be substantiated in Ibn Rushd's writings, that Ibn Rushd does not believe that mystical training can replace rational knowledge and that the mystic vision is not to be found at all in Ibn Rushd. Ibid. It is true that Ibn Rushd does not think that mystical training can replace rational methodology in the attainment of knowledge. But to argue that mystical vision is not to be found at all in Ibn Rushd would, in my view, be incorrect.

35. This passage, as well as the last passage in the previous quotation, is Elmore's translation in *Islamic Sainthood*, 50–53. F, 1, 53–54. The same desire—"How I wish I knew"—was expressed by Ibn al-ʿArabī years later when he was circumambulating the *Kaʿba*. There he heard the answer from a woman who would remain for him the theophanic figure of *Sophia aeterna*. See Corbin, *Creative Imagination,* 44. Concerning the interpretation of the encounter between Ibn al-ʿArabī and *Sophia* see Corbin, *Creative Imagination*, 140–145. Here it suffices to note that Ibn al-ʿArabī's wishful expressions do not signify necessarily the uncertainty associated with absolute lack of certainty, but rather a statement regarding the intrinsic self-transcendence of knowledge. The true mystic is always in a state of uncertainty. However, because of this very reason he is far removed from being content with the skeptic's conviction that attaining certainty in knowledge is impossible.

36. SPK, 284.

37. SPK, 384. F, 1, 325:16–22.

38. Addas, *The Quest*, 107. It is worth mentioning the three factors that determine the position of the individual in the Ṣūfī hierarchical order: the Law (*sharīʿa*), the spiritual path (*ṭarīqa*), and the Truth (*ḥaqīqa*). Realization of the Truth is what distinguishes the saints from individuals who belong to the levels of the knowledge of the Law and the knowledge of the spiritual path. See discussion in Hamid Dabashi, "The Ṣūfī Doctrine of 'the Perfect Man' and a View of the Hierarchical Structure of Islamic Culture," *Islamic Quarterly* 30 (1986): 122.

39. *Shorter Encyclopaedia of Islam*, 127.

40. Ibid. Qushayrī (d. 1072), the author of the *Risāla* defines the State in contrast to the Station (*maqām*) as follows: "According to the Folk [Ṣūfīs] the State is a meaning that descends on the heart without intention on the part of the Ṣūfīs and without investing any effort in bringing or acquiring it. . . . The Stations are acquired whereas the States are gifts that come from beyond Being. . . . The possessor of the Station is stabilized in his position, while the possessor of the State always transcends his state." Abū al-Qāsim ʿAbd al-Karīm al-Qushayrī, *al-Risāla al-Qushayriyya* (Cairo: Maṭbaʿat Muṣṭafā al-Ḥalabī, 1940), 34. On States (*aḥwāl*), Stations (*Maqāmāt*), and the difference between them in Ṣūfīsm see Seyyed Hossein Nasr, *Ṣūfī Essays*, 2nd ed. (Albany: State University of New York Press, 1991), 72–74.

41. Suʿād al-Ḥakīm, *al-Muʿjam al-Ṣūfī: Al-Ḥikma fī Ḥudūd al-Kalima* (Beirūt: Dandara, 1991), 334.

42. SPK, 100. F, 3, 198: 30.

43. SD, 60.
44. SPK, 4.
45. Ibid., 18.
46. SD, 86. F, 3, 396: 19–22.
47. Following Chittick, I would like to emphasize that in contrast with "existence" and "being," "finding," which is the literal translation of the word *wujūd,* has a necessary connection with awareness. That is why it is a better translation of Ibn al-ʿArabī's *wujūd.* SPK, 6. The Real cannot be found by means of rational deliberation, since the Real is finding and finding cannot be comprehended in terms of either/or, since it abides in a creative synthesis between existence and nonexistence. Such is also the state of those who are Realizers in the Knowledge of States, since they have become in the image of the Real. To say that the Realizers cannot be *found* means that they have become, like the Real, *beyond* existence and nonexistence.
48. SPK, 163. F, 1, 126: 6-8.
49. Ibn al-ʿArabī includes Plato among the Realizers in the Knowledge of the States. F, 2, 523:10. See also F, 2, 269: 22, where Ibn al-ʿArabī identifies the philosopher with the Realizer in the Knowledge of States. Ibn al-ʿArabī's reminder that the term *philosopher* means lover of wisdom, and his insistence that Plato possessed divine knowledge or knowledge of the States *(aḥwāl)* is sometimes ignored by scholars who present him as unqualifiedly critical of philosophical activity. Maḥmoud al-Ghourāb, for example, states that we should not try to link Ibn al-ʿArabī with the teaching of Aristotle or Plato because "the philosopher relies on intellect *(ʿaql)*, reflection *(fikr)*, and logic *(manṭiq)*, and considers these faculties to be the source of all his knowledge. On the other hand, Shaykh al-Akbar talks about Divine effusion *(al-fayḍ al-'ilāhī)*, and receiving *(talaqqī)*." Mahmoud al-Ghorāb, "Ibn al-ʿArabī Amidst Religion and Schools of Thought," in *Muḥyiddīn Ibn ʿArabī*: *A Commemorative Volume*, ed. Stephen Hirtenstein and Michael Tiernan (Rockport, Mass.: Element, 1993), 206. A more balanced view is presented by Franz Rosenthal, who concludes an article with the following statement: "The attempt is made here to let his statements speak for themselves and to see him as he might have seen himself . . . both a philosopher and a mystic." Franz Rosenthal, "Ibn ʿArabī Between 'Philosophy' and 'Mysticism,'" *Oriens* 31 (1988): 35.
50. There is no conjunction between *al-ḥaqq* (the Real) and *al-wujūd* (the Being).
51. Instead of *al-ḥaqq al-wujūd*, this (first) Path is called here *al-wujūd al-ḥaqq*. In my opinion, the purpose of reversing the order between the two terms is to qualify the identification between the Real and Being, as the identification becomes dynamic or active and does not boil down to a static or inert relationship.
52. F, 3, 141: 22-31.
53. Francis Macdonald Cornford, *Plato and Parmenides* (London: Routledge and Kegan Paul, 1951), 30–31. Ibn al-ʿArabī sides also with the impossibility of gaining knowledge of Absolute Nonbeing in his saying, "Knowledge pertains only to that which is, never to that which is not in an absolute sense, since this is devoid of form and is not limited by a quality." Ibn al-ʿArabī, *Kitāb Inshā' al-Dawā'ir* (Leiden: E. J. Brill, 1919), 11. What he says in the same work is consistent with what is brought in the present discussion. For he insists that the Real also cannot be an object for knowledge, since he is absolutely unlimited. Ibid., 15. Compare the discussion in the present chapter with

the discussion in the last section of chapter 5, especially in relation to the issue of the limits of rationalism.

54. *Shorter Encyclopaedia of Islam*, 583.

55. SD, 87. F, 4 106: 22.

56. Ibn al-ʿArabī says: "He who professes God's Unity is not fair, and he who associates others with Him has not hit the point. God is One not through the unification (*tawḥīd*) of the professor of His Unity nor through His *tawḥīd* to Himself. This is because He is One *in Himself* and, therefore, His Oneness cannot be fashioned, nor is the unity of His manyness unknown." The translation of this passage diverges slightly from Chittick's translation in *SD*, 336. F, 4, 107: 18–19.

57. Ibn al-ʿArabī, *The Bezels of Wisdom*, trans. R. W. J. Austin (New York: Paulist Press, 1980), 71–72. Alexander D. Knysh explains the doctrine on the basis of which Ibn al-ʿArabī's argument against the prophet Noah is established: "Ibn Arabi's argument rests on his doctrine of Divine manifestations, according to which God appears to the observer in both transcendent and immanent guises. In keeping with this doctrine, to discover the 'true' nature of God and His relationship with the World, the observer must renounce his rational outlook and give himself to the veridical 'direct vision' (*shuhūd*) and intuitive 'direct tasting' (*dhawq*). This new, higher knowledge can only be achieved by the human heart (*qalb*), an Arabic word whose lexical connotations point to 'motion,' 'fluctuation' and 'transformation.'" Alexander D. Knysh, "'Orthodoxy' and 'Heresy' in Medieval Islam: An Essay in Reassessment," *Muslim World* 83 (1993): 58.

58. TT, 281. The words in italics are my translation of *lā huwa 'illā huwa,* rendered by Van Den Bergh as *There is no reality besides Him.*

59. Ibn Rushd, *On the Harmony*, 32.

60. Ibid., 35.

61. TT, 215, emphasis added.

62. Ibid., 274.

63. Ibid., 215.

64. SPK, 110. F, 2, 483: 7

65. SPK, 74. F, 2, 307: 19–20.

66. Elmore, *Islamic Sainthood*, 53. For more on the encounter between Ibn al-ʿArabī and Ibn Rushd see Steffen Stelzer, "Decisive Meetings: Ibn Rushd, Ibn ʿArabī, and the Matter of Knowledge," *Alif* 16 (1996): 19–55.

67. William C. Chittick, "Ṣadr al-Dīn Qūnawī on the Oneness of Being," *International Philosophical Quarterly* 21 (1981): 172.

Chapter 5. The Barzakh

1. Martin Lings devotes a chapter in *Symbol and Archetype* to the Qur'ānic symbolism of water in which chapter he makes a brief allusion to the symbolic interpretation of Q 25:53. Lings does not mention Ibn al-ʿArabī in this chapter, but his discussion of the symbolic meaning of water in the Qur'ān and his mention of Q 25:53 might be relevant to the present discussion. He explains that the two bodies of water, the salt and the fresh, refer to the duality of the manifest and the nonmanifest, which is implicit in *al-Raḥmān*

(The All-Merciful), the Infinitely Good. The treasures of the waters of the nonmanifest and the waters of manifestation, which symbolize the attributes of transcendence and the attributes of immanence, comprise the two main aspects of the All-Merciful. Martin Lings, *Symbol and Archetype: A Study of the Meaning of Existence* (Cambridge: Quinta Essentia, 1991), 67–82.
2. ʿAlī, *The Meaning*, 731, 901–902, 1399.
3. Ibid., 901.
4. Examples: "And the herbs and the trees—both (alike) bow in adoration. (55:5) Then which of the favors of your Lord will ye deny? (55:6) Of Him seeks (its need) every creature in the heavens and on earth: Every day in (new) splendor doth He shine. (55:29) Soon shall We settle your affairs, O both ye worlds! (55:31) Then which of the favors of your Lord will ye deny? (55:32) O ye assembly of Jinns and men! If it be ye can pass beyond the zones of the heavens and the earth, pass ye! Not without authority shall ye be able to pass! (55:33) Then which of the favors of your Lord will ye deny?" (55:34). Ibid.
5. F, 1, 60: 27–34.
6. ʿAffīfī, *Mystical Philosophy,* 91. Wolfson brings Philo's mention of the Logos in his interpretation of the Platonic ideas: "When God by His own good will decided to create the world of ours, He first, out of the ideas which had been in His thought from eternity, constructed an 'intelligible world,' and this intelligible world He placed in the Logos, which had likewise existed previously from eternity in His thought. Then in the likeness of this intelligible world of ideas He created this 'visible world' of ours." Harry Austryn Wolfson, *Religious Philosophy* (Cambridge, Mass.: Harvard University Press, 1961), 31.
7. Naṣr Ḥāmid Abū Zayd, *Falsafat al-Ta'wīl*, 38.
8. In the following examination of the development of the notion of the Intermediate State in the Islamic canonical tradition I rely on Ragnar Eklund, *Life between Death and Resurrection according to Islam* (Uppsala: Almqvist and Boktryckeri, 1941). Hereafter cited as DR.
9. Ibid., 6. Ibn Rushd responded in a similar manner to Ibn al-ʿArabī's answer to his philosophical inquiry regarding the harmony between the method of mystical unveiling and the findings of the speculative thinkers. See discussion of the encounter between Ibn Rushd and Ibn al-ʿArabī in the previous chapter.
10. Ibid., 9.
11. Compare with the saint's words in Ibn al-ʿArabī story of his encounter with Ibn Rushd in the previous chapter: "This life and the Garden [in the hereafter] consist of the same bricks and the same structure, even though the one is made of clay . . . and the other of gold."
12. SD, 61. F, 3, 253: 15–19.
13. See n. 11.
14. SD, 363. F, 3, 13: 1–6.
15. See, for example, F, 3, 198: 28; 2, 384: 31; 2, 431: 28.
16. F, 2, 589: 29.
17. SPK, 103.
18. F, 2, 476: 29.
19. DR, 7.
20. F, 2, 295: 16–25. The notion that spiritual entities take on material forms in the barzakh is found in the Islamic collections of the narratives of the events that occur

after death. It is also found in the traditional Zoroastrian conceptions of the immediate happenings after death as the following citation demonstrates: "This is the visitation of a person described as having a beautiful face, lovely clothing, and (sometimes) a sweet fragrance, or as having an ugly countenance and exuding a noxious odor. Upon being asked to identify himself—'Who are you? I have never seen anyone more beautiful/ugly than you'—the person says either 'I am your good deeds' or 'I am your abominable deeds.'" Jane Idleman Smith and Yvonne Yazbeck Haddad, *The Islamic Understanding of Death and Resurrection* (Albany: State University of New York Press, 1981), 42.

21. To remind the reader that by "imaginal" Ibn al-ʿArabī means that which is a synthesis between the spiritual and the corporeal, which is more real than the imaginative impressions fashioned by the human mind.

22. SPK, 218. F, 2, 633: 11–14.

23. A famous theologian and mystic (d. 908). As Chittick points out, al-Ḥakīm al-Tirmidhī introduced 157 questions to be answered by those who claim to be Friends of God. Ibn al-ʿArabī answered these questions in *al-Jawāb al-Mustaqīm* [*The Straightforward Answer*], and later incorporated his answers into chapter 73 of the *Futūḥāt*. SPK, 396, n. 25.

24. F, 2, 82: 6.

25. F, 2, 82: 19–20. Here it is worth mentioning Sulimān Bashear's observation regarding Q 20:15, a verse that confirms that the coming of the Hour is imminent. Bashear says that the verse contains a key sentence whose variant reading expresses concern over the delay of the Hour. Those are the words *akādu akhfīhā/ukhfīhā* meaning: "I almost reveal/conceal it," as the verb *akhfā* conveys two opposite meanings. Bashear says that the two readings represented two opposing interpretations as one group of scholars continued to believe that the Hour was close while the other believed that the exact knowledge of the coming of the Hour belonged to God alone. See Sulimān Bashear, "Muslim Apocalypses and the Hour: A Case-Study in Traditional Reinterpretation," *Israel Oriental Studies* 13 (1993): 82.

26. F, 2, 82: 22-27.

27. DR, 82.

28. Ibid., 79. Not implying that the notion that stood behind the concept of the barzakh was absent in theology. This work expounds on two such notions, central to Islamic theological thought: the Muʿtazilites' "nonexistent" (*al-maʿdūm*) and the Ashʿarites' "states" (*aḥwāl*), which bear intermediate (barzakhī) characteristics.

29. Ibid., 86.

30. Franz Rosenthal, "Ibn ʿArabī between 'Philosophy' and 'Mysticism,'" 35. Ibn al-ʿArabī was, for sure, a reader of Ghazālī's *Iḥyā'*. See Addas, *Quest for the Red Sulphur*, 108.

31. Cited from Ghazālī, *Iḥyā'* in DR, 137–138. *Malakūtic* means angelic or heavenly; the word "*umma*" means (religious) community.

32. SD, 339. F, 4 99: 12-16.

33. F, 3, 198 : 23–28. As Chittick points out, imagination was employed long before Ibn al-ʿArabī by Islamic thinkers in interpreting the Islamic eschatological teachings. He mentions Ibn Sīnā, who emphasized the significance of imagination in acquiring knowledge and Ghazālī, who made extensive use of its explanatory possibilities. He insists, however, that Ibn al-ʿArabī's approach was unique in holding that knowledge of Imagination is a necessary condition for gaining any knowledge whatsoever. Chittick,

"Death and the World of Imagination: Ibn ʿArabī's Eschatology," *Muslim World* 88 (1988): 51–82.

34. I must make it explicit at the outset that in comparing Ibn al-ʿArabī's barzakh with Plato's Form, I am not trying to show that Ibn al-ʿArabī established his barzakh concept on the basis of Plato's theory of Forms. The following discussion of Plato's theory of Forms should be received as an attempt to present the theory as the philosophical background for Ibn al-ʿArabī's concept of the barzakh without, at the same time, making any far-reaching assumptions about any direct connection between the thought of Ibn al-ʿArabī and Plato's.

35. TCD, *Phaedo,* 100c.

36. TCD, xv.

37. According to Edith Hamilton and Huntington Cairns, "Plato's aim is to take the reader by steps, with as severe a logic as the conversational method permits, to an insight into the ultimate necessity of reason. And he never hesitates to submit his own ideas to the harshest critical scrutiny; he carried this procedure so far in the *Parmenides* that some commentators have held that his own doubts in this dialogue prevail over his affirmations. But the beliefs of mystics are not products of critical examination and logical clarification; they are, on the contrary, a series of apprehensions, flashes, based on feeling, denying the rational order." TCD, xv.

38. TCD, *Letter vii,* 344b.

39. TCD, *Parmenides,* 131c.

40. Parmenides says:

> Since, then, there is a *furthest limit,* [it] is completed,
> From every direction like the bulk of a well-rounded sphere,
> Everywhere from the center equally matched; for [it] must not be any larger
> Or any smaller here or there;
> For neither is there what-is-not, which could stop it from reaching
> [its] like; *nor is there a way in which what-is could be*
> More here and less there, since [it] all inviolably is;
> For equal to itself from every direction, [it] lies uniformly *within limits.*

Parmenides, *Parmenides of Elea*, trans. David Gallop (Toronto: University of Toronto Press, 1984), 73, emphasis added.

41. BWA, *Metaphys.*, 2. 5, 998a.

42. Ibn Rushd, *Tafsīr*, 138. Aristotle's *Metaphys.*, 1. 9, 991b: 31-37 reads: "Again, these thinkers must set up another genus of number as the subject of arithmetic, and also other genera, all of which are simply called 'Intermediate Objects' by some of them. But how is this to be done, and from what principles will these objects come? Or, why will these be between the things about us and the Ideas? Again, each of the Units in Two is generated from a prior Dyad, although this is impossible. Again, why is a Number, taken as a whole, one?" *Aristotle's Metaphysics*, trans. Apostle, 31.

43. BWA, *Metaphys.,* 2.2, 994b.

44. *Aristotle's Metaphysics*, trans. Apostle, 5.17, 1022a.

45. SD, 335. F, 3, 518: 1–12, 22–24, 27–29, emphasis added. The first passage is my translation.

46. Ibid., 2, 518: 12.
47. F, 4, 146: 11–12.
48. F, 3, 269: 26–27, 33–34
49. SD, 117. F, 3, 525: 26.
50. F, 3, 525: 28.
51. F, 3, 525: 29. I elaborated on this point in "Plato and Ibn ʿArabī on Skepticism," *Journal of the Muḥyiddīn Ibn ʿArabī Society* 30 (2001): 19–35.
52. F, 1, 304: 22–26, 29–30.
53. SPK, 215. F, 3, 116: 28–29.
54. Ghazālī, *The Niche of Lights* (*Mishkāt al-Anwār*), trans. David Bushman (Provo, Utah: Brighham Young University Press, 1998), 18.
55. In order to account for the participation of sensible things in the Forms, we posit an object to mediate between them. However, positing an intermediate object between the sensible objects and the Forms results in an infinite regress.
56. See definition of barzakh above.
57. See definition of barzakh above.
58. TCD, *Parmenides*, 131a.
59. F, 2, 476: 29–32.
60. F, 1, 184: 28–29.
61. F, 3, 339: 33
62. F, 3, 108: 14–17, 1, 130: 28–32
63. Michael Marmura, "Avicenna's Chapter, 'On the Relative,' in the *Metaphysics* of the *Shifā*," in *Essays on Islamic Philosophy and Science*, ed. Michael Marmura (Albany: State University of New York Press, 1975), 83-99. For a comparison between Ibn al-ʿArabī and Ibn Sīnā's conceptions of the relative see also Paul A. Hardy, "Response to Eric L. Ormsby," in *God and Creation: An Ecumenical Symposium*, ed. David B. Burrell and Bernard McGinnis (Notre Dame, Ind.: University of Notre Dame Press, 1990), 270.
64. Ibid., 78–88, emphasis added.
65. Ibid., 90.
66. Ibid., 93.
67. See definition of the barzakh above.
68. F, 2, 74: 18–19. The only means for identifying the Real is by discerning his absolute nondelimitation, and this cannot be discerned except through differentiating him from all delimited things. Through differentiating himself from all delimited things, that is, through relating himself negatively to the delimited things, the Real becomes manifest to our knowledge. See, F, 2, 518: 21.
69. F, 1, 183: 14–16, 19–23.
70. Corbin mentions also Ibn Sīnā, "who thought it possible for the pure intellect to demonstrate the existence of a Necessary Being outside of time, space, and form." See Corbin, *Creative Imagination*, 127.
71. Ibn al-ʿArabī, *The Bezels of Wisdom*, trans. Austin, 93.
72. SD, 131. F, 3, 547: 37–38.
73. SD, 131. F, 3, 547: 34–35. It is worth noting that the Arabic word *mawlā* means both "lord" (applied to God in the Qur'ān) and "slave."
74. F, 3, 546: 34–38.
75. SD, 128–129. F, 3, 546: 34–38.

76. Another possible reading is: "Similar to Nature, its power is in its actualizing, even though the entity is nonexistent in both."
77. Gerhard Böwering, "Ibn al-ʿArabī's Concept of Time," in *God is Beautiful and He Loves Beauty*, ed. A. Giese and J. C. Burgel (New York: Peter Lang, 1994), 75–76.
78. SPK 103, F, 2, 281: 3–4.

Chapter 6. The Third Entity: The Supreme Barzakh

1. PK, 363.
2. See, for example, Abū al-ʿIlā ʿAffīfī, "al-Aʿyān al-Thābita fī Madhhab Ibn ʿArabī wa-al-Maʿdūmāt fī Madhab al-Muʿtazila," in *al-Kitāb al-Tidhkārī: Muḥyiddīn Ibn Arabī fī al-Dhikra al-Mi'awiyya al-Thāmina li-Mīlādih*, ed. Ibrāhīm Bayūmī Madhkūr (Cairo: Dār al-Kitāb al-ʿArabī li'l-Ṭibaʿa wa-al-Nashr, 1969), 209–220.
3. The Ashʿarites held the doctrine of the States (*aḥwāl*), which possessed, like the barzakh, intermediate nature. Van Den Bergh draws our attention to the ambiguity of the term *ḥāl*. He explains that this term does not signify a thing or a material reality, but rather a fact, state, or event. He explains that the State is regarded by the theologians as something that is intermediate between reality and unreality, a meaning (*maʿnā*) or a property (*ḥukm*). He further adds that *maʿnā* can also mean "idea" in the Platonic sense. TT, 2: 3, n. 6.
4. SPK, 205. F, 3, 47: 29–31.
5. PK, 361.
6. See discussion of Wolfson's statement (in "The Kalām Problem of Nonexistents and Saadia's Second Theory of Creation") that in the tradition of the kalām the antemundane matter is referred to as a nonexistent that is still something. Masataka Takeshita, "An Analysis of Ibn ʿArabī's *Inshā' al-Dawā'ir* with Particular Reference to the Doctrine of the 'Third Entity,'" *Journal of Near Eastern Studies* 41 (1982): 249.
7. SPK, 84. Toshihiko Izutsu is one of the scholars who rendered *aʿyān thābita* as permanent archetypes. Izutsu, *Ṣūfism and Taoism*, 159–196.
8. According to Aristotle, Plato separated the Forms from the sensible objects that participate in them, thus departing from Socrates' view concerning the relationship between universals and particulars. Daniel T. Devereux points out that until recently scholars have accepted this view and its implications. Plato's separation of the Forms and the sensible particulars has been understood as implying that Forms are not immanent in particulars, as they are also ontologically independent from them. This view, Devereux says, has come under serious attack. Concerning the view that Forms are not immanent in particulars, critics witness that in some dialogues (*Symposium*, *Timaeus*) Plato seems to reject immanence while in others (*Phaedo*) he seems to regard Forms as *in* particulars. The critics have argued also that the claims concerning the ontological independence of the Forms cannot be supported and that the most that can be said is that Plato is committed to the independence of some Forms in some dialogues. Devereux emphasizes that "even supporters of the traditional view sometimes claim that Plato's notion of participation is incompatible with a strict doctrine of separation; thus his view may not have been as simple as and straightforward as Aristotle's statement implies." It must be noted, however, that Devereux is writing on behalf of the separation view. See,

Daniel T. Devereux, "Separation and Immanence in Plato's Theory of Forms," *Oxford Studies in Ancient Philosophy* 12 (1994): 63-64. I elaborated on the notion of the relationship between the Forms and the particulars that participate in them in "An Excursion into Mysticism: Plato and Ibn al-ʿArabī on the Knowledge of the Relationship between the Sensible Forms and the Intelligible Forms," *American Catholic Philosophical Quarterly*, 77 (2003): 497–517.

9. PK, 362.

10. Naomi Reshotko, "A Bastard Kind of Reasoning: The Argument From The Sciences and the Introduction of the Receptacle in Plato's *Timaeus*," *History of Philosophy Quarterly* 14 (1997): 121–137.

11. Ibid., 123.

12. Ibid.

13. TCD, *Timaeus,* 28b.

14. In the previous chapter I indicated that for Ibn al-ʿArabī, being (*wujūd*) is *finding*. I also pointed out that according to him, God cannot *be found*, in the sense that his Being cannot be unqualifiedly identified with a finite form of existence. Plato expresses the same thought here. For by saying that God cannot be found, he means that God cannot be known as confined within the limits of existence. He clarifies his meaning further by saying that even if we find God, we will not be able to communicate our finding to others, meaning that even if God can be found, that is, can be identified with being, His Being is the kind of Being that transcends (being) itself, which precludes all possibility of limiting Him by rational thought.

15. TCD, *Timaeus,* 19 a.

16. Ibid., 48 e.

17. Ibid., 49 c, d, e.

18. Ibid., 50 b 6 c 5.

19. Ibid., 52b: 2–4. "Spurious" is the translation of the Greek *nothos*, which is rendered by Reshotko, following Liddel and Scott's *A Greek-English Lexicon,* as "bastard."

20. Reshotko, "A Bastard Kind of Reasoning," 132. Reshotko concludes her article with an interesting statement: "Plato's statement that the Receptacle is introduced through a bastard sort of reasoning should not be taken as a negative statement concerning what we ultimately find in Plato's ontology. Plato is simply confirming his conviction that, when we do metaphysics, we don't have the luxury of discovering a priori or necessary truths. . . . When we do metaphysics, we risk everything. We cannot do metaphysics without taking the chance that we are dead wrong as we somehow . . . venture into completely unchartered territory—territory where assuming the existence of a legitimate compass is obviously and necessarily assuming far too much from the outset, and threatens to get us further lost rather than help us find our way." Ibid., 134–135. At Ibn Rushd's funeral Ibn al-ʿArabī uttered the following words: "Ah! how I wish I knew whether his hopes have been fulfilled." Years latter he expressed the same desire for knowledge in the following words: "Ah! To know if *they* know what heart they have possessed! How my heart would like to know what mountain paths *they* have taken." Corbin, *Creative Imagination*, 44, 140. In both situations, Ibn al-ʿArabī had but this idea in mind: When we do metaphysics we risk everything. We cannot expect that they (Lords, *a priori* truths) be introduced to us as a given. When *Sophia* answered Ibn al-ʿArabī's second wishful desire for knowledge she was only confirming this truth. In my view,

the lesson that we can learn from both Plato and Ibn al-ʿArabī in this respect is that knowledge is a matter of making or creating rather than reflecting or mere verifying. Therefore, the ambiguity involved in acquiring metaphysical knowledge should not be considered, as it has been in modern philosophical thought, as a defect or as something that we should extricate from our system of knowledge, but rather as something intrinsic to existence and knowledge.

21. F, 3, 397: 19.
22. F, 2, 47: 29-30.
23. SD, 58; F, 2, 682: 23–24.
24. F, 2, 671: 7.
25. For a discussion of this subject see Masataka Takeshita, "Encompassing Circles," 246.
26. F, 1, 253: 27–28. It is worth mentioning that Ibn al-ʿArabī is responding here to the same argument introduced by the theologians (he mentions Imām al-Ḥaramayn and Ibn al-Khatīb) against the existence of the infinity of relations, to which Ibn Sīnā responded by introducing his absolute concept of relation. See discussion in chapter 5.
27. F, 1, 119: 3–9; SPK, 136–137.
28. Ibn al-ʿArabī, *Inshā' al-Dawā'ir*, trans. Paul B. Fenton and Maurice Gloton as "The Book of the Description of the Encompassing Circles," in *Muḥyiddīn Ibn ʿArabī: A Commemorative Volume*, ed. Stephen Hirtenstein and Michael Tiernan (Rockport, Mass.: Element, 1993), 24–27. As Masataka Takeshita explains, the Third Thing as Primordial Matter can be interpreted as the antemundane matter from which God made the cosmos, or as supramundane or intelligible matter, which refers to God's undifferentiated knowledge of Himself. See "Encompassing Circles," 249.
29. ʿAbd al Razzāq Kāshānī, *Sharḥ Fuṣūṣ al-Ḥikam* (Cairo: al-Maṭbaʿa al-Maymūniyya, 1904), 239.
30. See Naṣr Ḥāmid Abū Zayd, *Falsafat al-Ta'wīl*, 78.
31. Kāshānī, *Sharḥ al-Fuṣūṣ*, 12.
32. SPK, 59.
33. Paul B. Fenton and Maurice Gloton, "The Book of the Description of the Encompassing Circles," 24.
34. Jammer, *The Philosophy of Quantum Mechanics*, 106.
35. As John T. Little explains, Ibn al-ʿArabī does not understand the Oneness of Being (*waḥdat al-wujūd*) in terms of passive existence. The term Being (*wujūd*) has for him the meanings of "to be found" and "finding." Since the Arabic *wajada* has two connotations, one pertaining to perception (finding) and the other pertaining to existence (found), *waḥdat al-wujūd* should be rendered as the Oneness of Being-Perception. John T. Little, "al-Insān al-Kāmil: The Perfect Man According to Ibn al-ʿArabī," *Muslim World* 77 (1987): 47. It is worth mentioning that the expression *waḥdat al-wujūd* is not to be found in Ibn al-ʿArabī's writings, and that it was a later reference by his followers to his metaphysical teaching.
36. F, 4, 107: 18–19.
37. F, 2, 633: 11–14.
38. Kāshānī, *Sharḥ al-Fuṣūṣ*, 12.
39. SPK, 63. Indeed one might argue (as W. T. Stace did) that absolute ineffability amounts to the total removal of the object of thought from our consciousness. See discussion in

C. J. Arthur, "Ineffability and Intelligibility: Towards an Understanding of the Radical Unlikeness of Religious Experience," *Philosophy of Religion* 20 (1986): 115. The problem of the relationship between ineffability and intelligibility is very complex and treating it in connection with Ibn al-ʿArabī's thought deserves an independent study. However, I have tried in this work to emphasize the paradoxicality intrinsic to Ibn al-ʿArabī's position regarding this subject.

40. SD, 169. F, 2, 289: 25–27.

41. Kāshānī, *Sharḥ al-Fuṣūṣ*, 47.

42. SD, 169. F, 2, 289: 28.

43. SD, 169, emphasis added; F, 2, 289: 29–33, 290: 1–2.

44. F, 3, 81: 33–35.

45. In Zen Buddhism this predicament is introduced by means of examples such as the following: "Kyogan (Hsiang-yen) said: 'Suppose a man climbing up a tree takes hold of a branch by his teeth, and his whole body is thus suspended. His hands are not holding anything and his feet are off the ground. Now another man comes along and asks the man in the tree as to the fundamental principle of Buddhism. If the man in the tree does not answer, he is neglecting the questioner; but if he tries to answer he will lose his life; how can he get out of his predicament?" Daisetz.T. Suzuki, *Zen Buddhism* (New York: Grove Weidenfeld 1964), 70. See discussion of the connection between silence and the mystical experience in James H. Austin, *Zen and the Brain: Toward an Understanding of Meditation and Consciousness* (Cambridge, Mass.: The MIT Press, 1998), 633.

46. F, 2, 290: 5–13.

47. The phrase *al-Insān al-Kāmil* (the Perfect Man) occurs for the first time in Ibn al-ʿArabī's *Fuṣūṣ al-Ḥikam*. The expression was employed by Ṣūfīs to denote the type of theosophist who has realized an essential oneness with God. Abū Yazīd al-Bisṭāmī (d. 874) speaks of the "perfect and complete" (*al-kāmil al-tāmm*), who passes away (*faniya*) from the divine names with which he has been invested to dwell in complete unity with God. The Perfect Man constitutes the central theme of ʿAbd al-Karīm al-Jīlī's work *al-Insān al-Kāmil fī Maʿrifat al-Awā'il wa-l-Awākhir*. See, *Shorter Encyclopaedia of Islam*, 170. See also Suʿād al-Ḥakīm, *al-Muʿjam al-Ṣūfī*, 158–163.

Chapter 7. The Perfect Man: The Epistemological Aspect of the Third Thing

1. SD, 172.

2. SD, 21. Chittick notes that the scholars of the canonical tradition consider this saying a forgery. He also notes that Ibn al-ʿArabī was aware of this, and that he claimed that the soundness of this tradition is established through unveiling, and not by way of transmission (*naql*). SPK, 14.

3. F, 2, 43: 34–35.

4. F, 4, 301: 15.

5. F, 4, 301: 16.

6. I have elaborated on Ibn al-ʿArabī's treatment of the subject of love in chapter 178 of the *Futūḥāt*, comparing it with Plato's treatment of the same subject in *Phaedo*, *Symposium* and *Republic*. I have attempted to show that according to both thinkers, love's

object is a nonexistent thing and that, therefore, love is not subject to finalized rational definition. See Salmān Bashier, "Plato and Ibn al-ʿArabī on Love," *Transcendent Philosophy* 4 (2003): 89–109.

7. F, 2, 327.

8. SD, 21–22. F, 2, 327: 9–13.

9. F, 2, 327: 15–20.

10. F, 2, 327: 27–28.

11. F, 2, 329: 21.

12. F, 2, 329: 22.

13. A process that reminds us of the story of Ḥayy in Ibn Ṭufayl's *Ḥayy Ibn Yaqẓān* [*Son of the Wakeful*], a story which resembles the history of the progressive development of the human soul from the state of animality to the highest level of spiritual achievement. Ḥayy's development is schematized in seven stages. In each stage the soul has a way of life and a method of inquiry affected by both its natural environment and its spiritual needs. Each stage culminates in a higher level of spiritual achievement. The soul's development culminates in the highest form of mystical knowledge that can be seen as a synthesis of the sense perceptual and the rational forms of knowledge. See Lenn Evan Goodman, Ibn Ṭufayl's *Ḥayy Ibn Yaqẓān* (New York: Twayne, 1972), 3–5.

14. According to Sahl at-Tustarī, a prominent *Ṣūfī* figure, the Day of the Covenant took place in Man's preexistence, which preceded his phenomenal existence. On the Day of the Covenant Man professed God's Oneness (*tawḥīd*), negating the affirmation of his own self. Man expressed his profession of God's Oneness by confessing God's Lordship (*rubūbiyya*), and his own being a servant (*ʿabd*) of His Lord. Gerhard Böwering, *The Mystical Vision of Existence in Classical Islam: The Qur'ānic Hermeneutics of the Ṣūfī Sahl at-Tustarī* (New York: Walter de Gruyter, 1979), 146.

15. F, 2, 331: 9–21.

16. SD, 249. F, 3, 398: 16–18.

17. *The Bezels of Wisdom*, trans. Austin, 56.

18. Izutsu, *Ṣūfīsm and Taoism,* 232.

19. Corbin, *Creative Imagination*, 314.

20. ʿAlī, *The Meanings*, 75–78.

21. Ibid., 314, n. 898.

22. F, 2, 278: 26–27. In this chapter (167), entitled "The Alchemy of Happiness," Ibn al-ʿArabī introduces one of his two ascension (*miʿrāj*) narratives in the *Futūḥāt.* Two persons, a follower of divine revelation (*tābiʿ Muḥammadī*) and a possessor of consideration (*sāḥib naẓar*) depart from the Elemental World in their quest for knowledge. They pass through the First Heaven in which they visit Adam; the Second Heaven in which they visit Jesus and Yaḥyā (John the Baptist); the Third Heaven in which they visit Joseph; the Fourth Heaven in which they visit Idrīs; the Fifth Heaven in which they visit Aaron; the Sixth Heaven in which they visit Moses and the Seventh Heaven (the Temple of the Heart), in which they visit Abraham. In each of these Heavens the Muḥammadan follower is granted divine knowledge, while the possessor of consideration is denied this knowledge. In the Seventh Heaven, the prophet Abraham does not even recognize the possessor of consideration. Finally, the Muḥammadan follower continues to the last station of the journey, the Lotus of the Limit (*Sidrat al-Muntahā*), while the possessor of consideration is forbidden from entering this Station. In chapter 367 of the

Futūḥāt, Ibn al-ʿArabī presents this journey through the Seven Heavens to the Lotus of the Limit as his own *miʿrāj*, in which he receives Culminating Revelation. James Winston Morris provided a translation and a commentary on Ibn al-ʿArabī's *miʿrāj*, as it is narrated in chapter 367. See James Winston Morris, "The Spiritual Ascension: Ibn ʿArabī and the Miʿrāj," *Journal of the American Oriental Society* 107 (1987): 629–652; and 108 (1987): 101–119.
23. F, 2, 278: 28–31. *Kaʿba* symbolizing the center of the world and the point connected to all points of all directions but to no specific direction. Scholars provide different translations of the terms *ʿaql* and *fikr*. Chittick renders *ʿaql* as "reason" and *fikr* as "reflection." Suʿād al-Ḥakīm renders *ʿaql* as "intellect" and *fikr* as "reason." Despite the differences in translation, scholars agree that Ibn al-ʿArabī does not reject *ʿaql* as such, but only its uncritical reliance on the faculty of *fikr*. For example, Suʿād al-Ḥakīm writes, "We ask why Ibn ʿArabī thinks that reason does not reach to the knowledge of God, and why he prevents it from using its mechanisms in the study of the Qur'ān, as the theologians have done. This is due, in my opinion, to two reasons which I put forward here. The first is that intellect to Ibn ʿArabī is a colossal force without limits, infinitely receptive to instruction, whatever instruction we give it, so long as that reason does not present obstacles, with its rules and limited logic. . . . Ibn ʿArabī's texts show us that intellect is not a chain, that it receives knowledge from instruction infinitely, and that it is reason which fetters it." Suʿād al-Ḥakīm, "Knowledge of God in Ibn ʿArabī," in *Muḥyyiddīn Ibn ʿArabī: A Commemorative Volume*, 269.
24. F, 2, 125: 34–35.
25. James Winston Morris draws our attention to a decisive distinction that Ibn al-ʿArabī draws between the individual's self-deluding imagination (*takhayyul*) and the Divine Imagination (*khayāl*), underlying all creation. He emphasizes that a proper understanding of the various dimensions of Ibn al-ʿArabī's teachings depends on acknowledging this distinction and the need for human beings to conform to the forms of Divine Imagination rather than following their self-imposed images. James Winston Morris, "Seeking God's Face': Ibn ʿArabī on Right Action and Theophanic Vision, Part 2," *Journal of the Muḥyiddīn Ibn ʿArabī Society* 17, (1995): 23.
26. F, 2, 126: 1–6.
27. Ibid.: 6–9.
28. Martin Heidegger, *On The Way to Language*, trans. Peter D. Hertz (New York: Harper and Row, 1971), 176.
29. Martin Heidegger, *Early Greek Thinking*, trans. David E. Krell and Frank A. Capuzzi (New York: Harper and Row, 1975), 64. The passage is quoted from Carl J. Kalwaitis, "The Origin of Paradox and its Relations to Philosophical Reflection," *Philosophy Today* 42 (1998): 371.
30. SD, 83, emphasis added; F, 3, 550: 4–7.
31. SPK, 379, emphasis added; F, 3, 105: 13–15, 19–21.
32. F, 3, 495: 31.
33. SPK, 29.
34. Ibid.
35. Izutsu, *Sūfism and Taoism*, 233.
36. Ibid., 254. Izutsu's translation is from Ibn al-ʿArabī's *Fuṣūṣ al-Ḥikam*, ed. ʿAffīfī, 113.
37. F, 2, 4: 33.

38. Stephen Hirtenstein, "Aspects of Time and Light," *Journal of the Muḥyiddīn Ibn ʿArabī Society* 6 (1986): 46–47, emphasis added.
39. Paul B. Fenton and Maurice Gloton, "The Book of the Description of the Encompassing Circles," 24.
40. F, 3, 287: 3.
41. Ibn al-ʿArabī says in the chapter entitled "The Wisdom of Rapturous Love in The Word of Abraham," in *The Bezels of Wisdom*, trans. Austin, 95, "I also know Him and perceive Him. Where then is His Self-sufficiency? Since I help Him and grant Him Bliss. It is for this that the Reality created me. For I give content to His knowledge and manifest Him. Thus did the message come, its meaning fulfilled in me."
42. *Fuṣūṣ al-Ḥikam*, ed. ʿAffīfī, 73. What a striking reminder of what Carl Jung says in *Aion*. See discussion in Donald H. Mayo, *Jung and Aesthetic Experience: the Unconscious as Source of Artistic Inspiration*, New Studies in Aesthetics, vol. 25 (New York: Peter Lang, 1995), 69.
43. For a full discussion of this subject see F, 2, chapters 32 and 33, especially: 216–220.
44. F, 2, 212: 1–7.
45. See chapter 7: "The Way," in Izutsu's *Ṣūfism and Taoism*, 375–397.
46. Izutsu, *Ṣūfism and Taoism*, 377.
47. Ibid., 378–379. I removed the parenthesis from the citation.
48. Ibid., 379.
49. Chittick points out that Ibn al-ʿArabī cites this verse more than any other to illustrate the radical ambiguity of existence. The verse was revealed after the battle of Badr, when the Prophet threw a handful of sand in the face of his enemies. SPK, 113. Notice the similarity between these words and the words of Khaḍir in his encounter with Moses: "I did it not of my own accord" (Q 16: 82).
50. F, 3, 525: 11–16.
51. The Word of the Real is the all-comprehensive object of His knowledge. It is the storehouse of all the immutable entities of all the possible things of the cosmos.
52. The Perfect Man is the Logos, or the Word which includes all other Logoi or words. The Logos is the active principle through which all divine knowledge is transmitted to all prophets. In virtue of being the Logos, the Perfect Man manifests the perfection of the Reality of Realities synthetically, while the world, which consists of the words, that is, the possible things that emerge instant by instant, manifests the perfection of the Reality of Realities analytically. See ʿAffīfī, *The Mystical Philosophy of Muḥyiddīn Ibnul ʿArabī*, 69.
53. John T. Little, "Al-Insān al-Kāmil," 49.
54. F, 2, 212: 5.
55. F, 2, 69: 9–16.
56. F, 2, 672: 16–18, 21–23.

Chapter 8. The Limit Situation

1. Some of the vocabulary employed in the translation, especially in passages in italics, is Chittick's translation. For a complete and more precise interpretation of the chapter please refer to SPK, 42–44.

2. Q 31: 27 reads, "And if all the trees on earth were pens and the Oceans behind it to add to its (supply), yet would not the Words of Allah be exhausted (in the writing): for Allah is exalted in power, full of Wisdom." ʿAlī, *The Meaning*, 1041.
3. Q 16: 40 reads, "For to anything which We have willed, We but say the Word, 'Be', and it is." ʿAlī, *The Meaning,* 647. In his interpretation of the verse, ʿAlī says that God's word is in itself the Deed meaning that there is no interposition of time between his Will and its consequences.
4. The property through which the ruling properties of the Lord and the vassal is determined is not affirmed through the Lord or the vassal alone but only through both. See discussion of the concept of relationship in chapter 5.
5. Compare with F, 2, 476: 29–32.
6. F, 4, 65: 24–35, 66: 1–22.
7. SPK, 128.
8. Ibid.
9. F, 3, 524: 27–31.
10. F, 3, 525: 1.
11. F, 4, 167: 1.
12. SD, 70; F, 4, 167: 7–9.
13. SD, 70.
14. SD, 71. F, 4, 167: 8–12, 22–23. I applied the term *being* whenever Chittick applied *wujūd.*
15. SPK, 155–156; F, 2, 619: 34–35, 620: 1.
16. SPK, 163. The following poetry lines from chapter 50 of the *Futūḥāt* are quoted from Avraham Abadi, "The Determinism Implicit to Change," in *Muḥyiddīn Ibn ʿArabī: A Commemorative Volume*, 142.

> He who claims to know that God is his Creator while not being perplexed,
> this is the evidence of his ignorance.
> None but God may know God, so take note in order that your facing will not
> be marred by heedlessness.
> The inability to comprehend perception is in itself a gnosis, and this is the
> conviction which prevails upon the intelligent.
> For He is the Divinity whose praises cannot be enumerated, He who is the
> Incomparable, to whom similitudes do not apply.

17. Nicholas of Cusa, *On Learned Ignorance*, trans. Jasper Hopkins (Minneapolis: The Arthur J. Banning Press, 1981), 52–53, emphasis added. Elizabeth Brient emphasizes the difference between this notion of our inability to know anything exhaustively expressed in the thought of thinkers such as Cusanus and the negative result arrived at by the purely skeptical position. She says that this position "forms the basis for an understanding of the project of knowledge acquisition as itself unbounded." See Elizabeth Brient, "Transitions to a Modern Cosmology: Meister Eckhart and Nicholas of Cusa on the Intensive Infinite." *Journal of the History of Philosophy* 37 (1999): 575–100. For more on Cusanus's conception of the infinitude of knowledge see Donald F. Duclow, "Pseudo-Dionysius, John Scotus Eriugena, Nicholas of Cusa: An Approach to the Hermeneutic of the Divine Names," *International Philosophical Quarterly* 12 (1972): 3.

18. Nicholas of Cusa, *On the Pursuit of Wisdom* in *Metaphysical Speculations*, trans. Jasper Hopkins (Minneapolis: The Arthur J. Banninig Press, 1998), 177–178.
19. See SD, 67.
20. *On The Pursuit of Wisdom*, 179.
21. Cusanus believes that among all thinkers only Plato, who "saw somewhat more clearly than did the other philosophers, said that he would be surprised if God were to be found—and would be even more surprised if, having been found, God could be made manifest." Ibid., 178. Cusanus is referring to the passage from Plato's *Timaeus* 28b.
22. Andrey V. Smirnov, "Nicholas of Cusa and Ibn ʿArabī: Two Philosophies of Mysticism," *Philosophy East and West* 43 (1993): 65–85.
23. Ibid., 66.
24. Ibid., 74.
25. F, 2, 476: 29–32. In my view, the notion that reality is both finite and infinite, not from two different perspectives but absolutely, is what constitutes the essence of the meaning of Ibn al-ʿArabī's response to Ibn Rushd's inquiry in their first encounter. Ibn Rushd asked Ibn al-ʿArabī whether the method of divine illumination accorded with rational interpretation, and his answer was "yes no," with no conjunction between the *yes* and the *no*. By joining the *no* to the *yes* without using the word *and*, Ibn al-ʿArabī was emphasizing the paradoxical nature of the combination of the opposites, a paradoxicality that posed a problem to Ibn Rushd's view of complementarity.
26. F, 3, 350: 20–23.
27. James Winston Morris, "The Spiritual Ascension: Ibn ʿArabī and the Miʿrāj: Part 2," *Journal of the American Oriental Society*, 108 (1988): 70–71. F, 3, 350: 29–32.
28. SD, 298. F, 3, 458: 6–9.
29. Murata, *The Tao of Islam*, 198.

Conclusions

1. See description of the incident in Addas, *The Quest*, 108.
2. F, 2, 523. It is worth noting that part of the criticism comes from persons who seek to defend Ibn al-ʿArabī so eagerly that they distance him from the philosophers only because philosophers were considered in orthodox Islam as not very much favored. Hence it seems suitable and ready handed for them to use all the material available in order to perform such a task.
3. Something that Chittick has warned about on several occasions. See, for example, SD, ix–xi.
4. Hence, I think that it is not by accident that Izutsu Toshihiko, the author of the comparative study *Ṣūfism and Taoism* chose to dedicate a separate part of his work to Ibn al-ʿArabī and then a separate part to Chinese Taoist philosophers.
5. And intentionally unsystematic at that. See discussion in James W. Morris, "Ibn ʿArabī's 'Esoterism': The Problem of Spiritual Authority," *Studia Islamica* 71 (1990): 42. Concerning some of the difficulties that confront the reader of the *Futūḥāt* and the preparation that its author requires from his readers, see James Winston Morris, "How to Study the *Futūḥāt*, Ibn ʿArabī's Own Advice," in *Muḥyiddīn Ibn ʿArabī: A Commemorative Volume*, ed. Stephen Hirtenstein and Michael Tiernan, 73–74. For more on some of the

methodological problems related to the *Futūḥāt* see Michel Chodkiewicks, "The *Futūḥāt Makkīyya* and Its Commentators: Some Unresolved Enigmas," in *The Heritage of Ṣūfism*, ed. Leonard Lewishon, 3 vols. (Oxford: One World, 1999), 2: 220–232.
6. This passage, to which Peter Von Sivers kindly drew my attention, is cited from *Textual Sources for the Study of Zoroastrianism*, ed. and trans. Mary Boyce, (Manchester: Manchester University Press, 1984), 45–46.
7. This is very much the case with Ibn al-ʿArabī's main example of the barzakh as the empty entity that separates between the sweet and the salt waters.
8. John D. Turner (trans.), "A Valentinian Exposition (XI, 2), with On The Anointing, On Baptism A and B, and On The Eucharist A and B," in *The Nag Hammadi Library in English*, ed. James M. Robinson (London: Harper and Row, 1978), 436–437.
9. TCD, *Parmenides,* 156, d–e.
10. See Allen R. Utke, "The Rainbow: A Universal Timeless 'Pointer' Toward Ultimate Reality and Meaning," *Ultimate Reality and Meaning* 19 (1996): 25.

Bibliography

Abadi, Avraham. "The Determinism Implicit to Change." In *Muḥyiddīn Ibn ʿArabī: A Commemorative Volume*, ed. Stephen Hirtenstein and Michael Tiernan, 142–162. Rockport, Massachusetts: Element, 1993.

Abrahamov, Binyamin. *Islamic Theology: Traditionalism and Rationalism*. Edinburgh: Edinburgh University Press, 1998.

Abū Zayd, Naṣr Ḥ. *Falsafat al-Ta'wīl*. Beirūt: Dār al-Tanwīr li'l-Ṭibāʿa wa-al-Nashr, 1993.

Addas, Claude. *The Quest for the Red Sulphur: The Life of Ibn ʿArabī*. Trans. Peter Kingsley. Cambridge: Islamic Texts Society, 1993.

Affīfī, Abū ʿIlā. "al-Aʿyān al-Thābita fī Madhab Ibn ʿArabī wa-al-Maʿdūmāt fī Madhab al-Muʿtazila." In *al-Kitāb al-Tidhkārī: Muḥyiddīn Ibn Arabī fī al-Dhikra al-Mi'awiyya al-Thāmina li-Miladih*, ed. Ibrāhīm Bayūmī Madhkūr, 209–220. Cairo: Dār al-Kitāb al-ʿArabī li'l Ṭibāʿa wa-al-Nashr, 1969.

———. *The Mystical Philosophy of Muḥyiddīn-Ibnul ʿArabī*. Lahore, Pakistan: Sh. Muḥammad Ashraf, 1964.

Afnan, Ruhi M. *Zoroaster's Influence on Greek Thought*. New York: Philosophical Library, 1965.

Afnan, Soheil. *Avicenna: His Life and Works*. London: George Allen and Unwin, 1958.

Akintola, Ishaq. "Creation Theories and the Qur'ān." *Islamic Quarterly* 36 (1992): 193–202.

Alī, ʿAbdullah Y. *The Meaning of the Holy Qur'ān*. 6th ed. Beltsville, Md.: Amana Corporation, 1989.

Alston, William P. *Perceiving God: The Epistemology of Religious Experience*. Ithaca and London: Cornell University Press, 1991.

Alwasī, Ḥusām. *Ḥiwār bayna al-Falāsifa wa-al-Mutakallimīn*. Baghdad: Maṭbaʿat al-Zahrā', 1967.

Aristotle. *Aristotle's Metaphysics*. Trans. Hippocrates G. Apostle. Bloomington: Indiana University Press, 1973.

———. *The Basic Works of Aristotle*. Ed. Richard McKeon. New York: Random House, 1941.

Arthur, C. J. "Ineffability and Intelligibility: Towards an Understanding of the Radical Unlikeness of Religious Experience." *Philosophy of Religion* 20 (1986): 109–129.

Austin, James H. *Zen and the Brain: Toward an Understanding of Meditation and Consciousness*. Cambridge, Mass.: MIT, 1998.

Bashear, Sulimān. "Muslim Apocalypses and the Hour: A Case-Study in Traditional Reinterpretation." *Israel Oriental Studies* 13 (1993): 75–99.

Bashier, Salmān H. "An Excursion into Mysticism: Plato and Ibn al-ʿArabī on the Knowledge of the Relationship between the Sensible Forms and the Intelligible Forms." *American Catholic Philosophical Quarterly* 77 (2003): 497–517.

———. "Plato and Ibn al-ʿArabi on Love." *Transcendent Philosophy* 4 (2003): 89–109.

———. "Plato and Ibn ʿArabī on Skepticism." *Journal of the Muḥyīddīn Ibn ʿArabi Society* 30 (2001): 19–35.

———. "Proofs for the Existence and the Unity of God in Greek and Islamic Thought, with an Emphasis on Ibn al-ʿArabī's Barzakh and Its Role in Proving God's Existence and Unity." *Transcendent Philosophy* 2 (2001): 29–51.

Battye, Nicholas. "Khiḍr in the Opus of Jung: The Teaching of Surrender." In *Jung and the Monotheisms Judaism, Christianity, and Islam*. Ed. Joel Ryce Menuhin. London: Routledge, 1994. 166–191.

Böwering, Gerhard. "Ibn al-ʿArabī's Concept of Time." In *God is Beautiful and He Loves Beauty*, ed. A. Giese and J. C. Burgel, 71–91. New York: Peter Lang, 1994.

———. *The Mystical Vision of Existence in Classical Islam: The Qur'ānic Hermeneutics of the Ṣūfī Sahl at-Tustarī*. New York: Walter de Gruyter, 1980.

Boyce, Mary, ed. and trans. *Textual Sources for the Study of Zoroastrianism*. Manchester: Manchester University Press, 1984.

Brandom, Robert B. Introduction to *Rorty and his Critics*, ed. Robert B. Brandom, ix–xx. Malden, Mass.: Blackwell, 2000.

Brient, Elizabeth. "Transitions to a Modern Cosmology: Meister Eckhart and Nicholas of Cusa on the Intensive Infinite." *Journal of the History of Philosophy* 37 (1999): 575–600.

Bunge, Mario. "Seven Desiderata for Rationality." In *Rationality: The Critical View*, ed. Joseph Agassi and Ian Charles Jarvie, 5–15. Boston: Martinus Nijhoff, 1987.

Burrell, David B. "Creation and Emanation: Two Paradigms of Reason." In *God and Creation: An Ecumenical Symposium*, ed. David B. Burrell, and Bernard McGinnis, 27–37. Notre Dame, Ind.: University of Notre Dame Press, 1990.

———. *Freedom and Creation in Three Traditions*. Notre Dame, Ind.: University of Notre Dame Press, 1993.

———. *Knowing the Unknowable God: Ibn Sīnā, Maimonides, Aquinas*. Notre Dame, Ind.: Notre Dame Press, 1986.

Bussanich, John. "Plotinus's Metaphysics of the One." In *The Cambridge Companion to Plotinus*, ed. Lloyd P. Gerson, 38–65. Cambridge: Cambridge University Press, 1996.

Carter, Michael G. "Infinity and Lies in Medieval Islam." In *Philosophy and Arts in the Islamic World*, Orientalia Lovaniensia Analecta, ed. U. Vermeulen and D. De Smet, vol. 87, 233–242. Leuven: Uitgeverij Peeters, 1998.

Chittick, William C. "Death and the World of Imagination." *Muslim World* 78 (1988): 51–82.

———. *The Heart of Islamic Philosophy: The Quest for Self-Knowledge in the Teachings of Afdal al-Dīn Kāshānī*. Oxford: Oxford University Press, 2001.

———. *Imaginal Worlds: Ibn al-ʿArabī and the Problem of Religious Diversity*. Albany: State University of New York Press, 1994.

———. "Mysticism vs. Philosophy in Earlier Islamic History: The al-Ṭūsī, al-Qūnawī Correspondence." *Religious Studies* 17 (1981): 87–104.

———. "Ṣadr al-Dīn Qūnawī on the Oneness of Being." *International Philosophical Quarterly* 21 (1981): 171–184.

———. *The Self-Disclosure of God: Principles of Ibn al-ʿArabī's Cosmology*. Albany: State University of New York Press, 1998.

———. "Spectrums of Islamic Thought: Saʿīd al-Dīn Farghānī on The Implication of Oneness and Manyness." In *The Heritage of Ṣūfīsm*, ed. Leonard Lewisohn. 3 vols. 2: 203–217. (Oxford: One World, 1999).

———. *The Ṣūfī Path of Knowledge*. Albany: State University of New York Press, 1989.

Chodkiewicz, Michel. *An Ocean without Shore: Ibn ʿArabī the Book and the Law*. Trans. David Streight. Albany: State University of New York Press, 1993.

———. *Seal of the Saints, Prophethood and Sainthood in the Doctrine of Ibn ʿArabī*. Trans. Liadain Sherrard. Cambridge, England: The Islamic Texts Society, 1993.

———. "The *Futūḥāt Makkīyya* and its Commentators: Some Unresolved Enigmas." In *The Heritage of Ṣūfīsm*, ed. Leonard Lewishon. 3 vols. 2: 220–232. Oxford: One World, 1999.

Corbin, Henry. *Creative Imagination in the Ṣūfīsm of Ibn ʿArabī*. Trans. Ralph Mannheim. Princeton, N.J.: Princeton University Press, 1969.

———. *Spiritual Body and Celestial Earth: From Mazdean Iran to Shiʿite Iran*. Princeton, N.J.: Princeton University Press, 1977.

Cornford, Macdonald F. *Plato and Parmenides: Parmenides' Way of Truth and Plato's Parmenides*. London: Routledge and Kegan Paul, 1951.

Cunningham, Francis A. "Averroes vs. Avicenna on Being." *New Scholasticism Quarterly Review of Philosophy* 48 (1974): 185–218.

Dabashi, Hamid. "The Ṣūfī Doctrine of 'the Perfect Man' and a View of the Hierarchical Structure of Islamic Culture." *Islamic Quarterly* 30 (1986): 118–130.

Devereux, Daniel T. "Separation and Immanence in Plato's Theory of Forms." *Oxford Studies in Ancient Philosophy* 12 (1994): 63–90.

Duclow, Donald F. "Pseudo-Dionysius, John Scotus Eriugena, Nicholas of Cusa: An approach to the Hermeneutic of the Divine Names." *International Philosophical Quarterly* 12 (1972): 260–278.

Eklund, Ragnar. *Life between Death and Resurrection According to Islam*. Uppsala: Almqvist and Boktryckeri, 1941.

Elmore, Gerald T. *Islamic Sainthood in the Fullness of Time: Ibn al-ʿArabī's Book of the Fabulous Gryphon*. Leiden: E. J. Brill, 1999.

Fakhry, Mājid. "The 'Antinomy' of the Eternity of the World in Averroes, Maimonides and Aquinas." *Le muséon* (1953): 139–155.

———. "The Classical Islamic Arguments for the Existence of God." *The Muslim World* 47 (1957): 133–145.

———. *History of Islamic Philosophy*. New York: Columbia University Press, 1983.

———. *Islamic Occasionalism and Its Critique by Averroes and Aquinas*. London: George Allen and Unwin, 1958.

———. "The Ontological Argument in the Arabic Tradition." *Studia Islamica* 64 (1986): 5–17.

———. "Rationality in Islamic Philosophy." In *Rationality in Question: On Eastern and Western Views of Rationality*, ed. Shlomo Biderman and Ben-Ami Scharfstein, 504–514. Leiden: E. J. Brill, 1989.

Feldman, Seymour. "Philoponus on the Metaphysics of Creation." In *A Straight Path: Studies in Medieval Philosophy and Culture*, ed. Ruth Link-Salinger, 74–85. Washington: The Catholic University of America Press, 1988.

Frank, Richard M. *al-Ghazālī and the Ash'arite School*. Durham, N.C.: Duke University Press, 1994.

———. "Kalām and Philosophy: A Perspective from One Problem." In *Islamic Philosophical Theology*, ed. Parviz Morewedge, 71–95. Albany: State University of New York Press, 1979.

Garber, Daniel. "Rationalism." In *The Cambridge Dictionary of Philosophy*, ed. Robert Audi, 673–674. Cambridge: Cambridge University Press, 1995.

Genequand, Charles. *Ibn Rushd's Metaphysics: A Translation with Introduction of Ibn Rushd's Commentary on Aristotle's Metaphysics, Book Lam*. Leiden: E. J. Brill, 1984.

———. "Metaphysics." In *History of Islamic Philosophy: Part II*. Routledge History of World Philosophies. Vol. 1, ed. Seyyed Hossein Nasr and Oliver Leaman, 783–801. London: Routledge, 1996.

Ghazālī, Abū Ḥāmid. *The Incoherence of the Philosophers*. Trans. Michael E. Marmura. Provo, Utah: Brigham Young University Press, 1997.

———. *Munqidh Min al-Ḍalāl* . Ed. Jamīl Salība and Kāmil ʿAyād. Dimashq: Maṭbaʿat Jāmiʿat Dimashq, 1960.

———. *The Niche of Lights*. Trans. David Bushman. Provo, Utah: Brigham Young University Press, 1998.

Ghorāb, Maḥmoud. "Ibn al-ʿArabī Amidst Religion and Schools of Thought." In *Muḥyiddīn Ibn ʿArabī: A Commemorative Volume*, ed. Stephen Hirtenstein and Michael Tiernan, 199–229. Rockport, Mass.: Element, 1993.

Gilson, Etienne. *Being and Some Philosophers*. Toronto: Pontifical Institute of Mediaeval Studies, 1949.

Goodman, Lenn E. *Avicenna*. London: Routledge, 1992.

———, trans. *Ibn Ṭufayl's Ḥayy Ibn Yaqẓān: A Philosophical Tale*. New York: Twayne, 1972.

———. "Three Meanings of the Idea of Creation." In *God and Creation: An Ecumenical Symposium*, ed. David B. Burrell and Bernard McGinnis, 85–113. Notre Dame, Ind.: University of Notre Dame Press, 1990.

———. "Time in Islam." *Asian Philosophy* 2 (1992): 3–19.

Gracia, Jorge E. "Interpretation and the Law: Averroes' Contribution to the Hermeneutics of Sacred Texts." *History of Philosophy Quarterly* 14 (1997): 139–153.

Gwynne, Rosalind W. "Al-Jubbā'ī, al-Ashʿarī and the Three Brothers: The Uses of Fiction." *Muslim World* 75 (1985): 132–161.

Habermas, Jürgen. "Richard Rorty's Pragmatic Turn." In *Rorty and his Critics*, ed. Robert B. Brandom, 30–52. Malden, Mass.: Blackwell Publishers, 2000.

Ḥakīm, Suʿād. "Knowledge of God in Ibn ʿArabī." In *Muḥyyiddīn Ibn ʿArabī: A Commemorative Volume*, ed. Stephen Hirtenstein and Michael Tiernan, 264–290. Rockport, Massachusetts: Element, 1993.

———. *al-Muʿjam al-Ṣūfī: al-Ḥikma fī Ḥudūd al-Kalima*. Beirūt: Dandara, 1991.

Haldane, John. "Scholasticism." In *The Oxford Companion to Philosophy*, ed. Ted Honderich, 802. Oxford: Oxford University Press, 1995.

Hall, Ronald. "Dialectic." In *The Encyclopedia of Philosophy*, ed. Paul Edwards. 8 vols. 2: 385–389. New York: Macmillan and Free Press.

Hardy, Paul A. "Response to Eric L. Ormsby." In *God and Creation: An Ecumenical Symposium*, ed. David B. Burrell and Bernard McGinnis, 265–275. Notre Dame, Ind.: University of Notre Dame Press, 1990.

Ḥāwī, Sāmī. *Islamic Naturalism and Mysticism: A Philosophic Study of Ibn Ṭufayl's Ḥayy Bin Yaqẓān*. Leiden: E. J. Brill, 1974.

Hegel, George W. F. *Phenomenology of Spirit*. Trans. Arnold. V. Miller. Oxford: Clarendon Press, 1977.

Hintikka, Jaakko. *Time and Necessity: Studies in Aristotle's Theory of Modality*. Oxford: Clarendon Press, 1973.

Hirtenstein, Stephen. "Aspects of Time and Light." *Journal of the Muḥyiddīn Ibn ʿArabī Society* 6 (1986): 31–49.

Honner, John. *The Description of Nature: Niels Bohr and the Philosophy of Quantum Physics*. Oxford: Clarendon Press, 1987.

Ibn ʿArabī, Muḥyiddīn. *ʿAnqāʾ Mughrib fī Maʿrifat Khatm al-Awlīyāʾ wa-Shams al-Maghrib*. Trans. Gerald T. Elmore, *Islamic Sainthood in the Fullness of Time: Ibn al-ʿArabī's Book of the Fabulous Gryphon*, Leiden: E. J. Brill, 1999.

———. *Fuṣūṣ al-Ḥikam*. Ed. Abū al-ʿIlā ʿAffīfī. Beirūt: Dār al-Kutub al-ʿArabī, 1946. Trans. R. W. J. Austin, *The Bezels of Wisdom*. New York: Paulist Press, 1981.

———. *al-Futūḥāt al-Makkiyya*. 4 vols. Cairo, 1911. Rep. Beirut: Dar Ṣādir, n. d. Rev. Ed. by O. Yahia. 14 vols. Cairo: al-Ḥayāt al-Miṣriyya al-ʿĀmma li'l-Kitāb, 1972–.

———. *Inshā' al-Dawā'ir*. Leiden: E. J. Brill, 1919. Trans. Paul B. Fenton and Maurice Gloton, "The Book of the Description of the Encompassing Circles." In *Muḥyiddīn Ibn ʿArabī: A Commemorative Volume*, ed. Stephen Hirtenstein and Michael Tiernan, 11–43. Rockport, Massachusetts: Element, 1993.

Ibn Rushd. *Faṣl al-Maqāl*. Trans. George F. Hourani. *On the Harmony of Religion and Philosophy*. London: Luzac, 1961.

———. *Kitāb al-Samāʿ al-Ṭabīʿī*. In *Rasā'il Ibn Rushd*. Maṭbaʿat Dāi'rat al-Maʿrifa al-ʿUthmāniyya, 1947.

———. *Tahāfut al-Tahāfut*. Trans. Simon Van Den Bergh. *The Incoherence of the Incoherence*. 2 vols. London: Oxford University Press, 1954.

Ibn Sīnā. *al-Ishārāt wa al-Tanbīhāt* . Ed. Solaymān Donyā. 4 vols. Cairo: Dār al-Maʿrifa, 1957.

———. *Danish Nameh*. Trans. Parviz Morewedge. *The Metaphysica of Avicenna*. London: Routledge and Kegan Paul, 1973.

———. *al-Najāt*. Ed. M. Kurdi. Cairo: Saʿadat Press, 1938.

Ibn Ṭufayl. *Ḥayy Ibn Yaqẓān : A Philosophical Tale*. Trans. with intro. by Lenn Evan Goodman. New York: Twayne Publishers, 1972.

Izutsu, Toshihiko. *Ṣūfism and Taoism: A Comparative Study of Key Philosophical Concepts*. Berkeley: University of California Press, 1983.

Jacobi, Renate. "The Khayāl Motif in Early Arabic Poetry." *Oriens* 32 (1990): 50–71.

Jammer, Max. *The Philosophy of Quantum Mechanics: The Implications in Historical Perspective*. New York: Wiley, 1974.

Janssens, Jules. "Al-Kindī's Concept of God." *Ultimate Reality and Meaning* 17 (1994): 4–16.

Jung, Carl G. "The Transcendent Function." In *Encountering Jung: Jung On Active Imagination*, ed. Joan Chodorow, 42–60. Princeton, N.J.: Princeton University Press, 1997.

Kalwaitis, Carl J. "The Origin of Paradox and Its Relations to Philosophical Reflection." *Philosophy Today* 42 (1998): 361–373.

Kant, Immanuel. *Critique of Pure Reason*. Trans. Norman Kemp Smith. London: Redwood Press, 1970.

Kāshānī, ʿAbd al-Razzāq. *Sharḥ Fuṣūṣ al-Ḥikam*. Cairo: al-Maṭbaʿa al-Maymūniyya, 1904.

Knysh, Alexander D. *Ibn ʿArabī in the Later Islamic Tradition: The Making of a Polemical Image in Medieval Islam*. Albany: State University of New York Press, 1999.

———. "'Orthodoxy' and 'Heresy' in Medieval Islam: An Essay in Reassessment." *The Muslim World* 83 (1993): 48–67.

Kogan, Barry S. *Averroes and the Metaphysics of Causation*. Albany: State University of New York Press, 1985.

———. "Eternity and Origination: Averroes' Discourse on the Manner of the World's Existence." In *Islamic Theology and Philosophy*, ed. Michael Marmura, 203–235. State University of New York press, 1984.

Leaman, Oliver. *Averroes and his Philosophy*. Oxford: Clarendon Press, 1988.

———. *An Introduction to Medieval Islamic Philosophy*. Cambridge: Cambridge University Press, 1985.

———. "Philosophy vs. Mysticism: An Islamic Controversy." In *Philosophy, Religion and the Spiritual Life*, ed. Michael McGhee, 177–187. Cambridge: Cambridge University Press, 1992.

Lings, Martin. *Symbol and Archetype: A Study of the Meaning of Existence*. Cambridge: Quinta Essentia, 1991.

Little, T. John. "al-Insān al-Kāmil: The Perfect Man According to Ibn Al-ʿArabī." *Muslim World* 77 (1987): 43–54.

Lynch, Michael P. *Truth in Context: An Essay on Pluralism and Objectivity* Cambridge, Mass.: MIT Press, 1998.

Marmura, Michael E. "Avicenna's Chapter, 'On the Relative' in the *Metaphysics* of the *Shifā*." In *Essays on Islamic Philosophy and Science*, ed. George F. Hourani, 83–99. Albany: State University of New York Press, 1975.

———. "Ghazālī's Attitude to the Secular Sciences and Logic." In *Essays on Islamic Philosophy and Science*, ed. George F. Hourani, 100–111. Albany: State University of New York Press, 1975.

———. "The Metaphysics of Efficient Causality in Avicenna." In *Islamic Theology and Philosophy*, ed. Michael Marmura, 172–187. Albany: State University of New York Press, 1984.

Martine, John B. *Indeterminacy and Intelligibility*. Albany: State University of New York Press, 1992.

Mayo, Donald H. *Jung and Aesthetic Experience: The Unconscious as Source of Artistic Inspiration*. New Studies in Aesthetics. Vol. 25. New York: Peter Lang, 1995.

Montada, Puig J. "Ibn Rushd vs. al-Ghazālī: Reconsidering of a Polemic." *Muslim World* 82 (1992): 113–131.

Morewedge, Parviz. "Philosophical Analysis and Ibn Sīnā's 'Essence-Existence' Distinction." *Journal of the American Oriental Society* 92 (1972): 425–434.

Morris, James W. "How to Study the *Futūḥāt*, Ibn ʿArabī's Own Advice." In *Muḥyiddīn Ibn ʿArabī: A Commemorative Volume*, ed. Stephen Hirtenstein and Michael Tiernan, 73–89. Rockport, Mass.: Element, 1993.

———. "Ibn ʿArabī'a 'Esotericism': The Problem of Spiritual Authority." *Studia Islamica* 71 (1990): 37–55.

———. "'Seeking God's Face: Ibn ʿArabi on Right Action and Theophanic Vision 2." *Journal of the Muḥyiddīn Ibn ʿArabī Society* 17 (1995): 1–39.

———. "The Spiritual Ascension: Ibn ʿArabī and the Miʿrāj 1." *Journal of the American Oriental Society* 107 (1987): 629–652.

———. "The Spiritual Ascension: Ibn ʿArabī and the Miʿrāj 2." *Journal of the American Oriental Society* 108 (1987): 101–119.

Murata Sachiko. *The Tao of Islam: A Sourcebook on Gender Relationships in Islamic Thought*. Albany: State University of New York Press, 1992.

Nasr, Hossein S. *Knowledge and The Sacred*. Albany: State University of New York Press, 1989.

———. *Ṣūfī Essays*. 2nd edition. Albany: State University of New York Press, 1991.

———. "Theology, Philosophy, and Spirituality." In *Islamic Spirituality: Manifestations*. 2 vols. 2: 395–446. World Spirituality, ed. Seyyed Hossein Nasr. New York: Crossroad, 1991.

Nettler, Ronald. " Ibn ʿArabī's Notion of Allah's Mercy." *Israel Oriental Society* 8 (1978): 219–229.

Netton, Ian R. *Allah Transcendent: Studies in the Structure and Semiotics of Islamic Philosophy, Theology and Cosmology*. London: Routledge, 1989.

———. "Theophany as Paradox: Ibn ʿArabī's Account of *al-Khaḍir* in his *Fuṣūṣ al-Ḥikam*." *Journal of the Muḥyiddīn Ibn ʿArabī Society* 11 (1992): 11–22.

Nicholas of Cusa. *On Learned Ignorance*. Trans. Jasper Hopkins. Minneapolis: Arthur J. Banning Press, 1981.

———. *On the Pursuit of Wisdom*. Trans. Jasper Hopkins. In *Nicholas of Cusa: Metaphysical Speculations*. Minneapolis: Arthur J. Banninig Press, 1998.

O'Shaughnessy, Thomas J. *Creation and the Teaching of the Qur'ān*. Rome: Biblical Institute Press, 1985.

Parmenides, *Fragments*. Trans. David Gallop. Toronto: University of Toronto Press, 1984.

Pines, Shlomo. *Studies in Islamic Atomism*. Ed. Tzvi Langermann. Trans. Michael Schwarz. Hebrew University, Jerusalem: Magnes Press, 1997.

Plato. *The Collected Dialogues*. Ed. Edith Hamilton and Huntington Cairns. Princeton, N.J.: Princeton University Press, 1994.

Priest, Graham. *Beyond the Limits of Thought*. Cambridge: Cambridge University Press, 1995.

Putnam, Hilary. *Reason, Truth and History*. Cambridge: Cambridge University Press, 1981.

———. "Richard Rorty on Reality and Justification." In *Rorty and His Critics*, ed. Robert B. Brandom, 81–87. Malden, Mass.: Blackwell, 2000.

Qushayrī, Abū al-Qāsim. *Al-Risāla al-Qushayriyya*. Cairo: Maṭbaʿat Muṣṭafā al-Ḥalabī, 1940.

Rahman, Fuzlur. "Essence and Existence in Ibn Sīna: The Myth and the Reality." *Hamdard Islamicus* 4 (1981): 3–14.

Reinhart, Kevin. *Before Revelation: The Boundaries of Muslim Moral Thought*. Albany: State University of New York Press, 1995.

Renard, John. *Seven Doors to Islam: Spirituality and the Religious Life of Muslims*. Berkeley: University of California Press, 1996.

Reshotko, Naomi. "A Bastard Kind of Reasoning: The Argument from the Sciences and the Introduction of the Receptacle in Plato's *Timaeus*." *History of Philosophy Quarterly* 14 (1997): 121–137.

Rinpoche, Sogyal. *The Tibetan Book of Living and Dying*. Ed. Patrick Gaffney and Andrew Harvey. New York: HarperCollins, 1994.

Rorty, Richard. Introduction to *The Linguistic Turn: Recent Essays in Philosophical Method*. Ed. Richard Rorty. Chicago: University of Chicago Press, 1967. 1–39.

———. *Philosophy and the Mirror of Nature*. Princeton: Princeton University Press, 1979.

———. "Response to Jacques Bouveresse." In *Rorty and his Critics*, ed. Robert B. Brandom, 147–155. Malden, Mass.: Blackwell, 2000.

———. "Response to Michael Williams." In *Rorty and his Critics*, ed. Robert B. Brandom, 213–219. Malden, Mass.: Blackwell, 2000.

———. "Universality and Truth." In *Rorty and his Critics*, ed. Robert B. Brandom, 1–30. Malden, Mass.: Blackwell, 2000.

Rosemann, Philipp. "A Change of Paradigm in the Study of Medieval Philosophy: From Rationalism to Postmodernism." *American Catholic Philosophical Quarterly* 72 (1998): 58–73.

———. *Understanding Scholastic Thought with Foucault*. New York: St. Martin's Press, 1999.

Rosenthal, Franz. "Ibn ʿArabī Between 'Philosophy' and 'Mysticism.'" *Oriens* 31 (1988): 1–35.

Sainsbury, Richard M. *Paradoxes*, Cambridge: Cambridge University Press, 1995.

Schimmel, Annemarie. *Deciphering the Signs of God: A Phenomenological Approach to Islam*. Albany: The State University of New York Press, 1994.

Shehadi, Fadlou. *Ghazālī's Unique Unknowable God*. Leiden: E. J. Brill, 1964.

Smirnov, V. Andrey. "Nicholas of Cusa and Ibn ʿArabī: Two Philosophies of Mysticism." *Philosophy East and West* 43 (1993): 65–85.

Smith, Jane I., and Yvonne Haddad Yazbeck. *The Islamic Understanding of Death and Resurrection*. Albany: State University of New York Press, 1981.

Stelzer, Steffen. "Decisive Meetings: Ibn Rushd, Ibn ʿArabī, and the Matter of Knowledge." *Alif* 16 (1996): 19–55.

Suzuki, Daisetz T. *Zen Buddhism.* New York: Grove Weidenfeld, 1964.

Sviri, Sara. "*The Obsession with Life: Jung, Khidr and the Ṣūfī Tradition.*" In *The Guild of Pastoral Psychology*, 1–16. Guild Lecture no. 273, 2000.

———. *The Taste of Hidden Things: Images on the Ṣūfī Path.* Inverness, Calif.: Golden Sufi Center, 1997.

Takeshita, Masataka. "An Analysis of Ibn ʿArabī's *Inshā' al-Dawā'ir* with Particular Reference to the Doctrine of the 'Third Entity.'" *Journal of Near Eastern Studies* 41 (1982): 243–260.

Teicher, Jacob L. "Avicenna's Place in Arabic Philosophy." In *Avicenna: Scientist and Philosopher*, ed. G. M. Wickens, 9–48. London: Luzac and Company, 1952.

Turner, John D., trans. "A Valentinian Exposition (XI, 2), with On The Anointing, On Baptism A and B, and On The Eucharist A and B." In *The Nag Hammadi Library in English*, ed. M. James M. Robinson, 435–442. London: Harper and Row, 1978.

Urvoy, Dominique. *Ibn Rushd* (Averroes). Trans. Olivia Stewart. London: Routledge, 1991.

Utke, Allen R. "The Rainbow: A Universal Timeless 'Pointer' Toward Ultimate Reality and Meaning." *Ultimate Reality and Meaning* 19 (1996): 22–39.

Walker, Paul E. "*Platonisms in Islamic Philosophy.*" *Studia Islamica* 79 (1996): 5–25.

Walsh, William H. "Kant." In *The Encyclopedia of Philosophy*, ed. Paul Edwards. 8 vols. New York: Macmillan and Free Press, 1967. 305–324.

Wasilewska, Ewa. *Creation Stories of the Middle East.* London: Jessica Kingsley, 2000.

Wasserstrom, Steven M. *Religion after Religion: Gershom Scholem, Mircea Eliade and Henry Corbin at Eranos.* Princeton, N.J.: Princeton University Press, 1999.

Weiss, Bernard G. *The Search for God's Law: Islamic Jurisprudence in the Writings of Ṣafy al-Dīn al-Amidī.* Salt Lake City: University of Utah Press, 1992.

———. *The Spirit of Islamic Law.* Athens: University of Georgia Press, 1998.

Whitehead, Alfred N. *Modes of Thought.* New York: Free Press, 1968.

Wolfson, Austryn H. *The Philosophy of the Kalām.* Cambridge: Harvard University Press, 1976.

———. *Religious Philosophy.* Cambridge: Harvard University Press, 1961.

Young, Peter. "Ibn ʿArabī: Towards a Universal Point of View." *Journal of the Muḥyiddīn Ibn ʿArabī Society* 25 (1986): 89–97.

Index

Abadi, Avraham, 183n16
Abraham, 117–18, 122
Abū Bakr (al-Ṣiddīq), 136
Abū Zayd, Naṣr, 76
act (activity)
  of defining, 87
  God's, 41, 78
  of the Perfect Mover, 54
actuality vs. actualization, 54–55, 65, 167n16
actualization, of love, 114
Addas, Claude, 26, 68
Aeon (*dahr*), 95
ʿAffīfī, Abū al-ʿIlā , 5, 76
Affirmation, 125, 68
  of similarity, 135
ʿAlī, ʿAbdullah, 76, 122
All-Merciful
  and barzakh, 76
  Breath of, 130–31
Allah, 77, 93–94, 105, 117, 123, 127. *See also* God
Alston, William, 14
antinomy, 8, 55, 151n27
antirepresentationalism, 20
argument, 12, 20, 31, 33–34, 37, 47–48
  of Chuang Tzu, 124
  for Forms, 99–100, 102
  against existence of relations, 93
  against polytheism, 118, 122
Aristotle, 7, 22, 31–35, 39–41, 45–46, 52–53, 56, 84, 86, 90, 97, 99, 106, 156n19, 158n32, 160n65
  Argument From The Sciences of, 99
  contradiction in his thought, 45, 56
  correspondence principle of, 35
  philosophical authority of, 22
Arnaldez, Roger, 30
articulation (*makhraj*), 131
ascension (*miʿrāj*), 131, 180n22
Ashʿarites, 8, 33, 46, 74, 97, 157n21, 162n23, 173n28, 176n3
associators (*mushrikin*), 71
attitude, 73
attributes, 104, 111

barrier, 11, 75, 102. *See also* barzakh
barzakh, 7, 12, 61, 75–78, 80–82, 84, 89, 90–92, 96–97, 102–3, 111, 128, 143–44, 152n2
  Arabized, 11
  definition of, 86
  as differentiator/unifier, 7, 11–12
  earthly, 81

grave as, 77
human being as, 116
Imagination as, 17
meanings embodied in, 79
paradoxical notion of, 11
Supreme, 108, 121, 124, 134
as undivided unity, 87, 90
World of, 11
bastard reason, 99, 101–2
beginning, 34, 47–49, 51, 55, 124
being, 70–71, 73, 82, 109, 114, 119, 124, 126
and becoming, 84
Parmenides's theory of, 32
as ultimate reality, 31. *See also* existence
bewilderment, 123
and regret, 126
Bohr, Neils, 151n28, 153n13
border, 145
boundaries, 63
breath
of All-Merciful, 130–31
human, 131
Knowledge of, 60, 65
of Life, 66
Burrell, David, 30, 40, 50

Cairns, Huntington, 13, 83, 174n37
Carter, Michael, 15–18, 153n17
causality, 32, 83
causation
and occasionalism, 36
priority of, 50
cause, 37, 46–47, 53, 50, 86, 100
center, 123
and *Kaʿba*, 118, 181n23
Chittick, William, 4–5, 7, 14, 44, 59– 61, 67–68, 73, 78, 98, 113, 120, 131, 133, 147, 155n63, 173n23
Chodkiewicz, Michel, 3
circle, 137
points on, 4
and time, 95, 107
Cloud (*ʿamāʾ*), 105
comparability, 73, 120, 135, 138
complementarity thesis, 8, 12, 107, 138, 151n28
comprehension, impossibility of, 136
configuration, 130, 135
of minds, 61
of perfect human being, 3–4
spiritual/natural, 115–17
consideration, 118, 180n22
continuity, 40, 114
between God and the world, 106
perspective of, 12
contradiction, 46, 150n16
and Ibn al-ʿArabī, 108
and Ibn Rushd, 107–8
Corbin, Henry, 11, 117
and history of religion, 25
as prophetic philosopher, 26
and religion after religion, 25, 27
correlation (*munāsaba*), 105, 110
correlatives, 47
correspondence, 19–20, 35, 129, 132
and Rorty, 22
cosmos, 98, 103, 110, 113
imaginal reality of, 68
knowledge of, 114
perpetual transmutation of, 65, 77
and Universal Reality, 104,
covenant with the Lord, 115, 180n14
creation, 32, 121
and breathing, 61
continuous, 35, 54, 158n41
interpreted allegorically, 30
as meaningless act, 38
moment of, 122
nontemporal, 37
and Philoponus's arguments, 34
renewal of, 78
tied to the Real, 130, 135
in *Timaeus*, 33, 84, 99–100
creation ex nihilo
and Ibn Rushd, 165n77
irrational (illogical), 32, 53
as miracle, 32
in Qur'ān, 29, 32

vagueness of, 30
creative imagination
human drive for, 16
Knowledge of, 61
Creator, Qur'ānic paradigm of, 29
Cusanus, 136–38, 183n17, 184n25

death, 75, 77, 80–82
greater/lesser, 82
of Newscholasticism, 6
of philosophy, 154n28
definition, 2, 5, 39, 83, 103, 110
Aristotle's theory of, 85
of barzakh, 87
and limit, 7, 56
of Real's existence, 106
of relation, 93
desire, 116
deviation, 126
dialectic, 150n16
dialectical argument, 44
dialectical method, 22
dialectical process, 126
difference, 73, 88
challenge of, 25
perspective of, 12
Postmodernist emphasis on, 6
root of things, 23
social, 26
differentiation (*farq*, *tafriqa*), 65, 102
as lower dimension, 5
root of things, 87
dimension, 5, 15, 65, 140
determinate, 65
miraculous, 32
disclosure (self-), 14, 65, 78–79, 89, 91, 120, 126, 137
distance, pathos of, 22, 27
divine
essence, 105
knowledge, 117, 140
love, 115
names, 98, 130
and secular knowledge, 167n18
Divinity (*ulūha*), 72, 94, 105–6
door, 140
duality, 90, 111
limit as, 7, 85–86

Eklund, Ragner, 77, 81
element, 103
Elmore, Gerald, 168n31, 168n33, 169n34
emanation, 53, 160n81
Ibn Rushd's rejection of, 53
encounter, 3, 26, 66
between Ibn al-ʿArabī and Ibn Rushd, 66–69
between Khaḍir and Moses, 60– 66
entity, 2, 8, 39, 50, 87, 91, 97, 99, 110
and barzakh, 11
liminal, 3, 7
middle, 41
spiritual, 79. *See also* fixed entity
epistemology, 27
epitome
of Aristotle's *Metaphysics*, 53
Perfect Man as, 122
essence (*ḥāqīqa*), 49, 53, 65, 90– 94, 108–9, 114
and existence (*wujūd*), 40–41
Essence of the Real, 61, 93, 110, 114
and discursive knowledge, 24, 137
independent, 94
nondelimited, 136
prior to being and nonbeing, 137
transcends representation, 107
unknowable, 109
unlimited by unlimitation, 109
eternity, 122, 126
eternity of the world, 34–35, 38, 49, 54
and Aristotle, 31
Ghazālī's rejection of, 38
Ibn Sīnā's argument for, 35
and theologians' arguments, 36, 133
existent (things), 4, 69, 74, 104–5, 109, 134
existence, 30, 35–41, 45, 47, 50–54, 89, 92, 96–98, 104–6, 108, 110–11, 113–14, 130–31
as absolute unity, 6
as accident, 40

engendered (*al-kawn*), 4, 5
entified, 104
identical to nonexistence, 88
relational, 110
things impossible of, 108
two kinds of, 50
underived, 106
experience
immediate, 64
mystical, 13

Fakhry, Mājid, 52–53
finding (*wujūd*), 107, 170n47
knowledge as, 25
finite, finitude, 33, 47–50, 54–56, 59, 91, 107–8, 110, 121–22
and infinitude, 107–8, 133–35
First (*al-Awwal*)
Cause, 15, 35, 53
and Last (*al-Ākhir*), 69, 91, 128, 139
Mover, 45. *See also* names
fixed (immutable) entity (*ʿayn thābita*), 61, 65, 89, 103, 137–38
fluctuation of, 78
individuations of, 103, 133
infinite, 129
and Plato's Form, 98
storehouse of, 132
form, 77, 79, 90–91, 103, 117, 120–21, 129, 133, 135
Frank, Richard, 38–39
Friend of God (*khalīl Allah*), 117

Garden, 66, 78
forms in, 87
rivers of, 77
Genequand, Charles, 53, 164n77
Ghazālī, Abū Ḥāmid al-, 33, 38, 43–52, 56–67, 81–82, 89, 94, 143, 173n33, 163n46
and dreams, 82
inconsistent practice of, 44
love-hate relationship of, 43–44
objections to philosophers, 45–48
and parity thesis, 50, 52
and rationalism, 46
Gilson, Etienne, 31, 40
God, 29–30, 37–50, 54, 61, 65, 71–73, 105, 108–9, 113, 117, 119, 120, 128
divested of attributes, 70
joins opposites, 69, 78, 91, 139
incomparable/comparable, 106, 108
incomprehensible, 72, 177n14
ontological priority of, 37
as perfect cause, 37
Presence of, 61
self-disclosures of, 78
timeless, 50
undefined, 138
Unity of, 71, 171n56
as unlimited Being, 105. *See also* Real
Goodman, Lenn, 32, 37–38, 40–41
grave, 77–79
as locus of manifestation, 79
Muḥammad's, 79
and snakes, 81
as third entity, 77
guidance (*hudā*), 126

Habermas, Jürgen, 21
Ḥakīm, Suʿād al-, 68, 181n23
heart (*qalb*), 77, 130, 171n57
and *Kaʿba*, 118
and reason, 113
Temple of, 180n22
heresy, 123, 153n17
Hertenstein, Stephen, 182n38
hidden knowledge, 2
hidden meaning
of Khaḍir's acts, 62
of Scriptures, 31

Ibn al-ʿArabī, 6, 8–9, 12, 14, 19–21, 24–25, 60, 65, 74, 76, 79, 84, 89, 90–91, 113, 115, 122–27, 131–33, 137–41, 143–47
and Abraham, 118
conception of state (*ḥāl*), 68
definition of barzakh, 86–87

definition of love, 114
on difference, 88
and dreams, 82
on essential limits, 103
on fixed entities, 97–98, 102
and Ghazālī's *Iḥyā'*, 81
and Ibn Sīnā, 94
on imagination, 7
and Khaḍir, 62
and Kharrāz, 78, 91, 139
on knowledge of relations, 93
and Liar, 17
and Noah, 71–72
on Paths of knowledge, 69–70
and Plato, 61
on rational faculties, 119–20
on reflection, 135–38
on the Real and the world, 104–7
on representation, 18
on Sainthood, 3
on types of thinkers, 69
on time, 4, 95
and Tirmidhī, 77, 80
on unknowability of Essence,108–10
Ibn Rushd, Abū al-Walīd, 12, 15, 17, 30, 36, 43–52, 54–57, 59–60, 66–69, 71–73, 85, 107, 143
on actuality, 54–55
defends rationality, 46–47
on God's priority, 59
and Knowledge of Mysteries, 67, 72
and methodological difficulties, 44
philosopher-believer, 71
on potential infinite, 47–48
on possibility and actuality, 52
and rational interpretation, 30
on the world as median, 49
Ibn Sīnā, Abū ʿAlī, 35–39, 41–42, 49–52, 74, 92–94, 106, 110, 143, 173n33,
emanationist account of, 53
on essence and existence, 92, 94
and imagination, 173n33
predicament of, 36
rational analysis of, 42
on specific unity, 110
tension in his position, 40
Ibn Ṭufayl, Abū Bakr, 44
identity, 103
ignorance (learned ignorance), 137–38. *See also* Cusanus
image
in mirror, 89
representation of, 18
imaginal encounters, 26
imaginal reality, 23
imagination
attitude of, 120
creative, 61
existent/nonexistent, 18, 89
as intermediate reality, 7
materialized, 80
meaning of, 166n15
Oriental, 7
Presence of, 82
and time, 96
Unbounded, 68
immutable entity, 98, 126, 131, 138. *See also* fixed entity
incomparability (*tanzīh*), 70, 73, 138
and comparability (*tashbīh*), 120
infinite, 33–37, 47, 49, 55–56, 59, 85, 91, 106–10, 114, 125, 130, 132–35
Aristotle's, 33–34, 158n31
greater than another, 34, 133
Ibn Rushd's actual/potential, 47
nonexistent, 36
occurrences, 37
unlimited in two directions, 47
infinitude, infinity, 121, 126, 134
and lies, 15–16
paradox of, 133
poses a threat to First Cause, 15
poses a threat to Islam, 16–17
instant (*al-ān*), 65, 121–22, 127–29
defines priority and posteriority, 55
and Plato, 146
intellect
finite, 136

insufficient, 59
and truth, 137
intermediate object, 84–85, 90, 174n42
intermediate state, 77
interpretation
allegorical, 72
as crossing over, 23, 154n49
irrational contents, 64
irrational in Moses's eyes, 62

Judgment
prejudiced, 63
rational, 64
Jung, Carl, 63, 182n42

Kaʿba, 48, 169n34, 181n23
Kalwaitis, Carl, 168n24
Kant, Immanuel, 155n64
Khaḍir, 3, 60–63, 65, 71, 166n9, 167n18
Kharrāz, Abū Saʿīd al-, 78, 91, 139
knowledge, 61, 66–67, 69–73, 86, 92, 116, 119, 135–38
assistance in, 130
of Breaths, 61
of cosmos, 114
of Perfect Man, 121
possessors of Khaḍir's, 65
of the Real, 122
Kogan, Barry, 48, 54–55

Language
game, 20,
symbolic form of, 22
Leaman, Oliver, 30, 39, 44, 51, 59
level
of abstraction, 102
of fixed entities, 105
of Reality of Realities, 108
of Third Thing, 108
of Uniqueness, 105
unity of, 110
liar, paradox of, 16–17, 24
lies (activity of lying), 16
and infinity, 15
and poetry, 15
light, of faith and reason, 109
liminal cases, 18
liminal definitions in music, 2
liminal reality of objects, 23
limit, 87, 103, 109, 122, 128, 140, 146
absolute conception of, 75
abstract nature of, 102
Aristotle's concept of, 7, 86
Being as, 124
of consideration, 63
as duality, 7
as essence, 7
false conception of, 86
God's Essential, 109
God's time as, 4
paradoxical definition of, 7
predetermined, 65
property of, 130
of rationality, 12–13
situation, 135, 139
staying within, 26–27
of time/space, 50
Lotus Tree of, 139, 180n22
as undivided unity, 102
limitation (*ḥaṣr*), 109, 125
of language, 17
and unlimitation, 108
Lings, Martin, 171n1
Little, John, 178n35
logical puzzles, 64
Lord (*rabb*), 140
favors of, 76
and slave, 150n17, 175n73
love, 113–16
definition of, 114
joins opposites, 115
to be known, 113–14
spiritual/natural, 115

Maker
and soul, 115
in *Timaues*, 100
manifest
and nonmanifest, 3, 116
domain, 129, 132. *See also* names

manifestation, 105, 114, 122, 129, 132–33
  and nonmanifestation, 121
Marmura, Michael, 36, 44, 92, 158n42
Martine, Brian, 64
matter
  Plato's eternal, 98
  preexistent, 97
Meeting of Two Seas, 61, 76
Middle (*wasat*), 125
miracle (*muʿjiza*), 157n21
mirror, 117, 121
  image in, 89
  imaginal, 12
  surface of, 89
moment
  of disclosure, 14
  present, 65
  transcended, 121
Morris, James, 181n25
Moses, 3, 60–63, 65, 71
motion, 54
Muḥammad, 125–28
Murata, Sachiko, 5
Muʿtazilites, 8, 33, 46, 73, 97–98, 157n24, 62n23, 173n28, 162n62
Mystical experience
  example of, 13
  religious and, 25

Names (Most Beautiful Names), 94, 105–6, 108, 117, 128, 140
  Manifest/Nonmanifest, 117, 139
  brought together, 69, 91
  represented by *kun*, 3. *See also* First
Naẓẓām, 34
necessary-of-existence, 51
necessity, two types of, 38–39
negation
  of Firstness, 127
  of negation, 124–26
  of Nonbeing, 127
  of similarity, 130, 135
  of thingness, 134
Netton, Richard, 29, 62
Noah, 72, 171n57
nonbeing, 32, 70, 124, 126–27
  absolute, 127
  qualified/unqualified, 32
  realized, 127
nonexistence, 39, 96–97, 104–6, 130
  Being unqualified by, 134
  relative, 127
  of time, 95
  transcends existence, 96, 121
nonexistent (thing), 36, 98, 104, 111, 130–31, 145
  neither existent nor, 69, 74, 95, 97
  as something, 8, 33, 97–99
nonmanifestation, knowledge of, 3
Nothing, metaphysical, 124–25

objects
  limited, 103
  sensible, 100–101
occasionalism, 36
Ohrmazd, 145
Ontological dependence on God, 38
Ontological division in *Timaues*, 99
Ontological tensions, 64
Ontological status of images, 89
opposites, gathering of, 104, 108
Other, (*khilāf*), 88

paradox
  Khaḍir's actions as, 62
  Liar, 16
  and opinion (*doxa*), 63, 168n24
paradoxical notion of limit, 145
paradoxical reality, 89
paradoxical tendency, 50
paradoxicality
  of relation, 107
  in Ibn al-ʿArabī's thought, 5
parity thesis, 50
Parmenides, 31–32, 70, 73, 84–85, 106, 174n40
Path (*ṭarīqa*)
  of knowledge, 69, 70
  of perfection, 126
  and Truth (*haqīqa*), 66

perfect human being, 3–4, 141
Perfect Man, 113, 117, 119–23, 140, 182n52
bindes the Real, 120
Gives assistance to the Real, 122
reasoning of, 124
permanence (*dawām*) of love, 114
permeation, 119
ontological, 121
phenomena, exterior/interior, 109
Philopunus, John, 33–34, 157n26
philosophers, 32, 36, 44–45, 47–48, 51, 67–68, 71
philosophers and theologians
controversy between, 29
possibility and necessity, 38
on eternity, 39
and Ibn al–ʿArabī, 67, 82
insufficient arguments, 48
limits of Being, 73
rational thought, 17
meaning of reflection, 69
philosophy
abandoning, 21
Ghazālī's attitude toward, 43–44
rationalizes mysticism, 12, 14
Plato, 12–13, 21–23, 83, 89, 91, 97–102, 146, 184n25
and Ibn al-ʿArabī, 22, 83
rationalist, 13, 174n37
represents the universal, 22
Rorty's enthusiasm with, 21
transcends the rational, 12, 101
Platonic Forms (ideas), 76, 83–84, 90–91, 98, 101, 103, 172n4, 176n8
Plenitude, Principle of, 51, 160n62
Plotinus, 164n70
poetry, considered fallible, 16
possible-of-existence, 51
and necessary-by-the-other, 39, 54
rational analysis of, 41
possible (things), 52, 119, 129, 131–37
dependent on the Necessary, 136
finite/infinite, 133
forms of, 135
possibility, 38, 51, 61
coextensive with reality, 52
in Aristotle's thought, 38
prediction, 99
present, 65, 96, 128, 133
presentation, experience of, 14
Prime Matter, 121
proofs, 73, 109
prophets, 2, 149n4
Putnam, Hilary, 19–20

quiddity (*māhiyya*), unattainable, 137

rainbow, 146
rational analysis, 111
rational consideration, 68
rational correspondence, 20
rational determinism, 64
rational faculty, 69, 73, 95, 119
rational formula, 126
rational interpretation, 31, 60
rational proof, 123
rational reflection, 116, 124, 138
rational thinker, 88–89, 109–10
predicament of, 63
rationalism, Newscholastic, 5, 150n19
Real (*ḥaqq*), 89, 121–22
Being of, 94, 133
dependent and independent, 114
jealousy of, 116
as liminal entity,134
limited by all limitations, 121
limited and unlimited, 139
neither limited nor unlimited, 104, 106
reality of, 66, 68, 105, 108, 133
self-disclosure of, 91
tied to creation, 136, 140
Word of, 126. *See also* God; Essence of the Real
reality, 103–6, 109, 116–17
imaginal, 101
rational, 101
of Realities, 108
Realizers (*muḥaqqiqūn*), 69
and Khaḍir, 60

and Plato, 170n49
sign of, 73
as states, 73
reason (reasoning), 102, 108, 119, 125
emphasized in Qur'ān, 31
follows reflection, 118
limited, 46
Receptacle, 99–102
Perfect Man as, 121, 177n20
as third thing,100
as unifying principle, 101
receptivities (*qawābil*), 80
reflection, 101, 118, 125
radical, 119
real meaning of, 69, 136
relatedness, 49
relation, 87, 93, 103–4, 106–9, 130–31
conception of, 92
of difference, 88
of fatherhood and sonship, 93–95
Ibn Sīnā's absolute, 92
knowledge of, 93
words as, 132
relationship, 104, 117
between eternal and temporal, 49
between finite and infinite, 49
between God and world, 42
musical knowledge of, 2
relativism, 6
religion (religious faith), 123
renewal of, 81
reports, of God's delimitation, 73
representation, 90, 121
element of, 13, 14
of given reality, 24
Ibn al-ʿArabī's theory of, 18
as veil of ideas, 22
Reshotko, Naomi, 99, 102, 177n20
Retreat, 66
root, 104–6
Rorty, Richard, 9, 18, 20–24, 26–27, 154n28
Rosemann, Phillip, 5–7, 151
Rozenthal, Franz, 81, 170n49
saints, 119
Seal of Sainthood, 3
skeptic
and knowledge, 24
Ghazālī as, 33–44
Rorty as, 20
Smirnov, Andrey, 137
sophist, 88, 150n16
soul, 115–16
Sphere of Life (*falak al-ḥayāt*), 104
stairs (*maʿārij*), 130
state (*ḥāl*), 103
and station, 68, 169n40
as intermediate reality, 8, 77
station (*maqām*), 68, 176n3
storehouse, 132
straight way, 123
substance, 40, 86, 98, 104
Ṣūfī, 14, 71
and rational thinkers, 11, 59
and revealed texts, 60
Suhrawardī, Shihāb al-Dīn al-, 23
Sviri, Sara, 14, 168n30
synthesis, 38, 65, 108, 116, 121, 150n16, 180n13

Teicher, Jacob, 42, 55–56
temporal origination, 122
theologians, 31–32, 35–36, 38, 41
things
compounded/uncompounded, 132
created, 101
intelligible/sensible, 99–100
thingness (*shayʾiyya*), 133
Third Thing (*al-shayʾ al-thālith*), 96, 99 104, 108, 178n28
threshold, 147, 153n27
throwing, 125
Tie, 131
time, 95–96, 133, 145
arises with the world, 50
in Aristotle's thought, 158n38
continuous/discontinuous, 35
as creative evolution, 56
as cyclical continuum, 107
dahr vs. *zaman*, 1, 150n11
essential vs. spatialized, 55

as limit, 35, 56
musical definition of, 2
preexistence in, 37
as straight line, 47
theologians' conception of, 35
Tirmidhī, Ḥakīm al-, 77, 79, 81, 173n23
Toshihiko, Izutsu, 117
transmutation (self-) (*taḥawwul*), 65
truth
correspondence theory of, 19
relative, 15
religious, 16
unity of, 59
Tzu, Chuang, 124

unification, (*tawḥīd*), 102, 111
active stance, 5
and difference, 5
unity
of Being, 71, 107
level of, 105
metaphysical, 7, 155n59
specific, 88, 110
unknown, 110
universality, 59
universe, 105
unveiling, 120
method of, 60
Urvoy, Dominique, 30

Van Den Bergh, Simon, 45
variegation (*talwīn*) and stability (*tamkīn*), 113
veil (*ḥijāb*)
of ideas, 22
Ibn Rushd behind, 67
visionary event (*wāqiʿa*), 80
Von Sivers, Peter, 151

Walker, Paul, 22
Wasserstrom, Steven, 25–27
water, 102
element, 31
solidified, 100
symbolism of, 171n1
two bodies of, 11, 75–76, 152n2
Way, 123
of Being, 70
Taoist, 124
Weiss, Bernard, 157n21
whatness (*māhiyya*), 109
Whitehead, Alfred, 12
will
divine vs. human, 45–46
God's, 65
Wolfson, Harry, 30, 33, 97
words
and things, 20
of God, 129–30, 132
infinite, 4
world, 107
of Barzakh, 11–12
finite/infinite, 59
of Imagination (*ʿālam al-khayāl*), 61
limited and unlimited, 8
as locus of manifestation, 78
as median (*wāsiṭa*), 48
origination of, 100
Rorty's reflection on, 21

Young, Peter, 6